# BLACK
# DRAMA

# BLACK DRAMA

The Story of the American Negro
in the Theatre

by Loften Mitchell

Hawthorn Books, Inc.    *Publishers*    New York City

# A PRAYER

When the final curtain falls
On the play known as my life,
I want no loud applause and certainly no tears.
I want only to cross the bridge once more
To my beloved Harlem.
I want only to move up 131st Street once again,
Turn up Lenox Avenue to 135th Street,
Then up to Seventh Avenue past the Lafayette,
The Tree of Hope,
Down to 125th Street and Seventh Avenue,
Then on to 116th Street, 113th Street,
Down to 110th Street and into Central Park.

When the earth is pulled around me,
Let me hear the sound of laughter,
For I shall be uttering prayers of thanks
For being from Harlem, for walking among the artists
Named in these pages and those not named.
Thanks for my parents, my wife, my children,
My brothers and my sister and other family members
Including those who make up that wonderful thing
Called mankind.

# Table of Contents

# Introduction

The seed for this volume was planted many years ago. When I was a boy in Harlem, the ten-cent movie houses were my windows to the world. But the movies did not project the stories I heard from older people—from Southern Negroes, West Indians and Northerners. Therefore, I found my visits to Harlem's vaudeville houses—the Lafayette, the Lincoln and the Alhambra—much more rewarding than moviegoing. At these theatres I saw vaudeville sketches, dramatic sketches and musical revues performed by black people. I identified with these artists and grew to love them.

The depression of 1929 ended my theatrical visits. Dimes were hard to get. My brother, Clayton, and I heard stories of boys buying daily newspapers for a penny, then selling them for a nickel. We went into the streets to sell papers.

I found my best sales backstage at Harlem's theatres. I met such artists as Ethel Waters, Fredi Washington, Dick Campbell, Muriel Rahn, Ralph Cooper, George Wiltshire, Juano Hernandez, John Bunn and Canada Lee. Invariably, I got into long discussions with them, and they were very good to me. They bought newspapers, then gave them back for me to sell elsewhere.

Those were difficult, depression years; yet these artists encouraged me to go into the theatre. And they told me wonderful stories of other black writers—of Bob Cole, Jesse Shipp and Paul Laurence Dunbar. They spoke, too, of Bert Williams, George Walker, Florence Mills, Bessie Smith and Josephine Baker. From them, too, I first heard of Ira Aldridge and James Hewlett. Anyone who believes the Negro theatre artist of those or earlier days was a handkerchief-head, a shuffling person of little education, should have known these proud, literate artists. The one thing these men and women did not tell me was the reason they were not truthfully presented in motion pictures. They didn't have to. I already knew that.

And so I set out to become a playwright, largely because I dared to dream the long dream and others dared to encourage me. I read every play I could get my hands on, and many of them were worthless. Later I discovered the plays of Shakespeare, O'Casey and Synge and the poems of Langston Hughes, Countee Cullen, Arna Bontemps and Paul Laurence Dunbar. I saw in the

1

theatre the elevation of human life and the hopes, the aspirations and image of the people I knew being projected to the world. I saw hope in the midst of hopelessness, progress in the place of frustration.

I saw, too, that some of the so-called finest plays in Western history contradicted everything I knew about black people. And insulted them. People seeing those plays on stage or screen or reading them could get angry enough to kill Negroes—just as I was angry enough to kill some white folks.

My father didn't shuffle to punch a white schoolteacher who had mistreated my brother. And he actually ran after a car in trying to catch a white driver who had yelled insulting remarks at my mother. My mother didn't wear bandannas, nor did she bow and bend to the whites for whom she managed an apartment building. I heard her use some language with them that would have shocked her church sisters—unless they used that language, too. And we youngsters didn't allow white gangs to attack us without retaliating with fists, sticks, rocks and lead pipes.

Andrew Burris, and later Zell Ingram and Glenn Carrington—leaders of boys' clubs to which I belonged—were no drawling characters. They and other dedicated Negroes were in the streets, building clubs, organizing meetings and bringing celebrated Negro figures to speak to us. We went to excellent concerts and lectures in Harlem. Contrary to a lot of present-day thinking, we knew of the Negro's participation in this nation's history long before we were out of our teens.

We knew, too, that Harlem was Africa-conscious. Anyone who states otherwise is ignorant and insulting to the nationalist leader Marcus Garvey, to J. A. Rogers, Claude McKay, Richard Moore, and the whole West Indian group that revitalized the black American's interest in Africa. Men like Frederick Douglass, W. E. B. DuBois, Carter Woodson, and groups like the Association for the Study of Negro Life and History resisted distorted views of the mother continent. The *New York Age* of 1906 used the term "Afro-American" consistently in referring to black people.

We knew, despite Hollywood, that while Europe was still a "barbaric land," Africans had learned to smelt iron, build monu-

ments and record human history. The oldest university in the
world was at Timbuktu, and its scholars were experts in mathe-
matics, astronomy and other sciences. One, Ahmed Baba, wrote
forty-seven books, all on different subjects. His personal library
of sixteen hundred books was destroyed when the Moors invaded
Timbuktu.

We knew, too, that Africans were welcomed in Europe as pos-
sessors of numerous skills. Historians—among them J. A. Rogers
and John Henrik Clarke—suggest that Columbus' knowledge of
a land to the west was due to his contact with Africans. They cite
the Africanesque features of many Mexican statues as evidence
of Africa's contact with the Americas long before 1492.

The suggestion that Negroes first reached America in 1619 is
a deliberate lie, created by those who would perpetuate the nontruth that the *only* black people to come to this continent were
slaves. Pietro, who captained one of Columbus' ships, was of
African origin, and so were many crewmen. Ponce De Leon had
a Negro with him when he landed in Florida on Easter Sunday,
1512. Balboa had Pedro Mexia with him when he discovered the
Pacific. A Negro named Estevanico was with De Narváez' expedition in 1527. He crossed the continent to Lower California, and
he later led an expedition that discovered what is now Arizona
and New Mexico. And Negroes either discovered or helped discover San Francisco, Los Angeles, Chicago, Wisconsin, Denver and
Pike's Peak.

The image of a people depends not only upon the prejudices
of others but also upon projection. These images shift as the
community shifts. In the nineteen-twenties and nineteen-thirties,
our community was seen by outsiders as a showplace, a center
of night life, a place for discovering "exotic Negroes" and new
art. In the nineteen-sixties Harlem is projected by well-intentioned
white and Negro artists as a slum, crowded with winos, addicts,
pushers, muggers, thugs and impoverished, angry, depraved, rioting Negroes. Harlem certainly has more than its share of these,
but it also has doctors, lawyers, artists, writers, cultural groups and
ordinary working people. You can't get into a Harlem bank without standing in long lines. Obviously *somebodies* there work for
a living. In fact, the reason the Bowery Savings Bank opened a

branch there is because the management learned there were more
postal savings in that area than in any other postal district. The
reality is that, like all places, Harlem has many sides.

The reality also is that this very young, very immature, naïve
nation and its power structure need a stereotype for a people it
has no intention of really freeing unless "they go along with the
program." So the big, big cowboy in the big, big house in Washington is compelled to give a little in terms of Anti-Poverty to
rationalize colored men fighting colored men in Viet Nam while
offering petty legalism for staying out of Rhodesia.

The present stereotype is thus assured—of the angry, depraved,
impoverished, rioting, dope-using Negro youth. The nation's rulers say: "We're doing them a favor, letting them die at war. And
we give them medals, too." And, of course, tired white souls say:
"Isn't it awful the way they riot and bite at the hand that tries
to feed them? They're better off in the army." Of course, no one
has thought about sending all-white troops to fight white Rhode-
sians or South Africans. The world situation was, of course, not
the same in my youth, but the attitudes were. The contempt for
Orientals and Jews did not help me think otherwise in younger
days.

While in high school I joined the Progressive Dramatizers
group at Salem Church, wrote sketches for it, then worked as an
actor for the Rose McClendon Players. The Pioneer Drama group
also produced some of my early sketches. But primarily I worked
as an actor—between dishwashing, delivering lunch orders and
standing in relief lines. Dennis Donoghue's *The Black Messiah,*
produced at the Nora Bayes Theatre in 1939, ended my acting
career. The critics said many performances were amateurish, and
they included mine.

Theatrical work for white actors had limitations then. For
black actors it was, to put it euphemistically, *beyond* limitations.
It took no genius to realize that a *bad* black actor had limitations
beyond limitations. By 1939 I had made two decisions: I was
going to write, and I was going to get far, far away from my
native New York and look at myself.

Through Andrew Burris I got a scholarship to Talladega College, which is thirty-two miles from Birmingham, Alabama. On a

bright September day in 1939 I left by bus, heading south for my first trip outside the big city. In the Richmond, Virginia, bus stop I saw the first "Colored" and "White" signs. I got that sinking feeling that only a black man in these United States can understand. I wondered if I hadn't stepped out of that proverbial frying pan into the equally proverbial, but much hotter, fire. I debated between returning to a New York Negro actor's starving life and sticking my anatomy further into the violently raging fire.

But I am a child of Harlem. The concrete sidewalks of 131st Street were the country lanes of my boyhood and 125th Street was the center of "town." Years of running and falling and hitting my head against the concrete made me hardheaded and unyielding. I lived with the belief that a bright tomorrow would dawn for me. I was not about to turn back. I felt that my parents must have known the same fear, loneliness and frustration when they left their rural North Carolina homeland to build a new life in the cold North. I remembered, too, that in my youth many newcomers could not adjust to the big city. Defeated, they returned to the Southland. I did not dare turn back and be seen on the streets of Harlem, not after the big sendoff I had gotten. I would have been disgraced, and Harlem is the *last* place one of its native sons wants to be disgraced.

I continued my journey, finding it uncomfortable, anger-provoking, but educational—especially for one who had decried "country hicks" in the big city. I learned about being a "city hick" in the country. I kept staring out the window at the white fields, wondering how snow could last under a blazing sun. A Negro woman next to me said: "Son, that ain't snow. That's cotton growing."

My next lesson was more devastating. I jumped off at a Georgia bus station, thinking I had arrived. After the bus pulled out, I learned I was one hundred and thirty miles from my destination, and the next bus would not appear for several hours! My "city" reasoning told me I was one hundred and thirty *blocks* from Talladega—so I set out to walk the distance.

The Georgia sun, red clay and tired feet combined to make me remember that it took twenty city blocks to make *one* mile. Twenty times one hundred and thirty miles happened to be more than I could mathematically compute—or walk. I thumbed a ride from a passing truck driver. He invited me into the rear of the vehicle, which was full of manure. The truck driver, the manure and I rolled into Talladega two days after I had left New York City.

I didn't like the town of Talladega and I didn't like the college. The town seemed like a page out of *Tobacco Road*, and the college was for me a small village unto itself. The very first thing I did on arriving was rush into the dormitory to make certain it had running water and a bath.

I disliked my classmates as much as I did the town. The truth is, I saw them as sons and daughters of Negro lawyers, doctors, teachers and other professionals who were middle class because of jimcrow. I did not realize that I was a supercilious New Yorker who thought the world ended when one crossed the Hudson and East Rivers. I also did not know jimcrow persisted while my classmates and I argued, but that in the end we would rally against it.

One day our freshman English professor, Maurice A. Lee, assigned research papers to be submitted by the end of the year. My friends foresaw long hours of library work that might have been used for socializing. I laughed at them. I hadn't lived in Harlem all of my life without getting the notion that I was "two-cents slick." I had talked to Professor Lee that very afternoon, explained that I wanted to write my paper on the Harlem theatre, and he was delighted. So was I—I knew this was going to be a "snap." Those wonderful performers who had helped me so much in the past were going to do so again—this time with my paper. I planned to sit down one night and write what I had heard them say. Like too many American students, I did not believe in hard work.

I outsmarted myself. Professor Lee liked my finished paper, but he suggested I should research this material thoroughly, then write a book. Much of the material, he said, had not been presented elsewhere. He added that it was the responsibility of some Negro to record these contributions faithfully, and he repeated a statement made, I believe, by John W. Vandercook that a race that doesn't know where it came from, doesn't know where it's going. I agreed with Professor Lee, readily, happily accepted the grade he gave me, stuck my research paper away and turned to other things. I had no intentions of getting caught up in excessive work—like writing a book.

The professor's suggestion haunted me for many years. After Naval service, I set out to work on a master's at Columbia. My two mentors, Barrett H. Clark and John Gassner, reminded me I had to select a topic for a thesis. At that very moment I had a play, *The Bancroft Dynasty*, scheduled for production. I pulled out my old college research paper and told my mentors I planned to write a history of the Harlem theatre. Both suggested that I write a history of the Negro in the American theatre; they added a few of Professor Lee's arguments and commented that white people need to know the meaning of black drama. They felt it regrettable that large numbers of Americans do not know one of the great influences of their culture.

I dodged and ducked while they persisted. Eventually, we compromised and I prepared a history of the groups that had attempted to build a permanent Harlem theatre. Later, through Professor Gassner, *Theatre Arts Monthly* commissioned me to prepare an article about these groups, and so I did. Then, I turned to the writing of two plays, *The Cellar* and *A Land Beyond the River*.

During the run of the latter play, Professor Gassner called on me to write an essay for the *Enciclopedia Dello Spettacolo*, published in Rome. This essay dealt with Negro "spettacolo," or performances, throughout the nation's history. In 1962, again through Professor Gassner, the *Oxford Companion to the Theatre* asked me to write on the Negro in the American theatre. While doing research for these works I came across that pioneer performer, Bert Williams, and I wrote the play now known as *Star of the Morning*.

The work for the present volume was creeping up on me. In 1965 James L. Hicks, then Executive Editor of the New York *Amsterdam News*, suggested that I contribute a series on the Negro theatre. This I did over a period of twenty-five weeks while arguing perennially with Managing Editor Jesse H. Walker. But he and I have been arguing for more than twenty years—a fact known to everyone in Harlem.

Then, another thing happened. The beautiful Marjorie Coulthurst Camacho and Horace Carter, an old friend, began to exchange ideas with me about doing a book based on the *Amsterdam News* series. Marjorie collected the entire series and delivered it to my agents, Jack Lewis and Aladar Farkas of the American Literary Exchange. They in turn brought the work to the attention of Robert Cunningham and George Caldwell of Hawthorn Books. Hawthorn bought the project, offered me a contract, which I signed, and paid me money which I had spent in advance. Since it is a known fact that people sue people for breaking contracts, I had no alternative but to write the book—especially since I couldn't give Hawthorn back its money. I turned out to be rather happy about the whole thing for I was invaluably assisted in the writing of this by my editors and by publisher Fred Kerner.

The tantalizing thought persists that, if I had really done a research paper for freshman English, I might not have had to write this book many years later. Nevertheless, I cannot resist thanking all of those who refused to let me get away with a "snap." As for those performers who were so very good to me, I hope this work in some way expresses my appreciation for the hope and encouragement they gave me when I needed both so very badly.

One note in conclusion: The history incorporated in these essays has been researched thoroughly and authenticated, and this is rare in other volumes about the Negro in the theatre for a very good reason: Many, many records have been buried in old trunks, attics and cellars. In addition, white historians in the past paid little or no attention to the Negro theatre artist. He was always a "neophyte," someone with promise who had not quite fulfilled himself. This resulted in conflicting dates and interpretations of theatrical events. The most blatant example of this was when a downtown daily wrote about *Bandanna Land* in 1908 and interpreted its setting, cast and meaning contrary to a report about the same performance by the critic from the *New York Age*. Then, there is an interesting book which describes the founding of the Negro Playwrights Company and mentions that playwright Owen Dodson had demonstrated his ability previously while serving at the Great Lakes Naval Training Station. The only thing wrong with all of that is Mr. Dodson was at Great Lakes during World

War II and the Negro Playwrights Company was organized before we entered the war.

While the history recorded here is accurate and factual, the thoughts, feelings and opinions expressed in these twelve essays are mine and I am accountable for them.

I approached this work from the point of view of the professional New York theatre, and this necessarily limits it. The wonderful contributions of the so-called tributary theatre are, of necessity, overlooked—which is a commentary on the professional theatre. I am reminded of Dr. Randolph Edmonds, currently chairman of the Drama Department of Florida A. and M. University. He has written forty-nine meritorious plays, all known to me from reading. It has been New York's misfortune to rarely see them.

A vital theatre group—the Free Southern Theatre—is also outside my experience; yet its work in bringing living theatre to Southern Negroes certainly deserves mentioning. Similarly the Negro's contribution to the films and to television is virtually overlooked. The whole area of show business, vaudeville and night club entertainment has of necessity been neglected here. However, if this volume stimulates another author to plow into these rich fields, I shall be extremely grateful—and feel much less guilty.

The saddest fact, however, is that, in spite of my efforts, I shall find that I left out someone—someone very important whose contributions deserve to be noted. For this I apologize. For this I can only say that black drama is like the night, filled with a million stars. Some of them may not be seen too clearly on any one night, but the night is as old as the earth, and it comes again and again. And the stars continue to shine—even those that are unseen.

Loften Mitchell
New York City

## Part One

## THE DAY BEFORE YESTERDAY

*I stood in the garden and cried*
*As I looked down on the flowers that would not grow.*
*I bent over and tried to pull the soil around one,*
*And the bush toppled.*
*It had no foundation because I, its planter,*
*Had not dug deep enough into the soil.*

# Chapter I

## *Of New York City in the Seventeenth and Eighteenth Centuries: Deliberate Distortion of an Image*

The Harlem of the nineteen-twenties was the scene of my youth. To this land north of 110th Street came Southern Negroes who fled from physical lynchings, West Indians who fled from economic lynchings and Northern Negroes who sought to escape the brutality they faced in Lower Manhattan. They brought with them their religiosity, their folkways and their dogged determination. They created in Harlem a small town where everyone knew everyone else. A youngster's misbehavior in any home earned him a beating there *plus* one when he got home. The cooking of chitterlings brought a curious neighbor to our door: "Mrs. Mitchell, you cooking chitterlings? . . . I thought you might need a little cornbread to go with them." A moment later a West Indian neighbor appeared with peas and rice. Another neighbor followed with homemade wine. What started as a family supper became a building party.

In this small-town atmosphere few people locked their doors. Those who did often found themselves locked outside with their keys inside. In the latter part of the decade we youngsters earned many nickels by climbing through open windows, opening doors and letting neighbors into their apartments. In fact, doing this became something of a status symbol: You were getting to be a big boy if you were called on to perform this service.

The first time I achieved status was when I stood on my father's shoulders, opened a woman's ground-floor window, climbed through and admitted her to her apartment. I rushed into the street, clutching the nickel she gave me. I shouted to my playmates: "Hey, you guys! See what I did!"

My father called to me, "Wait, boy! Take your time before you pass yourself! You better say, 'See what *we* did!' You stood on my shoulders—remember?"

I heard these words many times. I hear them now when people speak of the "New Negro," implying, of course, that it was all right to be unjust to the "Old Negro" for 346 years, whereas in this era of rapid communication, it is politically unwise to condone racial atrocities. I heard these words again when I researched the history of the Negro in the American theatre.

"You stood on my shoulders." And white American history hides the shoulders of slave insurrectionist Harriet Tubman, Sojourner Truth, Frederick Douglass, W. E. B. DuBois, Carter G. Woodson and others on which we stand. Our theatre fails to popularize their contributions, just as it failed James Hewlett, Ira Aldridge, Bert Williams, Florence Mills and Bill Robinson while singing of Booth, Cantor, Jolson and Ziegfeld. The theatre on this continent has been guilty not only of the double standard but of subverting the very concept of a great art form.

Theatre is discussed here in its broadest sense, in terms of the institution itself. Its beginning more than six thousand years ago was in ancient Egypt, on the banks of the Nile. One need only note the Sphinx' Negroid features to determine the race of the ancient Egyptians. For those who need further documentation, Herodotus—called by the Roman orator Cicero, the "Father of History"—wrote in his Book Two, Chapter 57, that the people of Egypt were black. His Book Two, Chapter 104, notes the people were "black and wooly-haired." Herodotus lived from approximately 484 to 425 B.C.

Since its founding the theatre has mirrored the life, customs, mores and habits of peoples; it has recorded human endeavor. Its purpose is to entertain and instruct; morals and customs have actually been changed as a result of religious, social and human implications in the theatre.

This institution has never been the sole property of any one group. It has been found among American Indians, South Sea Islanders, Australian aborigines, Central Africans, Greeks and Romans. A people's theatre, in short, is the living expression of that people, inextricably and inseparably intertwined with their present and past history.

In America the theatre has reflected the society which has stood on the Negro's shoulders, yet failed to acknowledge this. And these shoulders were strong ones.

Theatre in America was virtually nonexistent until the middle of the eighteenth century. Prior to that time the New World was being discovered, developed and violently disputed. This New World was a harsh, vast wilderness. Forty-four of the Pilgrim Fathers died their first winter in America.

The first white men needed help to perform the heavy labor required to develop this continent. Forests had to be felled, roads and cities built, crops planted. The Thirty Years' War and other senseless conflicts had depleted Europe's manpower. To develop the New World the Europeans had but one place to turn for labor. That place was Africa.

Turn to it the Europeans did, and they wrote in blood that savage crime known as chattel slavery. They dumped chained black Africans into slave ship holds, transplanted them from the dark beauty of their motherland and denied them their family ties, traditions and cultural continuity. Negroes were sold into both Southern and Northern areas of the New World.

Though black people had been in the New World from the time—or even before—it was discovered by western Europe, no one knows exactly when they reached New York City. It is recorded, however, that in 1626—when New York City was a Dutch outpost known as New Amsterdam—eleven African slaves were imported. These men were assigned living quarters on the fringe of what is now the Bowery. The eleven Africans built a wagon road to the upper part of the settlement—to a place called "Haarlem." Eighteen years later these Africans, with the support of rank and file colonists, petitioned the Dutch for freedom, received it, then settled in a swampland which they built into a prosperous community. That community is today known as Greenwich Village.

Race relations were relatively cordial in New Amsterdam. Color discrimination was practically nonexistent. Both races attended the same churches, drank in the same taverns and were buried in Trinity Church or St. Mark's cemeteries. Discrimination was in terms of class and caste. Even slavery in seventeenth-century New York was "integrated," since white slaves existed as well as black ones.

Black men were artisans, craftsmen, executioners; and many well-to-do Negroes owned slaves. Prominent Negroes of the times included Domingo Antony, who owned land on Canal Street; Catalina Antony, who owned land on what is now Pell Street; Annie D'Angelo, who owned the site of the original Madison Square Garden; Solomon Pieters, who owned thirty acres at 23rd Street and Fifth Avenue where the Flatiron Building now stands. Negroes owned, too, much of the land around what is now Astor Place, City Hall Park and the Woolworth Building.

Then—the British came. They seized New Amsterdam from the Dutch, named it New York, and instituted chattel slavery. Rigid slave codes were enforced during the remainder of the century. Color discrimination became a reality, and the rights of man were denied black people. In 1682 an edict was passed, stating that Negroes could no longer be buried in Trinity Cemetery. Land owned by Negroes was willed to the British Crown. The manumission of slaves became increasingly difficult.

Slave uprisings flared. Negroes—often assisted by Indians and poor white semislaves and slaves—set fire to any and every place. Fire was their chief weapon, and it was during this period that the New York City Fire Department came into existence. Though Negroes, Indians and poor whites were often burned at the stake, they struck repeatedly, burning the city to the ground. During the remainder of the century the British passed many restrictive laws, and the oppressed retaliated with fire, sometimes burning as many as three homes nightly.

This struggle continued into the eighteenth century. On April 7, 1712, a fierce African people, the Coromantees, seized weapons and went about the city setting fires and killing whites as they raced from their homes. White semislaves and slaves readily assisted Negroes, for they too were cruelly treated and sold on the auction block at Wall Street's slavemarket.

Slavemasters justifiably trembled with fear because there were only 880 New York families then and each had one to five slaves. In 1741 an African named Caesar led a slave uprising. That year, too, brought the discovery of the Great Negro Plot—a plot to set fire to the entire city and massacre all the whites. Four of the plotters were white people and they were hanged. Fourteen Negroes were burned alive, eighteen hanged and seventy-one shipped to the West Indies. The city proclaimed September 24 of that year as a day of thanksgiving for its narrow escape. But the firing of homes continued, and the next year another plot was discovered.

By this time, the local authorities, if they dared sleep in their homes at all, were having nightmares. The British knew they needed the Africans, but they also knew by then that Africans were neither submissive nor ignorant; nor were they the beasts that white rulers had so desperately attempted to label them. The ruling whites noted, too, the increasing sympathy and support flowing from poor whites toward the blacks. The authorities realized there was only one step left—the christianization and the education of the Africans.

If the times seemed to be filled with excitement, the American theatre did not reflect it. *Cato* by Joseph Addison was one of the earliest plays to be shown to white America in the year 1749. On April 27, 1767, *The Prince of Parthia*, said by many to be the first American play, was shown. The Negro as subject matter was introduced to the American theatre in 1769. This was in *The Padlock*, a comedy that had a West Indian slave named Mungo, who was a profane clown of little authenticity. Lewis Hallam, who supposedly sought realism in the American drama, played this role. In the words of that eminent author, Sterling Brown, "Hallam fathered a long line of comic Negroes in the drama."

*Candidates*, a play probably written before the American Revolution, had minor Negro characters. But it was John Leacock's *The Fall of British Tyranny* that projected Negroes in roles commensurate with their status in the New World.

*The Fall of British Tyranny*, which appeared in 1776, was the first American drama to take advantage of the turmoil that had existed in the New World during the period when it was being settled. It took into account, too, the difficulties Americans were having with the ruling British. In the course of this play Negro slaves agreed to kill their masters when freed. And this is exactly what happened offstage as well as onstage.

When the American Revolution began, it was a Negro named Crispus Attucks who became the first to fall in the Boston Massacre. Two Negroes, Peter Salem and Salem Poor, distinguished themselves during the early days of the Revolution. Throughout the early part of the Revolution, Negroes and whites fought side by side. One historian noted: "It looked as though Ethiopia had come to the rescue."

Color prejudice—that phenomenon which, since its inception, has always threatened America's stability—almost destroyed the country before it started. When the provincial forces were incorporated into the Continental Army, it became obvious to white masters that black slaves could not be used to fight for the freedom of white men. In November, 1775, all colored men were discharged from the army. It is said that the British nearly lost the war at that moment, for they celebrated, riotously, laughing at the way Americans had permitted their prejudices to trap them. Lord Dunsmore, British royal governor of New York and Virginia, immediately promised freedom and equality to all Negroes who joined him. And Negroes flocked to do so. Thousands joined up at Norfolk. Thousands more fled from their masters in South Carolina. Large numbers joined Lord Cornwallis—including some of George Washington's own slaves. The British armed them, and these Negroes harassed their masters, slaughtering them in their beds. They raided Savannah. In the Bronx a garrison of black men, known as the Negro Fort, held back their white masters. Some black men joined the Royal Navy. Some became pilots and one, Mungo, piloted the *Experiment* with fifty guns through Hell Gate into New York harbor, where he reinforced the British fleet.

Americans wept and wailed that the British had started a "race war." And John Leacock drew from this dilemma the material that was to treat the American Negro in the true light of his times. His play, *The Fall of British Tyranny*, looms as a parallel to those plays of the Greeks and Romans when the theatre dealt with contemporary ideas, thoughts and morals. And it is significant that, at the beginning of this nation's history, it did not want to hear these truths, in theatre or out of it.

Not too long after *The Fall of British Tyranny*, black men were welcomed back into the American army because George Washington realized that success of the war depended upon which side armed Negroes fastest. Five thousand black Americans fought in the Revolution on the American side. There were women patriots as well as men. Phoebe Fraunces, daughter of a New York West Indian Negro restaurateur, saved Washington's life by telling him a traitor had poisoned some peas intended for the General. In addition, Haitian Negroes played a prominent role in the war.

Yet, despite the historic role played by black people in America's war for freedom, the theatre was already engaged in efforts to dehumanize them. In 1786 the play *Robinson Crusoe and Harlequin Friday* appeared on the stages of America. The so-called Negro dialect is really an imitation of Daniel Defoe's pidgin-English much more than it is actual Negro speech.

In 1792 the play *The Yorker's Stratagem* was shown. This dealt with the marriage between a white New Yorker and a West Indian mulatto. But this was followed in 1795 by Murdock's *The Triumph of Love*, which introduced a shuffling, cackling, allegedly comic Negro servant. *The Politicians* in 1797 continued this stereotype. The course was therefore established—the course that was to lead the black man to be represented on the American stage as something to be ridiculed and a creature to be denied human status.

One can easily rationalize the dawn of this stereotype and declare that theatre people of America's early years were unsophisticated and often "lower class." But it is impossible and inconceivable that anyone who lived through the period described in these pages—who knew of Crispus Attucks and the role played by black soldiers in the American Revolution—could draw such Negro stereotypes without being deliberate. It was no accident then, and it is no accident now, that the stereotypes exist at the same time Negroes are prominently engaged in American wars.

White America saw what had happened to it during the Revolution. It saw its dependency upon the Negro, and it saw that the Negro had helped save this nation for all time. It saw, too, that this black man was a powerful force to be reckoned with, and this force had to be vitiated at all costs. And so what happened in the eighteenth century had a twofold purpose: a moral justification for continuing to enslave Negroes, and the destruction of these proud black people by making them beggars both inside and outside the American drama. It is the results of these deeds, written in infamy, that America struggles with today. And—though it may try to escape into Viet Nam, or even to the moon—that Day of Reckoning must be faced squarely or the New World shall grow old within a decade and die long before its time!

# Chapter II

## *Of the Nineteenth Century and the Rise of Minstrelsy*

The struggle of America today is the struggle for the survival of hope. Hope has been one of the cornerstones of the American Negro's existence. In his songs, his speech and his actions he has been the most avid seeker of the American dream. The question we face now in the midst of national and international despair is: At what point will America's most loyal citizen give up hope and turn his back upon the dream? What will happen when hope exists no longer, when the black man allies himself with the virulent waters of the stagnant, polluted mainstream?

On 130th Street in New York, between Lenox and Seventh Avenues, there lives a woman who personifies the hope of black people—Mrs. Alice Payton Brown, a short, thin woman who celebrated her 113th birthday on November 17, 1965. "Mother" Brown, as she is known in Harlem, was born a slave on the plantation owned by one Sam Holloman in Lexington, Virginia. I have known her for many years, and so has all Harlem. She walks the streets with her cane tapping the concrete, rhythmically, announcing her presence. While walking the streets with her, I have seen teen-agers who were standing on the corner cursing, suddenly stop and tip their hats as she walked by. I have seen winos hide their bottles when they feel her appearance. And I have seen the community's leading personalities say hello and bow to her.

Mother Brown's activities are legendary. On Sundays she is found at Friendship Baptist Church, where she serves as chief usher. On Mondays she takes flowers to hospitalized parishioners. On Tuesdays she appears at the Red Shield Day Center, where she participates in the Senior Citizens' Drama group. On Wednesdays she performs household chores, and Thursdays she is again at the Red Shield Day Center. Her Fridays are spent doing housework, and on Saturdays she meets with her church group and prepares for Sundays. In the spring and summer she tends a garden, which is in her backyard. She is mentally alert, blunt, determined, deeply religious and amazingly independent. Once I suggested that she might need some type of housekeeping service. I pointed out that any number of community agencies might supply this service. She looked directly into my face and said, "No, thank you."

"Oh, it won't cost you a penny," I said. "I'm sure of that."

"Ain't worried about no cost," she said. "Thank you just the same."

"Now, look," I said. "Maybe I didn't make myself clear—"

"Young man," she said, "I know every word you said. You said that 'cause of my age, I can get somebody to do my washing and cleaning and shopping. And I said no, 'cause Alice Brown ain't having nobody to do her work for her."

I was puzzled and I looked it.

"That's what's kept me on this earth so long," Mother Brown said. "That and God. All this exercise I get, picking up things and using my mind, keep me going. Ain't good for a body to lay up on the stool-of-do-nothing. Laziness has put more folks in the ground than you can keep count of. Some mornings I lay in bed and the devil tells me: 'You too tired to get up and go. You oughta just lay here a bit longer.' Well, I push him away and I get up and still go."

Life with Mother Brown has remained a series of amazing events. The day before her 108th birthday, I arrived at my office and found the elevator had broken down. My staff and I trudged to the fifth floor, blowing hard. We flopped into our chairs, worn out. Eventually, we heard the tap, tap, tap of a cane. Mother Brown had walked up five flights; she stepped into my office, took two deep breaths, then sat down to talk with me.

At the Salvation Army camp during the summer of 1964, the authorities sought the identity of the group that was leading Mother Brown up into the hills each morning. The result of that probe showed that Mother Brown was the ringleader. She took the group into the hills each morning to look at God's work and to offer prayers.

One cloudy afternoon I met her on 124th Street, bound for home. "It's going to rain," I said, solicitously. "Don't you want someone to walk with you?"

"I got someone to walk with me," she said, positively, starting to walk away.

"Who?" I asked.

"Jesus!" she flung back over her shoulder. And she turned the corner, her cane emphatically tapping the concrete.

Mother Brown has repeatedly described her days during slavery as being terrible, but she never ceased to hope she would be free. Her mother was the house cook, and she stole food from the table and brought it to the slaves' cabins.

"They made us like animals," she said. "Sometimes when old man Sam and his family had finished eating, we slaves would sneak into the house and just about knock one another down, snatching the crumbs from the table." Of slavery she added, "We was just dirt, just dirt. When colored folks died, they dragged 'em off to a corner of the plantation and dumped 'em in the ground." Then she broke into laughter: "And don't you know the biggest, sweetest strawberries you ever saw grew right on top of them dead colored folks' heads!"

One thing Mother Brown had made clear repeatedly: This was a cruel era in America's history. Whites did not simply mistreat blacks. They mistreated each other. The slavemaster's daughter lay dying of tuberculosis, and the master sent an undertaker into the bedroom to measure the daughter's body for a casket!

It was an era of hope, however, of eternal hope. At the age of fourteen Mother Brown was freed. With her mother she moved into the town of Lexington. There she did housework and saved enough money to leave for New York City. She left the South at the age of fifteen and never returned.

She rode the train to Hoboken, where she was met by a Negro who showed her to the New York ferry. She crossed the Hudson River on that ferry and was met there by another Negro who told her of a home, operated by the Quakers, on 30th Street. At this home Negro girls were fed and lodged until they found work. The problem wasn't getting work. It was getting paid for working. Numerous families hired Negro women, had them work in service and then, just before pay day, fired them. These women were then turned out, penniless, and they had to return to the house on 30th Street.

Mother Brown worked as a domestic, then later married and had three children. She has outlived her husband and her children, as well as her friends from her youth. But she trudges on, without complaining.

"I'm doing fine," she said. "Really making up for them bad

days. If I'd a let the devil talk me into giving up hope a long time ago, I wouldn't be around here now, enjoying these days."

Hope, eternal hope, that so characterizes Mother Brown's existence has been one of the strong motivating forces for all black people. During the slave era they cried out in spirituals for deliverance, longing to cross that Deep River over into the campground. A band of angels, they hoped, were coming for to carry them home. Freedom was always in sight and the shore always seen, though sometimes dimly. Adversity was a temporary thing, for my Lord delivered Daniel, why not every man? And this hope was sustained because Negroes invariably met some good white people who were genuinely interested in their welfare.

Nineteenth-century America, however, generally did little to sustain that hope. It had burned brightly in the black man's heart throughout the latter part of the eighteenth century when, in that Age of Enlightenment, Voltaire, Rousseau and Paine advocated the rights of man. And Americans declared that all men are created equal, Frenchmen shouted for liberty, equality and fraternity, and Haitian slaves struck for their freedom.

This hope blinded many people to the realization that America's founding fathers had no intention of extending the rights of man to either the poor black or the poor white. Rich whites demanded that one own property in order to vote. Since no modification was made for whites without property, certainly none could be made for Negroes, who were considered "three-fifths human."

The American Revolution was primarily a reform movement, a battle for control, not one for liberty and equality. It led directly to the establishment on this continent of the rule of white Anglo-Saxon Protestant property-holders. The founding fathers sought independence to perpetuate a slave system without sharing profits or paying taxes to a king. This desire led to the development in America of a direction for history, art, religion, politics and music— a direction bent on morally justifying a slave society by creating attitudes and myths that Negroes were "subhuman." It had its counterpart, too, in creating a dream among poor white people that they might one day be able to own slaves and be rich like the big planters. The poor white was fed race prejudice instead of bread. And he lived a barren life where he stared in awe at the rich white, bowed to him in spirit and in fact. Like the poor Negro,

*Bert Williams, as he appeared in the early years of this century.*
Brown Brothers

the poor white dreamed the long dream that the ruling oligarchy would never allow to become a reality for either group. But optimism and hope burned in their hearts and, as long as the dream was in view, neither turned from it. Indeed, they continued to go out and die for it.

This hope, this dream, was the basis for the formation of the African Grove Theatre in the year 1820. This group, established at Bleecker and Grove Streets in New York City, was spearheaded by James Hewlett, a West Indian Negro. The company performed Shakespearean dramas before mixed audiences as early as 1821.

James Hewlett was the first of the Negro tragedians. He was a many-talented man, and he sang and recited in hotels and at teas. One Mr. Brown, a former steward, invited Mr. Hewlett to recite at backyard parties. These parties attracted a large number of whites as well as free Negroes. Hewlett's artistry led directly to his founding the African Company.

Hewlett had been greatly influenced by the Park Theatre, one of America's oldest institutions. This theatre segregated Negroes, and it was from its gallery that Hewlett and Ira Aldridge watched white companies perform onstage.

The Park Theatre attracted many English actors. And it should be noted that their reception was not always polite. We have the words of Washington Irving to document the behavior of audiences. Irving speaks of sitting in the orchestra, watching a play in progress, then suddenly seeing something hurled from the balcony. He speaks, too, of the hoots, the catcalls and the many interruptions faced by performers.

This was an era of brutality, of bad manners and little respect for the rights of people, black or white. The aristocracy wanted to be divorced from the poor whites, and the poor whites resented it. They argued that this was a land where all men were supposed to be equal. Why, then, were some to "have" and others to "have not"? These questions haunted the minds of poor whites, who resented being treated like Negroes.

Hewlett and his African Company met a hostile press. Open references to the company's physical features, its elocution and its mannerisms fill the newspapers of that era. Apparently, Shakespeare's *Richard III* was a company favorite, repeatedly decried by the press. The company also had difficulty with white hoodlums who visited and jeered during showings. This problem became so acute that the management posted a sign stating that whites would have to be seated in the rear of the theatre because they did not know "how to behave themselves at entertainment designed for ladies and gentlemen of colour."

The police joined the attacks on the African Company. They raided the place repeatedly, interrupted performances and dragged actors off to jail. Sometimes the actors were reciting their lines as they were being carried away. And, upon the actors' release from jail, they returned and offered another performance.

What the police could not do was done by white hoodlums. They wrecked the African Theatre. This tore at the heart of James Hewlett, leaving a scar that was to make the great Ira Aldridge in later years refer to him as "Poor Jim."

Mr. Aldridge was the second of the Negro tragedians. With the destruction of the African Company, he felt there was little opportunity for a black actor on these shores. He sailed for England in 1824 and he was later acclaimed by European royalty. It is a comment on the era in which he lived that, while he was sailing for England, white British actors were sailing for America.

It is also worth noting that one year before Aldridge's sailing, white actor Edwin Forrest played the so-called plantation Negro on American stages. In 1828 another white performer, Thomas Dartmouth Rice, created the character "Jim Crow."

While these stereotypes dominated the American stage, Ira Aldridge played throughout Europe. He was particularly hailed for his Othello, his Macbeth, Lear and Shylock. Today his chair sits in the fourth row of the stalls at the Shakespearean Memorial Theatre, Stratford-on-Avon. Though he may be unknown to many white Americans, his black brothers know of him. James Weldon Johnson and a group of black Americans are responsible for installing the chair and its bronze plate. And there have been numerous theatre groups, societies and other organizations named in his honor. Authors Mildred Stock and Herbert Marshall have written a noteworthy book about him, entitled *Ira Aldridge, Negro Tragedian.*

The death of the African Company, the flight of Aldridge, his death on alien soil, and the present-day ignorance of Aldridge's

importance, all offer blatant evidence of reactionary forces successfully forcing a culture into oblivion. The deed was done—the deed
which was written in human blood, and this blood was to spill
over the years into the streets of Montgomery and Jackson and
Harlem. This deed educated America away from the Negro and
the Negro away from himself. This deed plunged the American
theatre into a dark age, from which it looked toward a Renaissance
that was to come only mechanically, never creatively. This deed
was to place the Negro in the position of fighting for his humanity,
of "proving" himself to himself and to the world. The blood from
this deed continues to flow from the knives wielded by cruel men
who are yet unable to face the fact that they are dealing with
human beings who demand truth where it has been denied and
justice where it has been made a mockery.

An art form is not always ahead of history, but a review of the
drama during the early nineteenth century indicates that it was
certainly assisting in undermining the Negro as a human being.
As early as 1802 a new tradition was hardening in America. Songs
in alleged Negro dialect were interspersed in A New Way to Win
Hearts, The Battle of Lake Champlain (1815) and Tom and
Jerry. In Tom and Jerry a spot is found for gay singing and dancing,
even in a Charleston slave market. In 1823—not too long after the
destruction of the African Company—Edwin Forrest's black-faced
acting in The Tailor in Distress was praised as "the first realistic
representation of the plantation Negro." Finding no white actress
willing to blacken her face to play opposite him, Forrest had to
hire an old Negro washerwoman.

"This squeamishness of white actresses did not last very long,"
writes Sterling Brown in his The Negro in the American Theatre
(Oxford Companion). "In the 1820's George Nichols popularized
'Zip Coon' and other songs and dances learned from Negroes in
the Mississippi Delta. George Washington Dixon impersonated
Negroes in songs like 'Coal Black Rose,' 'Long Tailed Blue,' and
in Negro burlettas. It became a rule to interpolate Negro songs in
theatre programs, whether farce or tragedy; they were sung by
circus clowns, sometimes from the backs of cantering audiences."

One of the first white performers to take advantage of the Negro
was Thomas "Daddy" Rice. In 1828, somewhere along the Ohio

River, Rice began to imitate the singing and shuffling of a Negro hostler. His skit was received with enthusiasm. In 1833 Rice expanded this act and included a four-year-old burnt-cork urchin whom he dumped from a bag onto the stage. This was Joseph Jefferson III, who proceeded to imitate Rice's dancing. Rice wove a number of these songs together into what he called *Bone Squash*, and he labeled it the "first Ethiopian opera."

Rice's popularity perpetuated further imitations of his work throughout the eighteen-thirties. P. T. Barnum, the circus magnate, exhibited Ethiopian breakdowns (a breakdown is a noisy, rapid, shuffling dance). The American Museum offered the Ethiopian Comic Statues, and Jim Crow, Esquire on Horseback, was a popular circus act. In 1843 Daniel Emmett, composer of *Dixie*, brought his Virginia Minstrels to the New York stage. These were white men with faces blackened. They wore gala costumes; they performed on the fiddle, banjo, bones and tambourine, telling jokes and ending with a general breakdown. And the great era of the minstrels was officially launched.

Both the minstrels and the spirituals were to have long-range effects on the Negro in American life. It is well that we pause here to discuss their origins.

It must be remembered that the African slave was shorn of his cultural heritage, his family ties, traditions and language. Mother Brown, the ex-slave, remarked numerous times that slaves were beaten for trying to teach young black children the African language. Mrs. Brown's own mother knew the language but dared not teach it to her daughter.

The Negro, therefore, had to learn a new language. Into this he poured the rhythms and images of his Africa. What developed then was an entirely new language, spoken in a drawl, but with a decided, rhythmic pattern. It was a pattern with both a musical and a vocal counterpart. Negro spirituals had a decided Africanesque influence. "I'm Gonna Tell God All My Troubles When I Get Home" has been documented by composer Lawrence Brown as an African work song made into a spiritual.

The Negro spirituals were more than songs of worship. They were protest-songs and signals—signals that the Underground Railroad was running tonight or that slaves could steal away to freedom. These spirituals, like Negro speech generally, had a "signifying" pattern—a sly one that said one thing to Negroes and another to their oppressors. In the heat of the day the slavemaster would sit on his veranda, drinking his mint julep and listening to his slaves, singing as they worked in the fields:

> *Steal away, steal away, steal away to Jesus,*
> *Steal away, steal away, steal away home,*
> *I ain't got long to stay here!*

Another group of slaves sang back:

> *Swing low, sweet chariot,*
> *Coming for to carry me home.*
> *I looked over Jordan and what did I see,*
> *Coming for to carry me home,*
> *A band of angels coming after me,*
> *Coming for to carry me home!*

Old master would smile at the religiosity of his slaves. What he didn't know is that one group of slaves was telling the other that the Underground Railroad was working that night. Many of those singing slaves didn't have long to stay there!

The Old Testament influenced Negro speech and song. The enslavement of the Hebrews was a point of identification in such Spirituals as "Go Down Moses":

> *When Israel was in Egypt land,*
> *Let my people go!*
> *Oppressed so hard they could not stand!*
> *Let my people go!*
> *Go down, Moses, 'way down in Egypt land,*
> *Tell old Pharaoh to let my people go!*

Here we see not only the influence of the early Hebrews, but the beginning of a decidedly American speech pattern. Israel is spoken of in this song as both a group and a person. We see the influence, too, of the African call and answer. One group sings of Israel in Egypt land, and the answerer calls, "Let my people go!" We see, too, the importance to the Negro of standing up, of being a man, for here he is oppressed so hard he cannot stand. We hear what was then a new expression, " 'way down," which means a far-off place, a bad place, specifically, hell. It should be noted, too, that we do not just tell Pharaoh; we tell "old" Pharaoh. "Old" here is used in the same vein as when we speak of Old Master, Old Mister Charlie, all used contemptuously.

The river runs deep throughout black imagery; this river is the Jordan. Negroes constantly sang and spoke of that land beyond the river, that deep river they wanted to cross over into the campground. The river and the sun—these figures of speech are in the writings of most modern black writers. Langston Hughes has the Negro speak of rivers. His soul has grown deep like the rivers. In my play, Negroes sing of "a land beyond the river" that we call the sweet forever. Lorraine Hansberry spoke of a raisin in the sun. South African-born Peter Abrahams calls himself a child of the sun. John Oliver Killens speaks of the southern sun, and James Baldwin of the absence of sunlight in the darkness of the ghetto.

These figures of speech are found in song, too. W. C. Handy hates "to see that evening sun go down" in his "St. Louis Blues." The early blues songs—the outgrowth of personal frustrations— are filled with references to darkness. And the word "blue" has made its way into the American majority language.

In the West Indies, Irish and Scotch brogues joined the Cockney dialect and mingled with the African tongue. A decided lilt was given to the speech of the West Indian Negro. This speech pattern, which is more British than the Southern Negro's, rose and fell with remarkable inflections. It was also a "signifying" speech, less bawdy and boisterous than the American Negro's, but equally sly and derogatory in speaking of the oppressors. The humor closely resembles that of the African. The West Indian speaks of a sly "mongoose," of "gwyne home 'cause I got the West Indian blues." In this speech and song pattern we hear of the "noonday sun," of "cutting cane with a bitter sweat to sweeten my tea in the morning." This is the basis of the calypso, the improvised song or poem, satiric in origin, created spontaneously as the West Indian decried his oppressors.

These speech patterns and usages—Southern Negro and West Indian—merged in the Harlem of the nineteen-twenties, and there developed a new language which was to influence significantly the entire American speech pattern and the theatre itself, as we shall see later.

The Southern Negro speech pattern and song, or interpolations of these, were used throughout the minstrel shows. The exact date of the origin of minstrels is unknown. There is a clue, however, in a water color, painted about 1790, known as "The Old Plant." This work, by an unknown painter, hangs now in the Ludwell-Paradine House in Williamsburg, Virginia. The painting shows a group of Negroes near a cabin, watching a banjo player, a drummer and dancers. This painting, in addition to those of William S. Mount, documents the Negro's creation of minstrelsy as sometime in the eighteenth century. In many circles it is argued that this form was created a few years after the arrival of slaves at Jamestown.

The same slavemaster who, in the afternoon, sat on his veranda listening to his slaves sing spirituals, sat in the evenings, listening to them singing, playing the banjo, dancing and telling jokes. He thought they were happy souls. He didn't know that they were, to use the vernacular, "telling it like it is."

An example of minstrelsy's thrust is included in the play *Star of the Morning.* Oliver, an elderly minstrel man, is talking to the leading characters, Bert Williams and his partner, George Walker. Oliver is about to leave and join the Touring Minstrels. Both Bert and George are impressed, but, as far as Oliver is concerned, it is just a job:

OLIVER: Ain't no success in going with Minstrels these days. Back there when I was a slave, though, it was. You know what minstrels was, boy? We did 'em on the plantation to poke fun at Old Master. We got that house Negro to stand up and say: "Gentlemen, be seated!" Then, we'd line up with Tams and Bones as the end men.

BERT: Tams and Bones?

OLIVER: That was the instruments they played. You think we could afford pianos?
   *(Remembering and reenacting)*
We used to take off on that house Negro 'cause he was the Master up and down.
   *(Imitating Tams)*
Tams would say: "Mistah Stafford, do darkies go to heaven?"
   *(Moves over, imitates Bones)*
Old Bones would say: "Yes, suh, Mistah Stafford. Do us darkies go to heaven?"
   *Moves back, imitates the house Negro)*

House Negro would say: "Now, why would you darkies be going to heaven? That's for white folks!"

*(Imitates Tams)*

Tams would say: "We just wanted to know who opens them Pearly Gates for white folks to get inside?"

*(All laugh.* OLIVER *becomes serious now)*

That's how it *was*. Them white folks come from up north and copied what we was doing. They made me a fool, and now I got to go out there and make money laughing at *me!*

Minstrelsy had a definite form. The first half of the performance had a group of at least seventeen men, all elaborately costumed, their faces blackened with burnt cork. These men sat in a half circle. At the center was the interlocutor, or master of ceremonies, a "straight man" who fed jokes to the comedians and was the butt of their replies. On the other side of the interlocutor were at least seven singers, dancers, monologuists or other featured performers. At the end of each line were the "end men," Mr. Bones and Tambo, so named for the instruments they played. The bones were used like castanets, and Tambo had a tambourine. Mr. Bones and Tambo were the leading comics.

A band was either in the pit or seated behind the performers. Each performance began with the interlocutor stating: "Gentlemen, be seated!" Ballads, comic songs, dialogue and dances followed in quick succession, and a "walk around" brought the first half to a close. The second half was the "olio." This was the less traditional form, more like later burlesque and vaudeville shows with sketches in which all the players were male.

"Though black-face minstrelsy started out with rudimentary realism, it soon degenerated into fantastic artificiality," Sterling Brown wrote in his essay, *The Negro in the American Theatre.* "It must be remembered that Ethiopian minstrelsy was white masquerade; Negro performers were not allowed to appear in it until after the Civil War; it was composed by whites, acted and sung by whites in burnt cork for white audiences. It succeeded in fixing one stereotype deeply in the American consciousness: the shiftless, lazy, improvident, loud-mouthed Negro, with kinky-hair and large lips, overaddicted to the eating of watermelon and chicken (almost always purloined), the drinking of gin, the shooting of dice and the twisting of language into ludicrous mal-formations. Life was a perennial joke or 'breakdown.' Black-face minstrelsy underestimated and misrepresented the American Negro in much the same way that the English drama treated the stage Irishman."

Only occasionally did minstrelsy involve a few sentimental plaints about the woes of slavery, even in the North. *Darling Nelly Gray* (1836) is a notable exception.

If the eighteenth century brought dreams of freedom to black people, the nineteenth burned these dreams in the smokestacks of the Industrial Revolution. The invention of the cotton gin and textile machinery created larger markets for cotton planters who, in turn, needed more land and more free labor. The number of slaves increased from 700,000 in George Washington's time to three million in 1850. Antislavery protests swelled and entered the theatre in the year 1831 when *The Gladiators* was produced. Although this work dealt with the uprising of slaves in ancient Rome, the author feared having his play produced in a slave state. His statement was that, in a slave state, he and his actors might be "rewarded with the penitentiary."

Outside the theatre the work of orator, writer and antislavery leader Frederick Douglass appeared. Born a Maryland slave around 1817, Mr. Douglass escaped to Massachusetts in 1838. In 1841 he became one of the speakers for the Massachusetts Anti-Slavery Society. Later he lectured in the British Isles for two years, and upon returning to this country in 1847, he bought his freedom. He founded the *North Star*, an abolitionist newspaper that fiercely attacked slavery.

The American stage and American fiction found full use of the antislavery theme during the eighteen-forties and -fifties. *The Captured Slave* and *The Branded Hand*, two abolitionist dramas, are known to have been written in 1845, but it is not known if they were produced. It was the appearance of *Uncle Tom's Cabin* in 1852 which created a sensation in terms of the antislavery theme. Six months after the publication of Harriet Beecher Stowe's novel, two adaptations were produced in New York City. Mrs. Stowe was opposed to the theatre on religious grounds, but she was unprotected by copyright and received no part of the huge profits made from the dramatization of her book. It was not until the fifth year of the play's amazing run that Mrs. Stowe attended a showing, and she did so incognito.

The work had many adaptations. Two appeared in Paris. In 1878 five London theatres presented the play concurrently. It has been America's most popular play, and from 1852 until 1931, it never left the boards. It has had notable revivals, among these George Abbott's *Sweet River* in 1936. It has also had influences in the modern theatre, like "The Small House of Uncle Thomas," which formed a significant part of *The King and I.*

George L. Aiken, adapter of the best-known version of *Uncle Tom's Cabin*, heightened the sentimentality and the melodrama. His treatment of the character Topsy lacked Mrs. Stowe's understanding, and it was, in fact, close to blackface minstrelsy. Eliza's crossing the ice was sheer theatrical sensationalism. And, over the years, the abolitionist edge to the play was dulled as the treatment moved toward melodrama and farce. Mrs. Stowe's second novel, *Dred*, had three adaptations—by C. W. Taylor, John Brougham and H. J. Conway—in 1856. While *Dred* had many good points as a novel, none of the dramatizations succeeded.

Despite their antislavery service, both *Uncle Tom's Cabin* and *Dred* helped further the stereotyping of the Negro in the American theatre. "More than the novel," says Sterling Brown, "the widely popular *Uncle Tom* plays have been too persuasive in supporting the generalizations that impish, light-fingered Topsy and the ideally forgiving and submissive Uncle Tom are 'typical Negroes,' and that it is only the mixed-blood Negroes who are, as a result of their biological inheritance, aggressive, intelligent and willing to fight for freedom."

*Uncle Tom's Cabin* is another example of the irony and the inconsistency of the Negro's role in American life. For one thing, its major character was based on a man named Josiah Benson, a minister, who escaped from slavery and took an active part in the Underground Railroad. He was in reality a militant, courageous man, but he became the prototype for Mrs. Stowe's leading character.

Mrs. Stowe was a good woman, deeply religious, but she could not understand—or did not want to understand—the aggressive, fighting Negro who hates much white-oriented thinking without hating all white people. She was not unlike many people who live today. And so the Reverend Mr. Benson became in print a submissive, all-forgiving loyal soul. And many abolitionists who were sincerely dedicated to destroying slavery preferred to believe this portrait.

History came full cycle. Negroes began to resent the character Uncle Tom, and his name became a source of contempt on the lips of black people. An "Uncle Tom," "Tom" or "Uncle" is the most inflammatory, insulting thing a black man can be called. In recent years there have been six court cases where Negroes have sued other Negroes for calling them "Uncle Tom"—and those who sued collected large sums for damages.

This characterization, this "Uncle Tom," was not only to inflame black people; it was to mislead white people completely in dealing with blacks. When the present Black Revolution began to rage, Negro ministers called for it to be nonviolent. Whites who had for so long seen what they believed to be submissive Negroes thought they could commit acts of violence without retaliation. They were in for many surprises, particularly in Clarendon County, South Carolina, Montgomery, Alabama, Birmingham, and Bogalusa, Louisiana. It is suggested here that, had the Southern whites really known the true character of black people and disbelieved the Uncle Tom concept, much of the present-day anguish and frustration might have been avoided.

The "tragic mulatto" became a stereotype in other abolitionist drama. In 1857 J. T. Trowbridge dramatized his novel, *Neighbor Jackwood*. In this work a beautiful octoroon escapes from Louisiana to Vermont. There she marries her Yankee benefactor. The revelation of Northern dislike for the Fugitive Slave Laws gives this play more reality and appeal than the dramatization warrants.

Negro author and antislavery agent William Wells Brown is credited with *Escape; or A Leap for Freedom*. This is reportedly the first known play by an American Negro. The work is not known to have been produced, but Mr. Brown gave readings of it in numerous places—readings that were warmly received. His comic scenes, unfortunately, are close to blackface minstrelsy, much more so than the author's personal slave experiences should have permitted. And his heroine is the octoroon beauty, the tragic mulatto.

In 1858 the Lincoln-Douglas debates stirred the nation into making slavery an issue. Playwright Dion Boucicault, called in many circles "potboiler par excellence," was not going to miss out on the topical nature of this. In 1859 he used the tragic mulatto as the central figure in his play *The Octoroon*. Boucicault obviously intended to write a typical work without offending North or South. He actually wrote two endings and his audience could take its choice. His heroine is Zoe, the octoroon, a tragic figure because she cannot marry the white man she loves. Zoe is a strange mixture of abjectness, of pride in her white blood and of forgiveness that equals Uncle Tom's. She is devoted to her dead white father who, incidentaliy, failed to guarantee her her freedom. The play brought Boucicault a great deal of money. It also brought a great deal of controversy.

When the work was revived more than one hundred years later by New York's Phoenix Theatre, wails of protest were heard from the lips of Negroes. The Phoenix actually held a conference devoted to discussing the merits of the play. Marc Connelly, author of *The Green Pastures* and self-appointed authority on the Negro in the drama, chastised those who objected to *The Octoroon*. He called many statements made by Negro theatre workers "the silliest things I've ever heard." The Phoenix Theatre went on to produce *The Octoroon* because it believed this was a part of the American drama, that "objectively, it should be produced for today's audiences." And the tragedy of today's theatre is that the Phoenix management never quite realized why it did not attract large Negro audiences in the future.

Had the Phoenix management cared to see, it would have known the Boucicault work brought Negroes countless insults by trying to convince audiences that it was a black man's white blood that made him intelligent—if he were considered intelligent. Black blood was painted as being "unclean." And *The Octoroon* was one of many plays that established the white beauty standard as dominant, irrefutable. The play was a disservice to whites who could not understand this was all a glorious lie, underscored again and again in the present century by such cinematic nonsense as *Imitation of Life* and such theatrical foolishness as *Mandingo*.

The concept of the tragic mulatto lingers today, and we see many whites flinch when the word "black" is used. Many of them quickly tell a tan-complexioned Negro: "You're not black." And the black man's reply to that is: "Not all white people are white. Some are blonde, brunette, swarthy-complexioned, olive-complexioned. By the same token, black people are fair-skinned, brown-skinned, black-skinned. What you do when you defensively look at me and say I'm not black is to snatch at my identity, to make black into a distasteful color. In other words, your white psychology is warping your thinking."

The tragic mulatto has brought pain to white society on yet another level. The society has failed to understand black men like Adam Clayton Powell, Malcolm X and Walter White. It has had to seek rationalization for their thinking, to attempt to paint them as people who are near-white, want to be white and, because they are outsiders, become militant. All of this is psychological hogwash because all any one of the three had to do was cross over the color line and pass, as many another American has done.

John Brown's historic raid on Harpers Ferry became the subject of J. C. Swayze's *Ossawatomie Brown* in the year 1859. Brown's Negro comrades were well represented and truthfully depicted on stage. They were neither the shuffling minstrels nor the forgiving Uncle Toms. They were men, fired with the desire to strike a blow for freedom.

The plays of the Civil War and the old South were generally vehicles wherein the Negro characters were either inconsequential or interchangeable. *The Guerillas* appeared in 1863, showing the faithful, loyal slave indignantly refusing freedom, which revealed to a Richmond audience its wish rather than a reality.

But this was the nineteenth century—the century of child labor and business expansion—the century that saw the Congress of Vienna attempt to restore the Divine Right of Kings. This century saw the bourgeoisie usurping power from the landowning aristocracy. This usurpation exploded into the American Civil War.

With that war's end came the Reconstruction era and its suggestion of real democracy for black and white alike. But an acquisitive, brutal frontier society demanded subservience and cheap labor. The pattern of the doublecross had already been established on this continent—first by the British when they instituted the color bar in early New York, then by the founding fathers when they ignored black people. Yet, despite these betrayals, the Negro remained loyal to this country. So—the Southern and Northern oligarchies in America married each other. Abetted by that drunken anti-Negro president, Andrew Johnson, the oligarchies conspired to put a badge on color and sell the Negro back to his oppressors.

W. E. B. DuBois in *Black Reconstruction* calls Andrew Johnson "the most pitiful character in American history." This poor white, in his youth, had hated the white ruling class, but because his prejudice prevented him from advocating the Negro's participation in land reform, Johnson turned from his early ideals and sold his soul to those who placed the Negro back in bondage. He went along with the program of pulling Federal forces from the South, which effectively sabotaged the Reconstruction and led to the long night of jimcrow and terror that still continues. This compromise with that which Johnson had so vehemently denounced led directly to his involvement with drink.

The compromise established America for what it is—a land peopled by a few aristocrats and those who want to become aristocrats. The latter stand eager for the former's good wishes and good graces. And these desires are so overwhelming that the would-be aristocrats sacrifice all burning desires in order to sit in parlors and cocktail lounges with the idle rich, drinking wines and liquors that block out early hopes and dreams long since dead.

The action of Andrew Johnson typifies the whole of bourgeois society. This group, composed of shop owners, factory owners and merchants, came into prominence during the Industrial Revolution. In this revolution serfs left the farms and settled in the cities. The industrial ruling group saw the opportunity to displace the farm owners and the planters, to take control of government, to institute changes beneficial to industrialization. But it saw too a group of people who represented the landed gentry, a group it had always wanted to emulate, and finally it settled for a "marriage" between the two—a marriage that was consummated in political circles. This marriage once again impeded the march of black people toward a measure of justice, liberty and freedom.

This marriage dictated that history books lie about the Negro and that the stage ridicule him. Legalized jimcrow encouraged lynch mobs to ride the Southern night. Since Negroes were seen as "not human," whites could strike them down and could attack their women and children. Some of America's status-seeking new immigrants sought to seek the favor of whites by joining in these attacks.

With this powerful offensive launched against black people, it is little wonder that the comic Negro appears in Edward Harrigan's *Mulligan* cycle of vaudeville sketches, sketches which deal with dialect-speaking Irishmen and Germans as well. Harrigan's *The Doyle Brothers* (1874) and *Pete* (1887) glorify the faithful old Negro servant. They were also unkind to the Irish and the German. This was an era when new white groups faced cruel distortions, too—an era that made many seek to be like the older Americans, to reach the least common denominator.

A notable exception to the caricatures of the day occurred in 1881 when Steele Mackaye's dramatization of Albion Tourgee's *A Fool's Errand* brought to the stage a sympathetic treatment of the newly freed Negro in a hostile Southland. But in 1882 the favorite tragic octoroon appeared again, this time in *The White Slave*, which rivaled *The Octoroon* in popularity. *For a Brother's Life* was shown in 1885, portraying Negro refugees from slavery in Union Army camps—a portrayal rarely seen since on American stages. Historically, it was the Negro slaves' exodus from the plantation that broke the South's economic back. And the Negro as soldier and sailor proved to be a decisive factor in bringing the South to defeat.

In 1892 Augustus Thomas' *Colonel Carter of Cartersville* emphasized the mutual affection between master and slave. The unconventional thing about this work was that a real Negro played the faithful servant. In 1893 the J. R. Grimer–Clay Greene play *The New South* documented the restless, uneasy side of life during slavery; James A. Herne portrayed Sampson, a Negro murderer. The octoroon was in vogue again in 1895, this time in *Captain Herne, U.S.A.* But a much more convincing octoroon reached the stage that same year when Frank Mayo offered his adaptation of Mark Twain's *Pudd'nhead Wilson*, an exposé of slavery. James A. Herne's play, *The Reverend Griffith Davenport*, was produced in 1899. It offered a soberly realistic view of slavery and its cruelties. In 1902 Winston Churchill's *The Crisis* described in vivid terms a slave auction.

But Thomas Dixon's *The Clansman* in 1906 reflected the prevailing attitudes of the day toward Negroes. This work, later filmed

as *The Birth of a Nation*, glorified the Ku Klux Klan and charac-
terized Negroes as brutes whose emancipation was a grave error.

Joseph S. Cotter, Sr., a Negro, wrote *Caleb, the Degenerate* in
the year 1906. This was an attempt to answer the Dixon work.
But the smearing attack is eternally more dramatic than any answer
—a fact known to any newspaperman who places the attacks on
the front page and the retractions in the midsection. And so Dixon's
smear outlasted and outreached Cotter's refutation.

In 1909 William Vaughn Moody portrayed the superstitious, religious fervor of Negro life and captured, too, its eloquence in *The
Faith Healer*. But it was the Edward Sheldon play *The Nigger* that
brought drama about the American Negro to searing heights.
Edward Sheldon is one of the most fascinating men the American
theatre has produced. He was a sincere, dedicated, intelligent, for-
ward-looking man. After *The Nigger*, he was to write other plays.
Particularly noteworthy are his *Romance* and his collaboration
with Charles MacArthur on *Lula Belle*. Although he was invalided
in his later years, those who knew him speak of him as a tower of
strength. They speak, too, of plays he helped others to write, plays
for which he refused to take credit.

In *The Nigger* Mr. Sheldon was sincere and angry, and he said
things the American theatre had never heard before. His play deals
with a man who is ostensibly white. This man advances to the
governorship of his state, then finds himself unable to help Negroes.
He confesses his race and pledges himself to the service of black
people. Throughout the play Mr. Sheldon added comments about
lynching, discrimination and miscegenation that created a sensation on the American stage. This sensation had other causes in
addition to the play's theme. The work appeared in 1910 when,
with the exception of Bert Williams, Negroes were not welcomed
in Broadway theatres as performers or patrons. This play about
and for Negroes was performed by an all-white cast. Harlem, then
becoming a black community, resented this; as a result, as we shall
see later, the first Harlem professional theatre companies came into
existence.

The year 1916 brought Michael Landman's *Pride of Race*, a
play with a miscegenation theme. The work proved to be less convincing, less boldly stated, and lacked the dramaturgy of Mr.
Sheldon's play.

Despite these works, the period of the 1880s and 1890s was primarily devoted to white projections of comic, stock characters in terms of Negro life. When the Reconstruction was sabotaged, the vote was taken away from the Negro. Jimcrow laws were introduced in Southern legislatures. The poor white was fed jimcrow instead of bread; he ate the crow and vomited it into the Negro's face. And he did this with the willing help of the American communications system!

Theatrically, the most significant development following the Civil War was the appearance of the Negro himself as an entertainer. He joined in the minstrel tradition; and in the words of James Weldon Johnson, he became a "caricature of a caricature" as he, too, blackened his face and imitated whites imitating Negroes.

Among the early Negro minstrel companies were Lew Johnson's Plantation Company, the Georgia Minstrels and the Colored Hamtown Singers. Famous Negro minstrel artists include Billy Kersands, Sam Lucas and James Bland, composer of "Carry Me Back to Old Virginny" and "In the Evening By the Moonlight." Charles Hicks, a Negro, organized the all-Negro Georgia Minstrels in 1865. He had trained musicians who actually played in concert halls. Hicks, however, had the usual racial difficulties in carrying his company through the Southland. Eventually, he permitted Charles Callender to take charge of the company. Later, the Frohmans became involved with this outfit. It was Gustav Frohman, incidentally, who originated the idea of Sam Lucas playing Uncle Tom in *Uncle Tom's Cabin*. And Mr. Lucas became the first Negro to play this role.

Minstrelsy was troublesome to Negroes. The inherent stereotypes have already been noted. True, it offered theatrical training to Negro performers. It left us vaudeville monologues, dance routines and the double forms of music—described by Isaac Goldberg as "music of the heels" and "music of the heart." Minstrelsy was also the first authentic American theatre form. But it was troublesome.

In the latter part of the nineteenth century a group of Negro theatrical pioneers sat down and plotted the deliberate destruction of the minstrel pattern. These men were Sam T. Jack, Bert Williams, George Walker, Jesse Shipp, Alex Rogers, S. H. Dudley,

Bob Cole, J. Rosamond Johnson and John W. Isham. And in destroying the minstrel pattern, these men were to help pave the way for the million-dollar musical pattern which today dominates the American theatre. What made these black men feel at this point in history that they could challenge an existing structure—a structure obviously rigged against them and of vital importance to the American elite? What made them feel they could earn recognition, a decent living, and win audiences to their sides when jim-crow barriers were being erected across the land? I asked **Mother Brown** this question.

"Hope!" she snapped, quickly. "I done told you before: If I'd a let the devil talk me into giving up hope a long time ago, I wouldn't be around here now, enjoying these days." Then, she mused: "Oh, yes. Lots of us hoped them boys into doing something. We got tired of sitting up in galleries and being buked and scorned. And when them boys started up their shows, we thought 'This is the Coming of the Lord!' "

The old woman's craggy features glowed. A smile creased her thin face as she recalled the moments of hope that had filled the hearts of the Negro in the cruel nineteenth century. And somehow as I looked at that face that had been beaten and bowed, I found myself believing that, while the struggle of America today is the struggle for the survival of hope, both will survive because the Negro survives!

# Chapter III

## Minstrelsy's Opponents

A Negro walked into a bus station in Cincinnati and bought a ticket to Kansas City. He turned from the ticket window and saw a fortune-telling machine. The Negro put a nickel in the machine and out came a card reading: "You are six feet tall and you weigh two hundred pounds. You are big, you are black, and you are on your way to Kansas City."

The Negro stared at the card in disbelief. He put another nickel in the machine and out came another card, repeating the exact words of the first one. The Negro shook his head, then looked across the station and saw an Indian woman. He strode toward the Indian, slipped her a quarter, then borrowed her shawl, slipped it over his head, then walked back to the fortune-telling machine. He covered his face with the shawl, and inserted another nickel into the machine. And out came the card. But, this time it read: "You are still six feet tall and you still weigh two hundred pounds. You are still big. You are still black, and while you've been fooling around with that damn Indian, you have missed your bus to Kansas City!"

The moral of this story is, of course, "Be yourself or else you're going to miss out on the real things in life." This moral is not unrelated to the American theatre. If the Negro theatre worker, trying be something other than himself, missed his bus to Kansas City, the white worker missed his train to Pittsburgh. Each has wallowed in the mud of uncertainty and insecurity, of seeking to put before audiences a face that was not his own. And because we have disliked ourselves, we have tried to project other images in terms of things and people.

The image of the confused man involved in that anecdote fits the opponents of minstrelsy; we must see them in that light or we miss the total sense of their failure. If we do not, we fail to understand why the noble efforts of Bert Williams, George Walker, Jesse Shipp and others were doomed to disappointment, tragedy and eventual failure. They hitched their wagons to the wrong star. They set out, not believing they were really human beings. They

*Charles Gilpin, the original* Emperor Jones *at the Provincetown Playhouse, 1920.*

Culver

set out justifying their existence, and their new and revolutionary
concepts were geared to gaining acceptance by those who laughed
at them in the first place and hated them, violently. An indication
of this was the refusal of Negro theatrical pioneers to incorporate
love scenes into their shows. Their argument was that whites would
not accept Negroes in love scenes.

The story of some of these pioneers deserves to be repeated here.
These men came into the American theatre at a time when minstrelsy was in vogue. They had in their hearts the long dream—the
dream of "making it," of pleasing white folks while doing so.
Their story must be seen against the total background of New York
City. The pattern of growth of this city has been consistently up-
ward, from the Battery to Wall Street, to 14th Street, to 23rd
Street, 34th Street, then 42nd Street. Improved lighting, transportation, building and industrial expansion were largely responsible for the city sprawling northward. By 1886 three elevated lines
reached Harlem, which was then a rural village. By 1886 there was
also full-scale immigration, and white Anglo-Saxon Protestant
Americans were not interested in living near these "foreigners."
Native New Yorkers fled to outlying areas, and in so doing they
developed Harlem into New York City's first suburb.

As New York moved uptown, so did the black population,
settling generally on the fringe of various neighborhoods. Negroes
were in Greenwich Village from the time the first Africans developed that community. They moved into the Chelsea area, on
into the neighborhood around Pennsylvania station, and then into
the fifties. These Negroes were not only domestics; they were
tradesmen, sportsmen, artists and other professionals. As early as
1900 the Hotel Marshall on West 53rd Street had been established
as a place one had to go—as a favorite among the successful Negro
artists of the day. Here, too, jockeys and prizefighters met. And
theatre fans—black and white—followed Negro theatre workers
into the place.

"Man!" said veteran actor-writer Sidney Easton, "when I first
came to New York, Bert Williams and George Walker took me
under their wings. Now, I was about as much out of the country
as a blade of green grass. When them cats walked into the Hotel
Marshall with their fine suits and their studs glistening, I *think*
the women passed out. The reason I say I *think* is 'cause I had
already passed out from just being there!"

According to Sidney Easton and others who were present, these were happy, glorious years not only for Negroes in the theatre, but for whites as well. Every city, town and hamlet in the United States had a theatre, and many had resident companies. Road tours were common things, and employment for actors was for fifty-two weeks a year. Mr. Easton said: "The only way I got a vacation was to turn down work for two or three weeks."

This was an era when America was in its preadolescence. Western states were entering the union. Railroads, coal, oil and steel were becoming monopolies. It was a big, growing country and it flexed its muscles menacingly. And it enjoyed itself. A wily man named Cornelius Vanderbilt built the Grand Central Station. A clerk named John D. Rockefeller wormed his way into the oil business, and Henry Ford brought low-cost cars to the so-called common man while Ford made an uncommon amount of money. Jim Fiske and the robber barons were making fortunes by cutting down smaller men, and Diamond Jim Brady was eating himself to death. Florenz Ziegfeld was overproducing and so were George Lederer and Charles Dillingham. Men were also dreaming of building the *Titanic*—a ship that could not sink. Wilbur and Orville Wright were about to take an airplane up over North Carolina and fly twenty-four and a half miles in less than a half-hour. Alexander Graham Bell was dreaming of the telephone. And Europe was an armed camp in this era when rapid communication was to become an industrial reality but never a human one.

This era saw the Negro dreaming with others. The plays of Clyde Fitch and Eugene Walter and David Belasco were the plays of the day. Their work was of little substance, but they satisfied a need for entertainment. Into this era, too, came poet William Vaughn Moody, and his play *The Great Divide* pitted the West against New England.

The black American's art and folkways began to influence the mainstream. The Blues were making their way up the Mississippi River. Jazz was stirring in New Orleans, and ragtime was a reality. The spirituals were rising from the religiosity to which they had been chained. And the Negro theatrical pioneer saw the truth of the minstrel pattern, of what it had become, and he set out to destroy this pattern.

It was a many-pronged attack. First, burlesque circuit manager

Sam T. Jack arranged *The Creole Show* along minstrel lines. However, he featured an innovation—a chorus of sixteen beautiful Negro girls who sang and danced. This show had its premiere in Boston in 1891, and later moved to Chicago where it was housed at Sam T. Jack's Opera House during the entire season of the World's Fair. In one form or another, *The Creole Show* was seen for a period of five years.

In 1895 a Negro named John W. Isham made another significant contribution. Mr. Isham had been an advance agent for *The Creole Show*. He organized and produced a show known as *The Octoroons*, a musical which broke further from the minstrel pattern. His next show, *Oriental America*, made an even greater break with minstrelsy. It did not use the traditional walkaround or cakewalk, but ended with an operatic medley. And Mr. Isham made other innovations. Instead of utilizing the comic burlesque performer, he engaged tenor Sidney Woodward, J. Rosamond Johnson and Inez Clough. Still another precedent was broken with *Oriental America*. It did not play the traditional burlesque houses generally played by Negro shows. It was presented at Palmer's Theatre, later to be known as Wallack's.

Theatrical activity flourished among New York Negroes. Worth's Museum stood at Sixth Avenue and 13th Street—not too far from the present site of the Village Presbyterian Church and Brotherhood Synagogue which houses the Greenwich Mews Theatre. Worth's housed a Negro stock company, spearheaded by Bob Cole. From all reports Cole was a brilliant man. He was well prepared, a good singer and dancer and an excellent actor. In the words of Sidney Easton: "He was a triple threat man. He could write dialogue, lyrics and music. And he could direct and act in his own shows, too. And if he wasn't doing any of those, some other manager had him doing something."

One of the times Cole was "doing something" was in *Black Patti's Troubadours*. Black Patti was the name given the great Sissieretta Jones, a rage in the concert field. Bob Cole wrote a show for her with an operatic finale. The show played for many years, at Proctor's 58th Street Theatre in New York and in many theatres in the larger cities of the North. It became, too, one of the large Negro shows to play the South in those days.

The year 1898 was particularly significant for the Negro in the

American theatre. Bob Cole wrote, directed and produced A *Trip to Coontown*, assisted by Billy Johnson. This was a musical with a plot—one that completely broke with the minstrel tradition and told a story through music, song and dance. It was produced at the Third Avenue Theatre in April, 1898. Some sources note the opening date as April 4, others as April 8. On September 12, 1898, the show opened at the Grand Opera House and had a run of eight performances. One of the cast members was Jesse Shipp, who would later write and direct many of the Williams and Walker shows.

Bob Cole was to team later with J. Rosamond Johnson, who with his brother, James Weldon Johnson, wrote "Lift Every Voice and Sing," known as the Negro National Anthem. With J. Rosamond Johnson, Cole wrote the first true Negro operetta, *The Shoofly Regiment*, and later *The Red Moon*. These were highly significant ventures, yet in 1953—more than a half century after their appearance—J. Rosamond Johnson told me he would not have written these works if he had it to do again. He spoke glowingly of Bob Cole and called him a remarkable man. But Mr. Johnson's goal in 1953 was integration. He felt any all-black show was doomed to failure. He spoke to me reluctantly, making it clear that I was stirring up trouble. He actually suggested that I leave him alone.

I pitied him. He had done so much, so very much; yet here he was, caught up in a tidal wave of present-day youth quests and the pages were falling rapidly from his calendar.

The year 1898 brought other significant ventures. Negroes were distinguishing themselves with Teddy Roosevelt's Rough Riders at San Juan Hill. They were also making their presence felt in the New York theatre. Will Marion Cook, father of Dr. Mercer Cook, former minister to Niger, wrote *Clorindy—the Origin of the Cakewalk* with poet Paul Laurence Dunbar. Mr. Cook was a great musician, trained under Joachim in Europe. He offered a fresh, great musical talent, and he showed what syncopation could be like when handled by an artist of worth. He was also alert enough to have lyrics by a poet of Dunbar's caliber.

*Clorindy* was produced by George W. Lederer, one of New York's leading musical producers. The work was shown at the Casino Roof Garden and it ran through the summer. Mr. Cook directed the orchestra and Ernest Hogan was prominently featured in the cast. This was the same Mr. Hogan who created "Rufus Rastus" and "The Oyster Man." Later he was to write the song—and to regret doing so—"All Coons Look Alike to Me."

Negroes were on the move now. Their theatrical life was ablaze, and they saw doors opening in houses they never dreamed of entering. They saw, too, not only Ernest Hogan, Bob Cole and Will Marion Cook, but also on the horizon, coming out of the west, a team that was to bring profound changes to the American Negro and the white theatre. That team was Bert Williams and George Walker.

Egbert Austin Williams, popularly known as Bert Williams, was the foremost Negro actor of his time. He was born in Antigua, British West Indies, in 1872. In his youth his family moved to California. Most authorities agree that the family moved because of the illness of his father on the recommendation of an island physician. No one seems to know exactly what type of illness he contracted, but it is known that the Williams family fortune waned. At any rate, Bert attended high school in California and dreamed of entering Stanford University. This was an economic impossibility, so he stuck his banjo under his arm and set out to find work in the honky-tonks of San Francisco. He was a skillful musician and was later to master a number of instruments.

In a San Francisco honky-tonk he met a tramp player from Lawrence, Kansas—George Nash Walker. They formed a team, known as Williams and Walker. The first idea was for Williams to play the straight man and for Walker to play the stooge and dance. However, they soon reversed their roles. Williams, an olive-complexioned Negro, donned burnt cork—but he did it with some misgivings.

Williams and Walker met writer-director-actor Jesse Shipp in Chicago, and they laid plans for working together in full-length musicals that would utilize the Negroes' gifts without resorting to minstrelsy. Williams and Walker then went on to Koster and Bial's in New York where they played for twenty-eight weeks—which surprised them more than it did their audiences.

They followed with their own shows—*The Sons of Ham*, which caused resentment on the part of many Negroes because of the blackface used, but the work was shown for two years. For that show, with the assistance of Alex Rogers, Williams wrote the song

"Jonah Man." *The Policy Players* followed, then *In Dahomey*, with a book by Jesse Shipp, music by Will Marion Cook and lyrics by Paul Laurence Dunbar. The latter reached Broadway in 1903.

An article dated April 7, 1903, entitled "We're Broadway Stars" notes that Williams and Walker both shouted "Hallelujah!" It took them seven years to get there, but they got there. They mention they were detoured in Second and Third Avenue spots and that Bert Williams used to say: "There's no such place as Broadway." George Walker told the article writer: "We're so used to it, all other towns seem like Hoboken." Bert, the honest man, said: "It was a pig in a clover puzzle to get here, but we got here!" They felt that Broadway represented the center of the universe. *Standard* and *Vanity Fair* reported: "*Dahomey* sets a pace for white comedians to follow in an entire absence of slapstick comedy and in a strict regard for only niceties in fun-making."

It should be noted that the entire Williams and Walker Company observed "only niceties" on and off stage. There were no love scenes in their scripts because they did not believe whites would accept the idea that Negroes could mate romantically. And the company had a booklet with strict rules on road conduct. These rules were seriously and strictly enforced, and there were fines for any cast member who broke them. George Walker, who played the strutting, city-slicker, overdressed Negro onstage, was a sensible man offstage. He declared: "The white man won't let us be serious!" And this same George Walker would, on January 25, 1906, call for an organization of colored performers.

In 1903 Hurtig and Seamon, managers for the Williams and Walker Company, took *In Dahomey* to London's Shaftesbury Theatre where it met with moderate favor, but the man who booked command performances at Buckingham Palace wanted *In Dahomey* for the birthday celebration of the young Prince of Wales. After their command performance, they toured the provinces. Williams and Walker became the rage of England. The whole nation learned the "cakewalk." While in Edinburgh, Williams joined the Masons—an honor he cherished until his death. After returning to America he made his famous comment: "It is no disgrace to be a Negro, but it is very inconvenient."

Before their next show Williams and Walker had an argument with their managers, Hurtig and Seamon, and this developed into a break. They were adamant, however, in keeping their company together. Large companies the size of theirs—over one hundred—found it particularly difficult at that time to find managers, but both Williams and Walker considered their company a "family." Eventually, the men found Melville B. Raymond, but in 1906 they had an argument with him over playing in first-class theatres.

Their next show, *Abyssinia*, was written by Jesse Shipp, Alex Rogers and Will Marion Cook with additional lyrics by Earle C. Jones. It opened at the Majestic Theatre on February 21, 1906. Featured were the company's favorites: Hattie McIntosh, Stella Wiley, Ada Overton Walker, Lottie Thompson Williams (Mrs. Bert Williams) and Charles Gilpin. *Abyssinia* told the story of George Walker taking a party of Americans to the land of his ancestors—to Abyssinia. The show had wonderful songs, opening with "Song of Reverence to the Setting Sun," a Rimski-Korsakov type number, then "Let It Alone," "It's Hard to Find a King Like Me," and "Here It Comes Again," the "It" meaning trouble.

The show also had wonderful satiric thrusts. Bert Williams, the ragged American "darky" wandered around through the splendor of black Abyssinia, reflecting contrasts between two cultures. During the play he takes some money George has given him to buy decent clothing and he buys a camel. He also is caught stealing a valuable vase, and for this he is taken before the Emperor. The punishment for this crime is the removal of one hand.

George assailed the imprisoned Bert: "Now, you went and done it! I brung you over here to Abyssinia where you can get some culture and you go walking through all this culture, looking like some vulture. I even take you swimming, half-hoping you gonna drown, but the water takes one look at you and it begins to frown. And it backs up to your—knees! What you gonna do? Huh? You know the punishment for what you done! They gonna cut off your hand. What you gonna look like with one hand and a nub, huh? What you gonna do then?"

Bert's reply was: "Oh, I'll put a hook on it!"

There followed the scene where Bert had to go before the Emperor. He became the poignant Negro for whom nothing went right at any time. And he sang "Here It Comes Again." Trouble was overhead, always looking for a place to light, and it generally lit on his head.

Bert's plea before the Emperor was poetically significant. "I ain't never done nothin' to nobody," he wailed in song. "I ain't never got nothin' from nobody no time. And until I get somethin' from somebody sometime, I don't intend to do nothin' to nobody no time!" And he literally stopped the show with music he wrote to Alex Rogers' lyrics—lyrics Bert could never remember, lyrics he had to carry with him on a small card or written on his glove.

*Abyssinia* was troublesome to the critics. They liked it, but they stated bluntly that it was a little "too arty." It was too Caucasian, some critics said, too serious. In other words, they wanted a fast-moving "darky show." But the work was highly successful, and after its New York run, it toured. However, it was the company's next show, *Bandanna Land*, which proved to be a smash hit.

*Bandanna Land* was produced February 16, 1908. This fast-paced musical was the forerunner of many another Negro and white show. It had a story, a point of view, wonderful songs and dances, and it was sharply satirical—although many whites did not "get the message," either by design or through ignorance, or both.

*Bandanna Land* satirized the "Negro-scare racket." In the show Williams and Walker decide on a quick way to make money. They buy up land in a well-to-do white section and move into a house. They proceed to give a number of parties, to raise hell, and the whites immediately agree to buy back the land at twice the amount the Negroes paid. It takes no genius to see the point the artists were making.

Toward the end of the play there is a scene that underlines the type of characters Williams and Walker played. Williams was the shuffling, slow man in blackface. Everything always went wrong for him, yet he was never as stupid as whites or Negroes thought him to be. Walker was the overdressed Negro, the "sharp cat," looking for a quick deal, always knowing he could fast-talk anyone out of anything. In *Bandanna Land*, after enough hell has been raised, a white man has invited Williams and Walker to his office to get the money whites are paying for their property. Walker sees a chance to get all of the money and leave Williams with none. The dialogue, paraphrased here, goes like this:

WALKER: I'll save you from getting up in the morning. Yeah. I'll do you a big favor. I'll go down to the white man's office and get the money and bring it to you. I'll be down at the white man's office about nine o'clock and I'll get you your share by 9:30. Where you gonna be at 9:30 A.M. tomorrow?

WILLIAMS: Right down there at the white man's office with you.

*Bandanna Land* was the last show Williams and Walker did together. A firsthand account of this last show is offered here as a result of a visit in 1955 along with veteran actor-producer-director Stanley Greene to the home of his uncle and aunt, Mr. and Mrs. Frank Wilson. Mr. Wilson was the great Negro actor who played the lead in *Porgy, In Abraham's Bosom,* and his plays, *Walk Together, Children* and *Meek Mose* are notable contributions to black drama. Mrs. Wilson was formerly a member of the Williams and Walker Company. She was one of the "Bon Bon Girls"—a part of the chorus that accompanied George Walker as he sang:

> *Bon Bon Buddie, the chocolate drop,*
> *That's me, that's me.*
> *Bon Bon Buddie, the chocolate drop,*
> *That's all I wanta be!*

Invariably, our conversation moved to the Negro in the American theatre. Mr. Wilson declared: "Negro theatre must get back to what Williams and Walker stood for. They took advantage of being Negroes—something we keep apologizing for."

Mrs. Wilson said of Williams and Walker: "They were such good men. George cut the fool on stage, but he was a smart man off that stage. One of the best businessmen I ever met! Once he and Bert sued their managers, and when George told the judge that he and Bert had earned forty thousand dollars the previous year, the judge nearly fell off the bench!"

She continued: "That Bert was one of the finest men that ever lived. A little too fine, I think, for those were days when everyone was struggling, scuffling and knocking each other down to get ahead. But Bert wanted *everything* for *everybody.* There wasn't a selfish streak in him. That's why his heart was broken—why he died so young."

Mrs. Wilson then repeated the story of the very end of the Williams and Walker Company. After the New York run of

*Bandanna Land,* the company went on the road and played a number of successful engagements. While in Boston one night, George began singing "Bon Bon Buddie." Suddenly, he began to sing in a thick-lipped manner, droning out the lyrics. Mrs. Wilson said she and the other cast member smiled, believing that George was improvising a new gag. Suddenly, however, they learned he was actually ill, that he had a stroke. It was at that very moment that George Nash Walker suffered the affliction that was to curtail his career.

George Walker went home to Lawrence, Kansas, where he died in 1911. Bert Williams went on to perform alone in *Mr. Lode of Kole,* a moderate hit, claiming that without his partner, he felt "like a rudderless ship." Williams divided his salary with George Walker up to the moment of Walker's death.

The winds of industrial change blew rapidly. Business expansion and the consolidation of power became potent factors, and control became a major item in the theatre. Big business appeared there as it appeared everywhere in American life.

Meanwhile, this land of patterns and fads yearned for "something new." Many critics declared: "The Negro musical comedy pattern is running thin." And so, with the consolidation of power, the tide of reaction rolled over the nation. The Negro was evicted from the Broadway stage. With the exception of Bert Williams—who was invited to join Abraham Erlanger's *Follies* in 1910—few, if any, Negroes worked on Broadway from 1910 through 1917. The gallant performers who had destroyed minstrelsy and created the American musical form found themselves again evicted from the mainstream and chased to upper Manhattan where they had to work alone.

Their heroic efforts were largely in vain. They had fought their revolution on the enemy's terms. They had believed what the enemy told them about themselves, and their works lie hidden, buried someplace beneath the debris of thought that told them they had to participate, to become involved in white theatre or else they were still in the "small time."

They fooled around with "that damn Indian." And they missed the bus to Kansas City.

# Chapter IV

## The Rise of the Theatrical Trust Syndicate and the Negro's Exile from Broadway

"Power does strange things to men."

These were the words of the late Malcolm X at the time of his historic break with Elijah Muhammed and his Muslim group. The last time I saw Malcolm X was a month before his death. At that time he elaborated upon this statement, citing the inevitable sabotage of revolutions throughout history.

When the Christian Church joined the Roman Establishment, it accepted the latter's mores and, indeed, became the agent of many of its dirty deeds. Martin Luther's followers and the Anglican Church, after breaking with Rome, also became allies of the political Establishment. In the American Revolution, cries of equality were dominant until peace became a reality. Robespierre, Danton and later Napoleon made a mockery of the French Revolution. The Industrial Revolution was similarly sabotaged by the bourgeoisie, which took control of the government from the landowning aristocracy and then allied itself with the aristocracy. In each instance, the evils that men did lived after them.

The American theatre is no exception. In 1896 the Theatrical Trust Syndicate was organized. This syndicate was spearheaded by Klaw, Abraham Erlanger, Charles Frohman, Al Hyman, Sam Nixon (or Samuel Nordlinger) and J. Fred Zimmerman. Its control of the theatre lasted for sixteen years.

The syndicate had good intentions. It originally sought to do away with theatrical wastage, to prevent exploitation and to bring organization into the theatre. It thrived in an era when big business was growing, when organization came to railroads, steel, oil and coal. The syndicate set out to control all bookings, hirings and firings.

But power does strange things to men. The desire for money ruined the syndicate's esthetic values and caused it to fight healthy competition. It hounded its opponents and unleashed painful reprisals upon any who challenged it. As it reached the height of its power, Mrs. Dwight Fiske proved "uncooperative." By exerting its influence, the syndicate made it possible for her to appear only in second-rate theatres. It also forced the great Sarah Bernhardt to appear in a tent. Both these actresses were assisted by Augustin Daly and David Belasco who, along with the Shubert family, fought the syndicate.

During its reign the syndicate noted, too, the rising tide of reaction against the Negro. Other business establishments had noted this, too, had taken advantage of it and had thus pushed the Negro back toward slavery. The American theatre did not follow the noble purpose of instructing, educating and entertaining. Under the syndicate's guidance, our theatre sought huge profits at the expense of a people.

Violent and vicious acts were committed against the black American. The 1900 race riot, New York City's fourth, was devastating. Atrocities continued until, in 1906, a call was made for the founding of the Niagara Movement, which met at Harpers Ferry and became the forerunner of the National Association for the Advancement of Colored People. Five demands were drafted, and these were preceded by this statement written by Dr. William Edward Burghardt DuBois:

"We will not be satisfied to take one jot or tittle less than our full manhood rights. We claim for ourselves every single right that belongs to a free-born American, political, civil and social; and until we get these rights, we will never cease to protest and assail the ears of America. The battle we wage is not for ourselves alone; but for all true Americans. It is a fight for ideals, lest this, our common fatherland, false to its founding, become in truth the land of the Thief and the home of the Slave—a byword and a hissing among the nations for its sounding pretensions and pitiful accomplishment. . . ."

This eloquence came too late, too late. Black America had been doublecrossed again as it had been in New York in 1664, in the American Revolution, after the Civil War and throughout the nation's history. But the period of this doublecross gave the Negro's enemies one important advantage—namely, time to organize their propaganda offensive, to wipe the Negro's contributions from the pages of history books, to make cheap distortions of his songs, to make his humor an instrument to use against him and his culture something inferior that should be destroyed.

This period saw the complete consolidation of the "white point of view" which declared "white is right." There existed, therefore, the silly songs of Stephen Foster, glorifying his old Kentucky home, his old Black Joe and his Swanee River from which Negroes ran as though it were the plague. There existed, too, Thomas Dixon's *The Clansman*, which echoed America's prevailing attitudes toward the Negro.

These prevailing attitudes put the Negro on the defensive, for he had to defend his person and his humanity. All of this permeated the American theatre and American life as long as the syndicate reigned. These prevailing attitudes were to send Negroes fleeing toward a community where they might find a measure of safety. These times were to see the Negro expelled from the Broadway theatre.

And it is these attitudes that flourish today, while the black American strives to recapture his heritage and his identity!

# Part Two

## YESTERDAY

*Yesterday is no elusive moment in time,*
*Suspended against a backdrop, hidden from view.*
*Yesterday is not the calendar's pages, torn and thrown*
    *away,*
*Nor is it the echo of a love-sigh long since dead.*
*Yesterday is today and today is yesterday—*
*The very ground on which we stand, the air we breathe,*
    *the things we feel and know.*

# Chapter V

## Harlem and Its Development by Negroes

There is a beautiful hill at the northern end of Central Park. This hill is grass-covered in the spring and summer, bare and brown in the autumn and cold and foreboding in the winter. But even in the winter when the earth is dark and cracked, you can look at that hill and know somehow that spring will come to it again and that the grass will be green. And, as you look, you know that spring cannot be denied, that it will come again and again.

From the top of that hill, you get a wide, clear view. You look directly down on 110th Street and Seventh Avenue. Then, as your eyes move westward, you see the Cathedral of St. John the Divine and Columbia University on Morningside Heights. You look straight up Seventh Avenue, and on a clear day you can see 125th Street, 135th Street and 145th Street, where the avenue runs on into the Harlem River. As your eyes gaze eastward they pick out the Triborough Bridge which spans the East River, connecting Manhattan, the Bronx and Queens. As your gaze moves downtown again, you see Fifth Avenue, then Lenox Avenue at 110th Street.

All of Harlem is before you when you stand on that hilltop. Harlem with its swanky apartment buildings, its monuments, its slums, its numerous businesses and its proud history. And its proud history is unique, like most of black American history—unique because it has been rarely stated.

After eleven Africans built a wagon road to Harlem in 1626, the community remained dormant for many years. True, some of the Revolutionary War battles were fought there, but the area itself was far, far uptown, away from the heart of the city.

Harlem in the mid-nineteenth century was a poor, rural village, populated by squatters in crude cottages. Improved transportation, lighting and building expansion soon transformed the area. By 1886 three elevated lines reached the community. White Anglo-Saxon Protestant Americans fled from the waves of immigrants that reached these shores. These well-to-do whites settled in exclusive Harlem dwellings and developed New York's first suburb. Many white Harlemites were careful to point out that they lived in Harlem, not New York City. In 1893 the white *Harlem Monthly Mazagine* saw the community as the future center of wealth, fashion, culture and intelligence. Harlem then was very staid, very comfortable, off to itself, away from the "ill-bred foreigners" who lived downtown with the "darkies."

The second phase of the Industrial Revolution was to show itself then. In the first phase the serfs left the rural areas and settled in the heart of the city, near the factories where they worked. They established living quarters beside the factory owners, who were then wooing the aristocracy. And the factory owners, the bourgeoisie, moved away from the heart of the city, to exclusive dwellings. But while the coming of the railroad centralized the city, the suburban lines and the growth of the automobile decentralized it. Though the bourgeoisie raced to suburban areas, the workers soon followed (in the second phase of the Industrial Revolution) and lived within proximity of their "masters."

So it was with the community known as Harlem. A sizable group of prominent New Yorkers settled north of 110th Street. Indeed, well into the nineteenth century, these people had their Negro servants visit them daily by sailing up the Hudson River from Lower Manhattan, from the thirties, the forties and later the fifties where black people lived.

Then, the news spread: In 1904 the Lenox Avenue subway was going to open. Wild speculation raged. Nearly all of Harlem's vacant land was sold. Buildings were built and then stood waiting to be rented. High rents discouraged the general population. Landlords competed for tenants for their empty buildings. They slashed rentals, for they faced financial ruin. Many expressed willingness to accept Negro tenants and collect the traditional high rents this group paid. Two Negro realtors, Philip Payton, Jr., and Solomon Riley, emphasized that home-hungry, harassed Negroes would pay twice the rents paid by whites. And the worried white realtors accepted their statements.

The first Negro families moved into the area, and a hastily formed Harlem Protective Association plastered the community with "For White Only" signs. Negroes continued to move into the area, and they met violence with violence. Bloody street-fighting raged on the streets between both races. And many of the whites began to move away.

The impatience of present-day Harlemites in terms of civil rights is directly related to the development of that black community. Older Harlem Negroes in the twenties, when speaking of the race problem, would say bluntly: "Look at the record from 1900 to 1906."

When I first heard that statement, I thought it was simply an expression, a rallying point. But now, in an age when Negroes are told to be patient in seeking their rights, to build for themselves as other groups have, it becomes necessary to review that period.

By 1900 Negro showmen had completely broken the minstrel tradition and "The Golden Age of the Negro in the Theatre" was proclaimed by many scholars. Yet there were rumblings of danger. In 1900 New York's fourth disastrous race riot flared. Roving white mobs flooded the streets shouting: "Get Williams and Walker!" Comedian Ernest Hogan had to lock himself in a theatre overnight to assure his personal safety.

In 1900 Booker T. Washington spoke at the Atlanta Exposition where he assured whites that in national disaster Negroes and whites would be together like a "closed fist," but in things social they would be "like the fingers on the hand." In 1903, from Atlanta, W. E. B. DuBois submitted a group of essays known as *The Souls of Black Folk*. One essay, *Of Mr. Booker T. Washington and Others*, took exception to Mr. Washington's views and held they were not representative of *all* Negro thinking. In that same volume Dr. DuBois wrote another brilliant essay in which he stated:

> "I have seen a land right merry with the sun, where children sing, and rolling hills lie like passioned women wanton with harvest. And there in the King's Highway sat and sits a figure veiled and bowed, by which the traveller's footsteps hasten as they go. On the tainted air broods fear. Three centuries' thought has been the raising and unveiling of that bowed human heart, and now behold a century new for the duty and the deed. The problem of the twentieth century is the problem of the color line."

The problem of the twentieth century is the problem of the

color line—the relation of the darker to the lighter races of men in Asia and Africa, in America and the islands of the sea, just as Dr. DuBois wrote in 1903. He also had hailed a "century new for the duty and the deed," but few wanted to listen to him. Negroes believed, as they had since the nation's founding, that real freedom would soon be theirs. The year 1906 shows how much they believed.

The *New York Age*, a Negro newspaper, carried an advertisement in 1906 noting that Philip Payton, Jr., had opened modern apartments on 134th Street in Harlem—with all modern conveniences except elevators and electricity. The rents ranged from twenty to thirty-two dollars per month.

The year 1906 found Negroes denouncing *The Clansman.* In January of that year Booker T. Washington wrote to the *New York Age,* denying he had advised President Theodore Roosevelt to remove all colored men from holding office in the South. The term "Afro-American" appeared in newspapers, and when "Negro" was used, it was with a small "n." The poll tax laws appeared in several states. Heflin of Alabama advocated jimcrow laws after Booker T. Washington and President Roosevelt ate together on a train. The *New York Age* noted in its report: "The bill will, of course, fail."

Virginia introduced jimcrow laws for its streetcars. The *Age* declared: "Few Afro-Americans will patronize these cars." Newspapers observed that a "revolt was kindling" when racial trouble broke out in South Africa. President Roosevelt declared that Negro and Indian music would contribute the only two schools of American music. Dr. Finch of the *New York Evening Post* denounced this statement. The *Age* agreed, however, while noting a penury of melody in Indian songs, and then added that ragtime is the basest form of degradation.

*In Abyssinia,* written by Jesse Shipp, Alex Rogers and Will Marion Cook with additional lyrics by Earle C. Jones, opened at the Majestic Theatre on February 21, 1906. Bert Williams sang "Nobody" and stopped the show.

This was the year, too, of the Boxer Rebellion. Stephen Phillips' play *Nero* opened in London with music by Samuel Coleridge Taylor, the Negro composer. Theodore Drury's Opera Company appeared at the 14th Street Theatre on May 28, 1906. Advertise-

*Florence Mills, one of the brightest stars of the twenties, came to Broadway in the review* Shuffle Along.

ments repeatedly declared there would be no color discrimination in the sale of tickets. And Ed Johnson was lynched after the Supreme Court ordered a stay of execution.

Clark Howell ran for governor of Georgia, and the Negro was disenfranchised there. Negroes were excluded from Civil Service jobs in the Philippines, and there were street fights in Maryland. Louisiana attempted to dismiss all Negro schoolteachers, and Negroes were burned in Springfield, Missouri, where Frederick Douglass had once been honored.

W. E. B. DuBois blasted Theodore Roosevelt at Hampton. The call went out, too, for the Niagara Movement, the forerunner of the NAACP. *The Shoofly Regiment* opened with book by Bob Cole, some lyrics by James Weldon Johnson and music by J. Rosamond Johnson.

In September, 1906, the Atlanta Outbreaks occurred. These lasted for two days, and thirty Negroes were "butchered." This was directly traceable to Hoke Smith's gubernatorial campaign. The *Atlanta News* boldly offered one thousand dollars per lynching. And Booker T. Washington pleaded for Negroes not to retaliate.

That same year Theodore Roosevelt sent to Congress a message in which he declared: "Rape is the greatest cause for lynching."

This was America in the Year of Our Lord 1906. It was a nation trying to turn back the clock, sabotage the Reconstruction era and sell a freed people back into a new form of slavery. The fact that nearly six decades later Negroes stood in Southern and Northern streets, demanding "Freedom Now," indicates how successful the powers were in creating this new slavery—one that gave a man a name, then thrust him into poverty, discrimination and the hell of jimcrow.

# Chapter VI

## *The First Harlem Theatre Movement: 1909–1917*

When I was in the sixth grade I won second prize in a citywide essay contest on fire prevention. I decided then that I was going to be a writer, and I reported this to my parents, who proudly told a West Indian neighbor of my decision.

This West Indian was an elderly man, a former sailor, who spoke in the vernacular of his island home. "Child," he told me, "you got to write about the things around you—the people, the monuments."

"What monuments?" I asked.

"What monuments?" he snapped. "Move your damn big feet and you'll see that you're standing on one! And take a good look because it won't be there a few years from now. They'll tear the blasted thing down and build a highway or a parking garage!"

Naturally, we all laughed at this. It was many years later when I saw the Hippodrome Theatre, the Center Theatre and other Broadway institutions demolished that his words began to have meaning. In reviewing the way we in this country destroy historic sights, one shudders at what the old West Indian said later that day. He told my father:

"Every time I go down to South Ferry, I wave good-bye to the Statue of Liberty."

"What you talking about?" asked my father. "You ain't going no place."

"No," said the old man, "but the Statue of Liberty just might be. Soon as some smart young engineer decides to build a bridge from Manhattan to Staten Island, he just might find that Lady Liberty is in the way, and that statue will come tumbling down for sure."

"That coffee my wife give you musta been spiked," my father said. He called to my mother: "Hey, Sugar, don't give him no more to drink!"

The Statue of Liberty still stands as of this writing, but many a theatre does not—including the first Harlem theatre. This was the Crescent, located at 36-38 West 135th Street, built in the year 1909. What stands there now is Lenox Terrace aparments, without the slightest inscription any place to indicate that the Crescent once occupied the site.

The moving force behind the Crescent Theatre was a man named Eddie Hunter. Mr. Hunter was born in New York City in 1888. His family lived in the fifties, where a Negro colony thrived. At an early age Mr. Hunter's mother took him to a Bert Williams show. The youngster was greatly impressed and he decided to embark upon a theatrical career.

In his youth Mr. Hunter operated an elevator at 1211 Madison Avenue. When service was slow, he attempted to write plays. One night the great opera star Enrico Caruso appeared and wanted to know what the elevator operator was writing. Young Mr. Hunter told him, and Mr. Caruso requested permission to read his work. Mr. Caruso was impressed, and he brought the young man's work to the attention of his hosts, a Mr. and Mrs. Shubert, unrelated to the theatrical family of that name. The Shuberts sent their son nightly to teach Mr. Hunter mastery of the English language.

Mr. Hunter then begged theatrical manager "Frenchy" Elmore to book him into the Lincoln Theatre, which was located at 56 West 135th Street. This was then a "Nickelette" house—the earliest motion pictures offered in the Harlem area. Young Mr. Hunter and his partner, James Howard, were hired to "sandwich" original comedy acts around these early movies. They earned forty dollars a week and sometimes they did five and six shows daily.

Later Mr. Hunter teamed with Harry Fidler and played the William Fox theatres. Family difficulties forced Fidler to leave the act, and Hunter teamed with Thomas Chappelle. They played the Fox, Loew's and Keith circuits.

Another period of idleness followed, and Mr. Hunter began operating an elevator again, this time in a building on 137th Street near Eighth Avenue. Martinson and Niber, two liquor dealers, were tenants in that building, and when Mr. Hunter heard they were starting the Crescent Theatre, he asked them for work. Both laughed and insisted he was an elevator operator. When the young man offered to work without salary, Martinson and Niber were impressed. They engaged him to present his act, *Going to the Races*, at the Crescent in 1909.

In Mr. Hunter's words, "That show was talking pictures before they talked." Hunter and Chappelle started the program with a live discussion of races. Then they stepped to one side while motion pictures of horses were shown on screen. They made various comments in the meantime. And the climax of the act was the revelation that Hunter had bet on a mule!

This successful work led Martinson and Niber to engage young Hunter to produce the Crescent shows. For this theatre Mr. Hunter wrote and produced *The Battle of Who Run, Why Husbands Leave Home* and *Subway Sal.*

The Crescent's work was not confined to comedic ventures. A notable production, *The Tryst,* was produced there in 1909. This was the work of the pioneer composer Harry Lawrence Freeman, popularly known as H. Lawrence Freeman. Mr. Freeman was an opera composer for four decades. Parts of his *Nada* were performed by Johann Beck and the Cleveland Symphony Orchestra in 1900. After the turn of the twentieth century Mr. Freeman offered *Valdo, The Octoroon*—based on M. E. Bradden's story—*An African Krall, Voodo, Althalia,* and *Vendetta,* which appeared at the Lafayette in 1923. His repertoire also included *The Flapper, Uzziah, The Prophecy, The Plantation* and *Leah Kleschna* from the play made famous by George Arliss and Katherine Fiske.

The variety of programs presented by the Crescent drew heavily on the nearby Lincoln Theatre's following. Tim Moore, Cook and Stevens and other headliners were hired by the Lincoln to win back lost audiences. When the Lincoln finally emphasized a movie policy with low rates, it grasped a firm hold on the community. And the Crescent closed its doors.

Martinson and Niber then leased the Lafayette Theatre, which was built by John Mulonski in 1912. The building stood at 132nd Street and Seventh Avenue. Martinson and Niber took their Crescent shows there, along with Eddie Hunter. For a time Mr. Hunter produced shows there with Lester A. Walton. After leaving the Lafayette, Mr. Hunter wrote the Broadway show, *How Come?,* seen in 1923. Along with Andrew Trimble and Norman Astwood he played Loew's American, then went to London and wrote three editions of *Blackbirds.* He returned to the United States, toured with Lew Leslie's *Blackbirds* and—when the Depression gripped the nation—went into real estate.

I have spoken to Mr. Hunter by telephone in recent years, and he seems to be in good health. When I last saw him, in the nine-teen-fifties, he was managing seventeen apartment buildings in the Sugar Hill area, living comfortably and, on special occasions, performing for local groups. Mr. Hunter still was the lively, ener-getic man with the rapid-fire delivery so well remembered. We sat in his living room, sipping cocktails, and he spoke enthusiastically of his belief that a permanent Harlem theatre would exist one day. He declared that what has retarded the Harlem theatre move-ment is the attempt of "middle-class Negroes to be just like white folks." This attempt, he stated, makes many members of the black bourgeoisie reject our unique traits. He insisted that the day will come when the black working class will reject the model life being designed for it by others. This, he said, will lead to a con-centrated effort to revitalize the Negro culture as it really is, not as hostile forces want it to be.

No site in Harlem has as much theatrical meaning as the corner of 132nd Street and Seventh Avenue. Here once stood the Lafay-ette, previously noted as having been built in 1912 by John Mulon-ski. Nearby, at 131st Street and Seventh Avenue, stands the stump of the Tree of Hope, donated by that great dancer Bill "Bojangles" Robinson. This Tree of Hope stood outside the Lafayette Theatre, and it was so named because, as legend has it, an unemployed actor once lingered beneath the tree, hoping for work. A theatri-cal manager is said to have approached him and offered him a job. Thereafter, crowds of unemployed actors stood beneath that tree, sometimes blocking the way of passersby.

Since traffic is more important than human beings and tradi-tions, when Seventh Avenue was widened, the Tree of Hope had to be cut down. Bill Robinson took the stump of the tree and en-shrined it in the middle of Seventh Avenue at 131st Street.

Long before this area became a theatrical center, the Crescent, and later the Lincoln, had attracted large sections of the growing Negro community. When the Lincoln's vaudeville and movie fea-tures became responsible for the Crescent's closing, Martinson and Niber were determined to continue their efforts. They leased the Lafayette and, with Eddie Hunter, they brought to this theatre the type of material previously presented at the Crescent. The material did not draw too well. The Lincoln, in the meantime, housed vaudeville, movies and legitimate plays. One of the first Negro plays presented in Harlem, if not the first, was given at the Lincoln in 1914—Henry Cramer's *The Odd Man's Boy.* S. H. Dudley also wrote and produced several shows there. His *The Smart Set* was an outstanding venture.

Martinson and Niber's lease at the Lafayette lasted from 1912 through 1914. When they gave up the lease in 1914 it was taken over by a Mr. Morgenstern and Lester A. Walton. Mr. Walton, a St. Louisan, had worked as drama critic for the *New York Age.* From 1914 until 1916 he kept the Lafayette supplied with musicals and other shows. Working with him were such men as Eddie Hunter and Flournoy Miller and Aubrey Lyles, who later contributed so greatly to the success of *Shuffle Along.*

J. Leubrie Hill's *Darktown Follies* opened there in 1913, and it became the theatre's first smash hit. Scores of whites journeyed to Harlem to see it. Florenz Ziegfeld was among those who witnessed *Darktown Follies,* and he bought the Finale for his own use in his *Follies.* Thus the stamp of white approval was placed upon the Lafayette. E. S. Wright and Margaret Brown were seen in *Othello.* When Flournoy Miller and Aubrey Lyles' *Darkydom* appeared in 1915 the premiere was attended by many whites in coaches. This prompted one critic to note: "It looked like a Broadway opening." Sketches from *Darkydom* were also sold to Broadway producers.

During this entire period Lester Walton was constantly booking shows from the Lafayette into Washington's Howard Theatre and Philadelphia's Dunbar. The road paid well then, and he worked closely with John Cort, the builder of New York's Cort Theatre. At the time that *Darkydom* opened, Mr. Cort went into bankruptcy. Bookings for the show were canceled from Minnesota to California. Mr. Walton, however, believed in the vehicle and sank his own money into it. *Darkydom* was a hit and it brought many returns. But by this time, Mr. Walton's lease on the Lafayette was expiring, and he gave up managing the theatre.

A significant venture occurred during the period when Mr. Walton was away from the Lafayette. This was Ridgeley Torrence's *Three Plays for a Negro Theatre,* produced at the Old Garden Theatre, April 5, 1917, outside the Harlem area. Its production outside Harlem deserves some comment. The American standard has continuously been a white one; therefore, anything all-black is "inferior" and not "truly recognized." Many well-intentioned white people—and black people—insist that total acceptance from white society is necessary to "make it." This is true today and it was true in 1917 when, despite the existence of three theatres in Harlem, Torrence's plays were presented downtown.

Mr. Torrence's triple bill resulted from a 1914 double-bill production by Emilie Hapgood and Dorothy Donnelly for the Stage Society. One of the features on this bill was Mr. Torrence's *Granny Maumee*. Enthusiastic critics urged Mr. Torrence to write more plays about Negro life. So, in 1917, *Granny Maumee* was joined by *The Rider of Dreams* and *Simon the Cyrenian* to make up the bill that came to be known as *Three Plays for a Negro Theatre*. This was Robert Edmond Jones' first directional effort. Featured in the cast were Inez Clough, Opal Cooper, and Charles Gilpin. Triumphant announcements followed that the Negro had "his foot in the door again." The United States entered the First World War the very next day, and the enthusiasm for Torrence's work waned.

Torrence's dramas must have played better than they read. Certainly the opinions of such authorities as James Weldon Johnson and Edith Isaacs are not to be discounted. But Mr. Torrence's written text is embarrassingly clumsy, his Negro speech earthbound, and his themes seem remote from the actual experience of black people on this continent. While Torrence may have assisted in paving the way for the Negro to reenter the downtown theatre, he also assisted in fathering a long line of neostereotype characters that ranged from the Emperor Jones to Abraham to Porgy to those of the present. Apparently, Torrence struck a norm that appealed to white theatregoers.

The drama of battle overshadowed any theatrical ventures during the First World War. With the war's end came new dramatic developments. In 1919 Lester Walton was called back to manage the Lafayette. This time he brought with him Anita Bush, the talented actress who had started a stock company at the Lincoln Theatre, and Charles Gilpin. The first production under this new leadership was *The Octoroons*—not to be confused with a half-dozen or more other plays produced under this name. This first production officially launched the organization that came to be known as the Lafayette Players.

The Lafayette Players were probably the outstanding Negro

theatre group of their time. They did dance-dramas, remade variations of popular plays and original plays. These plays were shown on a weekly basis. Musicals, such as Eddie Hunter's *How Come?*, were presented for runs. One thing must be stated about the Lafayette Players: Theirs was basically a "me-too" organization— one devoted to showing white folks that I, too, can play roles that you think are yours alone, that I, too, am human. It was, in short, a defensive organization, unsure of what might have been unleashed had it said: "I am black, so what? This is me, and this is my creative effort."

The community supported the Lafayette. Its musicals were particularly well received. The theatre's chief competition came from low-cost movie houses which were making inroads into all legitimate houses at that time.

After Mr. Walton left the Lafayette in 1921, he continued to produce plays, working as a journalist, and he served as Minister to Liberia from 1936 until 1946. I knew and admired him greatly. The last time I saw him was in the summer of 1953. I climbed the steps to his apartment in the Dunbar. He greeted me with a big smile that filled his moonlike, reddish brown face. His shoulders sagged just a bit and some of the bounce had gone out of his walk, but his mind bristled with new activities. He poured cocktails and we sipped them while we talked theatre.

His primary interest then, he reported, was the Coordinating Council of Colored Performers. This was a group to which I belonged—a group dedicated to integrating the Negro in television work. Mr. Walton felt that television was the area in which Negroes must strike now. The legitimate theatre and the motion picture medium were by no means dead, but one could not deny the potential of television, especially as long as it remained something immediate, on the spot. He foresaw amazing news coverage by television, and predicted it would be able to send news pictures back to New York from the far places of the world—and on the same day.

I listened with great interest as he spoke. He went on to state that television was going to bring remarkable changes to the modern world. Because it could flash pictures of what had happened one hour before to the entire world, there would be hesitancy on the part of bigots to perform antiracial acts in a world that was predominantly nonwhite. He predicted that colonial powers—and America itself—would be forced to devise new methods of dealing with colored peoples.

He also said, quite bluntly, that he believed that the white communications media realized this much more so than the darker peoples of the world—*and that this was going to be the very last medium into which the Negro could walk, as either performer, director, writer or producer.*

I listened to him then, yet today I wish I had listened more carefully. So it is with human knowledge. The professor is invariably talking about the *meaning* of the fall of the Roman Empire, and romantic students are seeing themselves driving chariots through a city uncluttered by the problems of the modern world. Mr. Walton was talking about the *meaning* of today's events, and I wanted to talk about theatre as it was, as it had been, and so I guided the conversation toward his attitudes and thoughts about that institution.

His feelings were—in the past and present—that Negroes must write the Negro dramas. This had been the underlying theme of his entire theatrical career. He cited Alex Rogers' *Old Man's Boy*, one of his productions, as an indication of his efforts. He mentioned, too, his 1928 production of Frank Wilson's *Meek Mose*, financed by Otto Kahn and shown on the Broadway stage. *Meek Mose* was not a commercial success, but Mr. Walton showed me numerous congratulatory letters from notable scholars, all of which indicated the show was an artistic success.

When we turned to discussing Mr. Walton's withdrawal from the Lafayette, he stated that the Coleman brothers had become managers of the house. They brought in vaudeville shows and motion pictures. It was some time after that that Frank Schiffman assumed control of the theatre. Many years later it became an empty building. Today the structure is one of Harlem's many churches.

In evaluating the importance of the Lafayette, Mr. Walton said it had bridged the days of Williams and Walker with the present period. He noted the numerous actors who had gained invaluable training at the Lafayette, and said that without the existence of that theatre, many would have not benefited at all. Mr. Walton saw, too, a possible return to Harlem of a similar theatre group.

He felt that the movies had had a great deal to do with the

decline of the Lafayette as a legitimate house. He pointed out that he simply could not operate professionally and charge prices comparable to those charged for motion picture showings.

He claimed that to build a permanent Harlem theatre we must take that art form away from so-called intellectuals and bring it to the people of the community. The hope of the theatre, he stated, is in expanding and reaching the masses, particularly the Negro masses.

He expressed the hope that, when the Negro theatre of tomorrow becomes a reality, someone might mention his name and note that the Lafayette once existed. I have interviewed people for many years and written numerous columns about them. Rarely has sentiment intruded upon an interview, but this time it did. I could not resist telling him that I knew his name would live as long as thoughts of a Negro theatre lived.

We had several talks after that, all generally along the lines noted previously. Several times I saw his daughter at various gatherings; she always invited me to visit and I always said that I would. But time is a strange phenomenon in this complex and changing world, and those relatives and friends we cherish are always going to be seen the very next week. And so it was here. The last time I talked with him was by telephone in 1965 when I called to inquire of his health. He said he had been ill and that he wanted to see me. "Do come and visit me," he urged.

"I promise," I said. "I'll be there within the next two weeks."

I never saw him again. He died the very next week.

# Chapter VII

## *1917–1929: The Black Renaissance, Broadway, the Harlem Theatre and the Road*

Pappy Harmon was one of the most colorful personalities who lived in Harlem during the nineteen-twenties. He was a tall, wiry man, and the weight of more than sixty years made his broad shoulders sag. White hair jutted from beneath his cap and framed his very black face. His old-fashioned overalls were creased and worn and his shoes run over at the heels.

Daily you could see Pappy and his horse, Maude, riding up 131st Street, pulling a wagon, sometimes filled with junk, sometimes with vegetables and at other times with fruit or fish. My father said you could tell the day of the week just by Pappy's appearance. If it was Friday, he sang out:

> Fry those porgies nice and brown,
> Come on down, only five cents a pound.
> Fishman, yay—
> Fresh fish today!

Many of the people who lived on our block didn't like Pappy Harmon. He was a "little too much." Some of our West Indian neighbors thought he was a throwback to the vendor of the islands. Many Southern Negroes felt he represented the salesman of the black communities—the type the authors of *Porgy and Bess* attempted to recreate in the Crab Man. Our white neighbors who had newly fallen in love with black people thought he was a stereotype, and therefore not of the same school as "their Negroes."

But Pappy went on selling his wares and caring for Maude. He was a rather silent man until he got into a long conversation with our doctor, Charles Augustin Petioni. It was through Dr. Petioni that my father struck up an acquaintance with Pappy. My father reasoned: "As busy as Doc is, if he got time to stand and talk to anybody for a half-hour, that man's just got to be worth *something*."

Pappy was a New Yorker who had been born in Greenwich

Village. He was in show business until 1910, when the wave of reaction excluded the Negro from Broadway. Finding other types of work dull and monotonous, he bought a wagon and began peddling. He told me once that he liked it because it gave him a chance to get around, to see a lot of people and find out what human beings were thinking.

"You never know unless you're out there among people just what's going to happen next," he said again and again. "You go hide someplace and you can find yourself kicked right out of a lot of places—like the theatre."

How Pappy gained possession of his horse, Maude, was described to me by my father. Maude had been formerly owned by a cruel Negro peddler who beat the horse mercilessly. One day the peddler was standing, talking to Pappy on the corner of 131st Street and Fifth Avenue. The peddler, for no reason, grabbed his whip and began to lash Maude's back. Pappy grimaced each time the whip landed. The horse let out a series of noises and looked back at her master. The whip landed again and again. Pappy, who had been a ventriloquist at one time, "threw his voice." It seemed as if the horse said: "Negro, don't you hit me no more!"

The peddler had his whip in the air, ready to land another blow. He paused as the voice came again: "Negro, I said for you not to hit me no more!"

The peddler screamed, dropped the whip, then started running down Fifth Avenue. He reached 125th Street, and although Negroes were beaten if they crossed it in those days, the peddler continued running. No one knows just how far he actually ran, but the stories that floated back to Harlem had him in Virginia, running every time he saw a horse. Pappy never confirmed or denied any of this, but my father insisted every word of it was true.

Pappy was devoted to Maude and to his pigeons, which he kept on the roof of the Fifth Avenue building in which he lived. Many times he took me up on the roof with him and he would cut his pigeons loose: "All right, children," he told them. "Come home safe."

He told me he called them his "children" because his wife and two children had all died long before he moved to Harlem. They were victims of influenza during the Spanish-American War. He had, therefore, only his horse, his pigeons and his books and papers.

And books and papers he had in abundance. They cluttered his small, two-room apartment, which was on the second floor front. I remember the small coal stove that sat in the center of the room, his old rocking chair and his small table. But most of all I remember his walls, which were covered with newspaper accounts. From these walls I learned Charles Gilpin appeared in John Drinkwater's *Abraham Lincoln* in 1917. This was considered historic because, with the exception of Bert Williams, Negroes did not work in the downtown theatre between 1910 and 1917. From these walls, too, I learned the Negro was considered a "natural" for the theatre in 1920. There developed in America a phenomenon that can only be described as "dramatic nationalism." Just as Sean O'Casey, J. M. Synge and Yeats and other Irishmen rejected European theatrical standards to build a truly Irish theatre, writers Eugene O'Neill, Philip Barry, Sidney Howard, Elmer Rice and others rejected European and puritanical standards. These men sought to deal with America in realistic terms. The Negro theatre artist benefited from this dramatic nationalism when Eugene O'Neill's *The Emperor Jones* opened at the Provincetown Playhouse in Greenwich Village in 1920.

For all its dramaturgical excellence, *The Emperor Jones* remains ludicrous. O'Neill managed a large measure of suspense, and there is something imposing about Brutus Jones, the ex-Pullman car porter, ex-convict, proclaiming himself Emperor of a West Indian island. As we see Jones "bleeding" the island people, robbing them just as he saw "white quality folks" do when he was a Pullman porter, we see the Negro who has accepted white standards. But unlike the whites who accept white standards, Jones is compelled to flee for his life, to race through jungles, and find himself reduced to nakedness, a tortured soul, hounded by drum beats.

This play, while offering one of the most magnificent roles for a Negro in the American theatre, is the first of a long line to deal with the Negro on this level. O'Neill obviously saw in the Negro rich subject matter, but he was either incapable or unwilling to deal directly with this matter. He chose, therefore, the Negro who would do the same things whites would do under similar circumstances—namely, establish an empire and exploit the people.

Well, to judge by recent developments, it becomes obvious that black people do *not* do what whites do when they assume power. Black people have few records of reprisals against white colonialists. In Kenya, where the Mau Mau was a potent factor, whites were not destroyed when freedom came. Nor in Nigeria and other African nations, with the possible exception of the Congo, where attacks were deliberately fostered by imperialists.

By having Jones react as he does, O'Neill implicitly suggests there is really no need to look toward the freeing of black people because, once freed, they will do the same thing as whites. This line of thinking is not as far from that in *The Birth of a Nation* and Jean Genet's *The Blacks* as the authors would have us believe.

Despite the objections to *The Emperor Jones*, one must note that, until that time, with the exception of the Harlem ventures, the Negro had been generally a comic character on stage. With *The Emperor Jones* the black man planted his feet firmly on the nation's stage and demanded to be dealt with seriously. And Charles Gilpin's great performance in the title role catapulted him to stardom.

The success of this play also split the Provincetown into factions. Some wanted to move the work to Broadway and others, led by Jasper Deeter, did not. As a result of this split Jasper Deeter founded the now famous Hedgerow Theatre in Moylan, Pennsylvania.

*The Emperor Jones* reigned, but *Shuffle Along* was on the horizon. This musical by Flournoy Miller, Aubrey Lyles, Noble Sissle and Eubie Blake would reach Broadway with a stellar cast and launch the period that became known as the Negro Renaissance. *Shuffle Along* did anything but shuffle. It exploded onto the stage. This revue, written by Negroes, produced and directed by Negroes for Negro audiences, ignored white tastes and imitations. Noble Sissle and Eubie Blake provided the score which had such hits as "Love Will Find A Way" and "I'm Just Wild About Harry." Paul Floyd directed a cast that could make up a "Who's Who in the Negro Theatre." The great Josephine Baker was in the chorus.

Eubie Blake and Noble Sissle told the story behind *Shuffle Along* one night in late 1965—at a party that could be described as a "name-dropper's delight." Among the guests were James Farmer, saxophonist Bud Freeman and Allan Morrison.

"Noble and I had been composing, leading bands and so on," said Mr. Blake. "One day we met Flournoy Miller and Aubrey Lyles, who wrote the sketches for *Darkydom*. They heard our music and Lyles said, 'You're our Sullivan and we're your Gilbert.' "

The four men wrote *Shuffle Along*. The cast was assembled in New York and arrangements were made to open at Washington's Howard Theatre.

"We had trouble getting fares for the cast," Mr. Sissle remembered, "but somehow we scratched the money up. We played two weeks in Washington, then we moved into the Dunbar in Philadelphia. And we played to standing room only. By the time we moved to New York's 63rd Street Theatre, the big city was ready for *Shuffle Along* and *Shuffle Along* was ready for the big city."

The leading female role was played by an actress named Florence Mills. Miss Mills had been a child prodigy. She was in the second company of Williams and Walker's *The Sons of Ham*. She had played various Harlem nightclubs with notable success, and when actress Gertrude Saunders became ill, Miss Mills replaced her in *Shuffle Along*. And like the show itself, she was sensational.

Pappy Harmon always told me that the treatment accorded Florence Mills indicated the lopsided nature of the American double standard. I did not really know the meaning of his words, but in those days—like most of the kids on my block—I thought Pappy Harmon knew everything. If Pappy said the Yankees would win the pennant, that Babe Ruth would hit a homer, that there'd be no war this year, I believed him.

The meaning of his statement was made clear to me one afternoon in 1965. I met George Wiltshire, the veteran actor, Sam Theard, composer of "I'll Be Glad When You Dead, You Rascal, You," and actor Ed Harding. We stood on the corner of 125th Street and Eighth Avenue and indulged in what is known in Harlem as "Black Communion." That communion comes when a group of black people get together and begin to talk and exchange ideas. It needs no church, no outer structure, yet there is a very real ritual. One person is going one way, the other another way, and still another is going another way. All happen to be in a hurry, yet they have time to stop and talk. I suspect that "Black Communion" has profited numerous taxi drivers trying to get late Negroes to early appointments.

At this particular session, George Wiltshire lamented the anonymity accorded Negro artists. As he pursued this theme, he said:

"They have shows eulogizing Fannie Brice, Eddie Cantor, Jolson, but, where, oh, where is the story of Bill Robinson, Fats Waller, Bessie Smith, Butterbeans and Susie? Where is the story of Florence Mills? All we have about her is the song, 'Memories of You,' written by Eubie Blake and Andy Razaf. That girl's life was like Andy's lyric—a rosary of tears."

Mr. Wiltshire's words stirred memories of Florence Mills. My mind raced back to the Harlem of the nineteen-twenties when her name was on the lips of everyone in the community. People sat in parlors, on stoops, or stood in hallways, trying to find words that might describe her. Such terms as "birdlike," "bell-like," "exciting," "beautiful" and "great" were applied to her, but these terms always seemed inadequate.

I was sitting on our stoop one evening during the nineteen-twenties, and the neighbors and my parents spoke of Miss Mills. They argued about adjectives that might apply to her. In the midst of the discussion, Pappy Harmon walked down the street on his way home. He stopped for a moment, listened to the talk, then asked:

"What's the matter with you all? Someone here was just looking for a white person to compare Florence with? Why do we always have to have a white person to remind us of ourselves? I got mad when they named Sissieretta Jones 'Black Patti.' Why can't we say there ain't no words for Florence Mills? Let's just say—she's Florence Mills."

Pappy turned away in obvious disgust, grunted a mute goodnight, then started toward his Fifth Avenue apartment. My neighbors continued to argue, and to chastise Pappy Harmon. But as the night began to creep around us and the street lights were turned on, they finally agreed that there were no words to describe Florence Mills. She was Florence Mills and that was a fact.

Miss Mills blazed a trail across Broadway during and after *Shuffle Along*. She remained with this show for a year, then producer Lew Leslie's *The Plantation Revue* claimed her. This was first tried out in a Harlem nightclub, expanded, then moved to Broadway on July 17, 1922. The next year Leslie took her to England, where she captivated British audiences in *From Dover to Dixie*. This vehicle was later retitled *Dixie to Broadway*, and it opened at the Broadhurst Theatre on October 29, 1924. As she

did throughout her career, the small, effervescent, lovely star captivated her audiences and earned another personal success.

In 1926 Miss Mills was back in the Harlem she loved. *Blackbirds*, written especially for her, opened at the Alhambra Theatre,
126th Street and Seventh Avenue. It played for six weeks; then
Leslie took the show to Paris for six months. It then played London, and the story is told that the Prince of Wales saw it sixteen
times.

Harlem—and New York itself—waited for Miss Mills to come
home and open *Blackbirds* in the big city. They waited to hear
her sing her song, "I'm a Little Blackbird Looking for a Bluebird."
They waited in vain, for a delayed operation for appendicitis
claimed her life.

Lilyn Brown Wilson, actress and friend of Miss Mills, looked
out the funeral car and, amidst tears, pointed a finger into Lew
Leslie's face: "I guess you're satisfied," she told him. "You worked
her to death."

Mr. Leslie cried: "I didn't, I didn't. I kept telling her to get
that operation, but she said she didn't have time. She had too
many people waiting for her."

All Harlem cried. I know. I was there. Thousands of people lined
the streets, watching the funeral procession. And an airplane flew
over the city, releasing a flock of blackbirds.

It was from the newspapers on Pappy Harmon's wall that I
first learned of the Negro Renaissance. I knew there was a Renaissance Theatre on 137th Street and Seventh Avenue and that there
was a ballroom of that name above the theatre, but the exact
meaning of the term was to come to me years later when Langston Hughes so ably defined it in his autobiography, *The Big Sea*.
This, in Mr. Hughes' words, was "when the Negro was in vogue."
Whites journeyed to Harlem nightly and frequented cabarets
and nightclubs. A thriving business belonged to the Harlem "host."
This host was a man who printed cards indicating where he
could be reached. When Mr. and Mrs. Rich White Folks visited
New York, they telephoned the host, who arranged to escort
them through Harlem. The fees for this type of service were
remarkable.

In addition, Negro arts flourished. Books were written by and
about Negroes. Jazz swept the nation, and the Savoy Ballroom

on Lenox Avenue attracted all the great bands. New dances blossomed from the community's streets—the Charleston, the Black Bottom and the Lindy Hop.

Harlem of the Renaissance was a direct part of America itself.

This nation, in its preadolescence during the Industrial Revolution, had expanded its borders and linked together two oceans. Railroad tracks had been laid, wireless developed, and the automobile and the airplane became realities. The nation went to war in April, 1917, "to make the world safe for democracy." Young Americans sailed across the Atlantic and boldly asked war-weary Europe: "Where's this shooting gallery?" And by November of the following year this young upstart of a nation had beaten the German war machine to its knees. The doughboys came home, floating on the waves of optimism and euphoria that rolled over the land. There was to be "no more war." The nation was big now, half-grown, and like too many adolescents, it mistook its size and strength for maturity and manhood. It ignored the cries of other nations to join in forming a League of Nations. America turned its back on involvements with others and sought its own destiny.

But a nation does not mature rapidly, especially one dedicated to quick, easy living, to acquiring and displaying wealth. The hustle and the bustle of those who sought to acquire dollars and glory brought a built-in energy and signs of eventual destruction. This was the era of big things. Babe Ruth set new baseball records as his big bat propelled balls out of parks. He was responsible for the building of Yankee Stadium, described even today by commentator Red Barber as "the *big* ball park." William S. Hart could shoot faster than any cowboy in the old West, our movies said, and Tom Mix was able to beat up three badmen at one time. The movies told glorious lies of our covered wagons traveling west, meeting Indians and killing them. On Broadway Florenz Ziegfeld produced big, big shows that glorified the American girl. Big cars belonged to those who could afford them, and big gangsters fought over the right to sell bootleg liquor and needled beer. It was, in short, an era that could only exist in a youthful, or at most an adolescent nation.

The country craved excitement, and it took flings with various cultural groups. It was only natural that the Negro would become

A *great actress of the twenties, Rose McClendon appeared in* In
Abraham's Bosom *and other important plays.*

"in vogue." Thrill-seekers met the so-called New Negro in the Harlem of the nineteen-twenties. And this Harlem also held numerous Southerners and West Indians who, having heard that their relatives became rich during the First World War, deserted their homelands and journeyed to the North, to Harlem, Harlem, U.S.A.

Harlem was heaven, then. Negro artists captured New York. Many had white patrons with money to spend, and they spent lavishly. The steps of the people of Harlemtown were light and gay. For many black and white Americans, this was the millennium.

While America enjoyed itself during the twenties, other voices tried to say other things about this culture. Some of these voices were not particularly noteworthy, but at least they attempted to be heard.

Eugene O'Neill was certainly one of those voices. His efforts in dealing with Negroes appear more sincere than skillful. His *Dreamy Kid*, shown at the Provincetown, dealt with Negro super-stition and gangster life. Admittedly, this was an early play, but it showed none of the powerful characterizations that emerge in *Desire Under the Elms, The Iceman Cometh, Mourning Becomes Electra* and his other work. He was simply not on familiar ground in his plays of Negro life.

No one particularly cared then, for a lot was happening. That fine actor Frank Wilson had his first play, *Sugar Cane*, produced during the nineteen-twenties. Ernest Howard Culbertson's *Goat Alley* reached the Bijou Theatre on June 20, 1921. The great Bert Williams died in 1922. *Strut, Miss Lizzie* by Creamor and Layton reached New York via Chicago on June 15, 1922. Nan Bagby Stephens wrote *Roseanne*, and Paul Robeson made his first profes-sional stage appearance in Mary Hoyt Wiborg's *Taboo*. It has already been noted that Florence Mills starred in Lew Leslie's *Plantation Revue*, which moved into the 48th Street Theatre on July 17, 1922. And, on April 16, 1923, Eddie Hunter's *How Come?*, featuring jazz musician Sidney Bechet, was shown at the Apollo Theatre.

Meanwhile, in Harlem, Lester Walton left the Lafayette, and Frank Schiffman bought it. Vaudeville proved to be increasingly popular there, and soon that theatre was showing a motion picture "sandwiched" by specialty live numbers.

Raymond O'Neil and Mrs. Sherwood Anderson brought Chicago's Ethiopian Art Players to Harlem, and when the community was unkind to this group, the producers moved their work to Broadway in May, 1923. One of the plays, *The Chipwoman's Fortune*, was the work of that serious, talented Negro playwright Willis Richardson. It was particularly well received, and so was *Salome* with Evelyn Preer. A jazz version of *The Comedy of Errors* was less fortunate.

Noble Sissle and Eubie Blake were heard from again on September 1, 1924. Their *Chocolate Dandies* opened on Broadway. This tuneful, fast-moving show had Josephine Baker in a small role.

The most notorious theatrical event of 1924 was the Provincetown's production of Eugene O'Neill's *All God's Chillun Got Wings*. Paul Robeson and Mary Blair played the leads in this show. The script, published prior to production in the *American Mercury*, dealt with a Negro intellectual who marries a "lost" white woman. Yellow journalism blazed. Headlines, editorials and news stories sought to destroy the work. Fears of racial trouble spread. Nevertheless, the production opened, and the tense opening-night audience was ready for anything. The critics disliked the work. They were many steps behind Negroes, who hated it.

In discussing *All God's Chillun Got Wings*, I am reminded of a conversation I overheard between my father and Pappy Harmon. A popular speaker had appeared at a Harlem church, and he wondered why a greater number of citizens did not appear. My father echoed the speaker's lament. Pappy Harmon answered them both:

"Harlem ain't got just one problem," he said. "It's got so many that sometimes—while it's being attacked on one front—it's also being attacked on another."

So it was with *All God's Chillun Got Wings*. O'Neill brought to the stage a Negro intellectual who marries a white woman who is not only outside of his race but outside of his "class." The hero of this play would have had trouble had he married a black woman on the level of the white he married.

Whether O'Neill knew or understood that cannot be decided here. He was, however, talking about interracial marriage, and Negroes were fighting to be free, to eat regularly, live decently and get white feet off their necks.

The Harlem revival of O'Neill's *The Emperor Jones* at the

Lincoln Theatre during the twenties illustrates this. The great Jules
Bledsoe played the Emperor, and Langston Hughes tells us that
when Bledsoe ran through the jungle, Negroes shouted from the
audience: "Man, you come on outa that jungle! This is Harlem!"

That may sound folklorish, but it is also one of the reasons the
theatre became a middle-class luxury, for it avoided speaking to
people in terms of the truth of their daily lives. It was, therefore,
easy for people to turn from the lies and fairy tales placed on the
American stage to those manufactured by Hollywood, especially
since the latter were considerably less expensive.

We see then that from 1821, when the African Theatre was
wrecked by hoodlums, the American theatre charted a course that
reeked with dishonesty. It was a course that sought to sell audiences prejudices toward black people—a course easily followed
because many whites had been denied status in their own lands,
and now they sought it by denying it to black people.

Negro pioneers—Williams and Walker, Cole and Johnson and
others—stepped in to revolutionize theatrical concepts regarding
the Negro. But they fought their revolution on the grounds of
the oppressors. They used the same weapons—the blackface, the
low comedy—and did the things whites would pay to see Negroes
do. They used for their reasoning the belief that whites would
not accept them any other way. These Negroes, then, were true
to the first American Revolution. They engaged in a reform
movement, not a revolution. They fought a defensive action, rather
than an offensive one. The wrecking of the African Company,
therefore, reached down through the years from 1821 and rever-
berated into the 1920s and beyond.

This reverberation was felt in Negro-authored plays as well as
ones by whites. Garland Anderson's *Appearances,* which appeared
in 1925, is often spoken of as "the first Negro-written Broadway
drama," despite the fact that Willis Richardson's *The Chipwoman's Fortune* was shown in May, 1923. Mr. Anderson's work
reflected more tenacity on his part than dramatic skill. The play
left the boards after a short run.

Tim Moore, later to become famous on television as Kingfish
in the Amos 'n Andy series, appeared on Broadway in *Lucky
Sambo.* That period also saw productions of *My Magnolia* and
*Deep River* and a revival of *The Emperor Jones* with Charles

Gilpin and Moss Hart—the same Moss Hart who was to become a prominent dramatist, direct *My Fair Lady* and later write *Act One*.

In 1926 Paul Green's *In Abraham's Bosom* opened at the Provincetown Playhouse. Mr. Green had previously earned a measure of acclaim in New York City. His *The No Count Boy* was brought to the city by the Carolina Playmakers, and it won the Little Theatre Tournament Award. For *In Abraham's Bosom* he had a distinguished cast, led by Rose McClendon, Abbie Mitchell and Jules Bledsoe, who was later succeeded by Frank Wilson. The play won the Pulitzer Prize for 1926. For all of Mr. Green's sincerity and dramatic skill, *In Abraham's Bosom* is not a great play. It seems to have little relationship to the plight of the American Negro at that point in the nation's history. He presented to us a man named Abraham who attempted to "elevate" his people through education. In the midst of all of this, Abraham has trouble with black people and white people and, of course, he ends up by killing a white man.

That same year, 1926, Flournoy Miller and Aubrey Lyles followed their *Shuffle Along* with *Runnin' Wild*. This show, produced by George White, introduced the music of James Johnson to theatre audiences. A. Harrington Gibbs wrote the title song of this work, which ran for eight months. *Runnin' Wild* also introduced the dance called the Charleston to Broadway audiences.

Miller and Lyles were great performing artists as well as creative writers. Teamwork, timing, respect for each other, respect for audiences and genuine talent dominated their routines. Much of their work has been copied by other comedians, particularly the skit in which Miller says to Lyles:

MILLER: Man, I was just over to that house and I saw—
LYLES (*interrupting*): I saw him yesterday and he said—
MILLER: Did he say that? Why, I was told—
LYLES: I heard that, too, but I thought—
MILLER: I thought so, too! (*Then*) The thing I like about you is, a man can always get into a good conversation with you!

No report does this routine justice. Split-second timing, inflection, gesture and sheer artistry surrounded it. And this was not "handkerchief-head stuff." These men were telling audiences that Negroes have a dialogue with each other and you can laugh at it if you like, but you'd better listen to it.

Miller and Lyles also wrote *Rang Tang*, which featured Daniel Haynes and Evelyn Prior. On February 27, 1928, their *Keep Shufflin'* opened. Aubrey Lyles died in 1933 and Flournoy Miller went on to the West Coast, where he lives today.

The year 1926 brought still another play about Negro life. This was David Belasco's production of *Lula Belle*, written by Charles MacArthur and Edward Sheldon. This was the same Charles MacArthur who, with Ben Hecht, would later write *The Front Page, Twentieth Century, Jumbo* and *Ladies and Gentlemen*. And this was the same Edward Sheldon whose *The Nigger* created a Broadway sensation in 1910, and whose *Romance* proved a popular favorite.

*Lula Belle* had an interracial cast. Lenore Ulric played a prostitute and Henry Hull was a Negro barber. Evelyn Prior was the second lead, and she was later succeeded by Edna Thomas. The play was colorfully produced, but it was sheer melodrama that did no more than capitalize on the popularity of Harlem during that era.

The year 1927 brought *Porgy*, written by DuBose and Dorothy Heyward, based on Mr. Hayward's novel of the same name. Its cast included Frank Wilson, Georgette Harvey, Jack Carter, Wesley Hill, Rose McClendon, Evelyn Ellis, Leigh Whipper, A. B. Cromathiere, Richard Huey and Percy Verwayne. *Porgy* later became the basis of the opera, *Porgy and Bess*. That same year Ethel Waters reached Broadway in Earl Dancer's production, *Africana*.

Lew Leslie ushered his *Blackbirds of 1928* to Broadway the following season. This starred the great dancer Bill "Bojangles" Robinson, Adelaide Hall, Ada Ward and Johnny Hudgins. Such song hits as "I Can't Give You Anything But Love," "I Must Have That Man" and "Diga Diga Do" were featured in this show, which ran for five hundred performances. The following year Mr. Leslie brought his *Blackbirds of 1929* to Broadway, and this featured the music of Eubie Blake.

In 1929 a stark melodrama named *Harlem* opened. This was the work of that fine Negro writer Wallace Thurman, in collaboration with William Rapp. The short-lived play was directed by

Chester Erskine, and it featured Isabell Washington and Inez Clough. It was a startlingly realistic drama of Harlem life, of its evils as faced by a mother in an uptown flat. In many ways James Baldwin's portraits of Harlem are decidedly reminiscent of Thurman's—a fact cited often by Arna Bontemps in his discussions of the modern black writer's relationship to the Negro Renaissance.

These plays produced during America's adolescence are not unrelated to the present crop of dramas about black people. These were either fast-moving musicals or folk plays that generally depicted the Negro in conflict with himself and his people. Few, if any, faced the direct problems of the Negro grappling with the power structure.

Adolescent pimples appeared on the nation's face. These were pricked, and scars and blemishes were left. They remain to date.

Sometimes I think there are human beings who know they are destined to die young. These people pour every ounce of energy into living. They create, build and organize in rapid-fire tempo. I think, too, there are periods of history that are much the same. The nineteen-twenties was one. That decade with its breathtaking pace was crammed with social, cultural and political activities as it raced towards its death.

Death is final but never meaningless. A seed is placed in the ground and it sprouts anew. And the nineteen-twenties left many seeds. Not only was the Negro on Broadway stages, but he had theatres in Harlem and on the road as well. He had such producers as S. H. Dudley, Tutt Whitney, J. Homer Tutt and Irving Miller, and had that phenomenal organization known as Theatrical Owners and Bookers Association, or T.O.A.B.A.—or "Toby-time." It was also jokingly and affectionately known as "Tough on Black Actors"—much as one laughs at a good job with such signs as: "You Don't Have to be Crazy to Work Here, But It Helps."

This organization booked Negro performers into houses across the nation. It must be remembered that around the turn of the twentieth century there were about five thousand theatres in the United States. Almost every city boasted one or more resident companies, and these theatres attracted great stars from the New York stage. The arrival of the talking picture brought a decline in the number of these theatres, and by 1940 there remained only about two hundred professional theatres in the entire country. But these theatres were there in the days of "Toby-time," and veteran actor George Wiltshire declares that endless work made it possible for actors constantly to polish their techniques. The rise of the movie medium and the growing influence of white managers destroyed "Toby-time." But it left us many fine veterans who paved the way for others.

The latter part of the nineteen-twenties saw Dr. W. E. B. DuBois organize the Krigwa Players in connection with *Crisis* magazine, the official publication of the NAACP. Dr. DuBois feared for the death of the Negro folk play, and he advocated a drama written by Negroes, produced by Negroes and supported by Negroes. The Krigwa group won a place in the Little Theatre Tournament and competed for the David Belasco trophy. It did not win the trophy, but its production of Eulalie Spence's *The Fool's Errand* won one of the Samuel French prizes for being the best unpublished script in the contest. Such works as Willis Richardson's *Compromise*, Georgia Douglas Johnson's *Broken Banjo and Blue Blood* and Eulalie Spence's *Brothers and Sisters of the Church Council* were in Krigwa's repertoire.

The year 1928 brought another venture to Harlem. Regina Andrews, Dorothy Williams, Gladys Reid, Benjamin Locke, Inez R. Wilson, Jessie Fawcett and Harold Jackman spearheaded the founding of the Harlem Experimental Theatre. Its repertoire included *Plumes, A Sunny Morning, Duchess Says Her Prayers, The No Count Boy, Little Stone Ladder, Prodigal Son, Rider of Dreams* and *Climbing Jacob's Ladder.*

On June 20, 1929, the Negro Art Theatre was born at Abyssinia Baptist Church. Spearheading this venture was the present Congressman, Adam Clayton Powell. Laura Bowman was in the cast of *Wade in the Water.* And during the nineteen-twenties the Harlem Community Players produced Edward Smith's *Release* in the auditorium of the 135th Street Library.

On July 30, 1929, the Dunbar Garden Players offered *Before Breakfast* and Alice Brown's *Joint Owners of Spain* at St. Mark's Church. Eulalie Spence was the director.

It was high summer by then, and the year moved along, seemingly toward the usual exciting moment. But there were ominous signs. The New York Yankees had won the American League pennant in 1926, 1927, 1928. But, somehow, in 1929 they weren't breaking down fences. Babe Ruth's big bat still boomed balls into the seats, and Lou Gehrig was hitting with remarkable power. But the Philadelphia Athletics were winning games with a consistency that worried many people. On the street corner we youngsters heard many old-timers shake their heads and wonder if this weren't the end of an era.

It should be noted here that the image of the New York Yankees baseball team differed sharply in the nineteen-twenties from its image at present. The New York Giants, then playing at the Polo Grounds in Harlem, represented the "aristocrats." That team had a large number of hostile Southern whites playing for it and Harlem youngsters were not welcomed there with the hospitality we found at Yankee Stadium. Our allegiance was, therefore, to the Yankees and when they won, we won. And now that they were losing, we were losing.

After one particularly disastrous Yankee series I went looking for Pappy Harmon. I knew that all he had to tell me was that the Yankees would win the pennant, and then they would win it. When I reached the corner of 131st Street and Fifth Avenue, I saw a crowd milling around in front of the building where Pappy lived. I caught my breath, and suddenly the plight of the Yankees seemed of little significance. I dashed across the street and found my father in the center of the crowd.

"You, boy! You go on home," he said. "Right now!"

"What's wrong, Pop?" I pleaded. "What's wrong?"

"They found Pappy Harmon dead this morning," a man told me. My father glared at the man, then urged me again to go home.

I walked away. My tears blinded me momentarily, and I leaned against the lamppost on Fifth Avenue. Through the mist that filled my eyes I saw dimly that several men were coming out of the building, carrying Pappy's books and papers. They dumped these into his wagon, then one started leading Maude away. Maude trudged, slowly, continually looking back until she had turned the corner. A moment later another group of men brought a covered figure out the door and placed it in a big car. The car drove off and the crowd began to drift away.

Later that afternoon I sneaked into the backyard of the building where Pappy Harmon had once lived. I climbed the fire escape to the roof, then walked across it and cut his pigeons loose.

They soared westward toward Lenox Avenue, then beyond it. As they crossed Seventh Avenue they seemed to meet with a group of blackbirds, and I remember that I wondered if Pappy's pigeons and Florence Mills' blackbirds hadn't met up there in the sky to make a long, long journey together.

# Chapter VIII

## *The Depression Years: Propaganda Plays, the Federal Theatre, Efforts Toward a New Harlem Theatre*

When the stock market crashed in 1929, Variety's headline declared: "Wall Street Lays an Egg!" This apt headline was first shown to me by Dick Campbell, the actor-singer, who was later to become a producer-director and theatre builder. At that time Mr. Campbell was a tall, thin, pleasant young man, playing the Alhambra Theatre. He had just played 219 performances of *Hot Chocolates*, a revue written by Andy Razaf, with music by Thomas "Fats" Waller and Harry Brooks, directed by Leonard Harper. This revue opened at the Hudson Theatre on June 20, 1929; and along with Mr. Campbell, that old veteran of the Negro theatre, Eddie Green, was prominently featured.

Mr. Campbell, as of this writing, is Director of Information and Development for Operation Crossroads Africa—the group founded by the Reverend James Robinson which is the prototype for the Peace Corps. In addition, Mr. Campbell is Chairman of the newly formed Committee on Desegregating the Arts. This, in itself, is a commentary on the Negro in the theatre, since Mr. Campbell is in his fourth decade of attempts to bring a measure of equality, justice and truthful representation to the American theatregoer and theatre worker.

Dick Campbell was born fighting. He was an end on his college football team; and when he went into theatre, he harassed agents, producers and managers as though they were opposing players. He challenged any attack on his dignity. One blazing example of this was when he and his late wife, Muriel Rahn, were booked into a Philadelphia house for $150 weekly. The manager cried "poor" and suggested that Campbell and Rahn accept $75. Unions were not what they are today, and many managers got away with such stunts. This one didn't. Mr. Campbell called the police. He also called the Fire Department, and both showed up at the theatre at the same time.

"Where's the fire?" asked the Chief.

"I'm the fire!" screamed Campbell. "I want our money. All of it!"

"I don't see any fire," said the Chief.

"Then, look at me!" Campbell roared. "I'm burning up."

"Why'd you call the police?" asked an officer.

"Because I'm being robbed!" yelled Campbell. "And burned up, too!"

The police, the Fire Department and the "poor" manager had a conference. And Campbell and Rahn got their money.

Mr. Campbell stands as one of the truly majestic figures of the nineteen-thirties. He was there, dreaming of a bright future for the Negro theatre worker, just as James Hewlett did in the early nineteenth century, Bert Williams in the latter nineteenth century, Lester Walton and Eddie Hunter in the early part of the twentieth century, and the Lafayette Players after World War I. And very few Negroes in the modern theatre do not trace their beginning back to association and training with Dick Campbell.

His role is peculiarly American, for if the Negro performers now in theatre and on television don't know of the fights Mr. Campbell and his associates waged to open doors for them, they can take satisfaction in the realization that not too many whites know the suffering and agony of their pioneering parents. And they will never know until the true stories of these lives are faithfully projected from our stages and screens.

I always remember Dick Campbell as he was on the very first day I sold him a newspaper backstage at the Alhambra Theatre. He was ready to laugh easily, and to joke about things being "so tough that roosters are walking around hens, counting the eggs they are laying."

During those early depression years you could hear headliners talk about times being hard. These performers tried to maintain their dignity and status, but there simply were not the jobs around that they once had. And so they dreamed many dreams—of new shows that would soon open, of great roles to come and of plays yet to be written. Dick Campbell looked at them as he listened, and more than once I heard him say that a new day was dawning, that there would never be a return to the days that had passed. He reiterated that the time had arrived for the building of a Harlem theatre, unique unto itself, *for* the people of Harlem and supported by *them*.

One night an elderly performer upbraided him: "Young fellow, you're the one dreaming. We've got to get back downtown where the money is. The white folks have all the money."

Mr. Campbell said: "I just heard a man out there on 125th Street. He said that white folks can always figure out a way of keeping Negroes from downtown. First, they were beating up Negroes down there. Now, with this depression, Negroes are afraid to walk downtown—afraid that all those white folks who lost their money are jumping out of skyscraper windows and they just might land on colored folks' heads!"

Roars of laughter filled the backstage area. But such humor was short-lived. Panic raged. Tears flooded the nation's eyes as the economic depression clawed the souls, minds and bodies of all who lived during that era. The scars from this clawing remain with us today, making us frightened in the midst of abundance and unimaginative in a period of readjustment when we should be boldly inventive.

Joblessness reigned in the nineteen-thirties. Once proud men stood on 125th Street with signs on their coat lapels, reading: "Unemployed. Please buy apples." But few people had money to buy even an apple.

Families who could not pay their rent saw their furnishings put out on sidewalks. Poverty forced many families to move eighteen times within nine years. Homes for these families became dark, dank, shifting rows of tenements, totally lacking in permanency and security. Homeless men wandered across the nation, eating from garbage cans, if they found any filled. Once proud workers lived in "Hoovervilles"—the name given to the collection of shacks they erected in vacant lots along river fronts. And black women "shaped up" on the Bronx slave market—which means they stood around, waiting for white women to approach them and offer them a day's domestic work at twenty-five cents per hour. Meanwhile, in Washington, President Herbert Hoover declared prosperity was just around the corner, that soon there'd be a chicken in every pot.

Local movies and stage shows were suddenly out of one's financial reach. Though the theatre was just across the street, financially it was a million miles away.

Dusty Fletcher appeared at the Alhambra in a vaudeville skit, "Suprise Me." Apus Brooks, Sandy Burns, George Wiltshire, Sidney Easton and Johnny Hudgins appeared there, too, along with countless headliners. Backstage performers kept dreaming of days to come, of glorious days. One night the talk began to circulate about a play that was going to open on Broadway in February, 1930. The name of that play was *The Green Pastures*. A lot of actors were enthusiastic about its chances, but Dick Campbell asked a grave question. "From what I know of that script," he said, "I don't know which is going to claw the Negro image the most—that play or this depression."

*The Green Pastures* opened at the Mansfield Theatre on February 26, 1930. Marc Connelly based his play on Roark Bradford's burlesque stories, *Old Man Adam and His Chillun*. The work, labeled "an attempt to see certain aspects of a living religion," describes a Southern Negro child's image of the Creation. God, for the child, is "De Lawd"—a frock-coated, ten-cent-cigar-smoking preacher, witnessing the fish-fry, the crap-shooters, sinners and Noah wanting a second keg of liquor to balance his Ark. Black blood flowed in those pastures as white knives ripped at the Negro image.

Such Negro theatre veterans as Jesse Shipp, Homer Tutt, Tutt Whitney, Wesley Hill, Daniel Haynes, Oscar Polk, the Hall Johnson Choir and Richard B. Harrison tried valiantly to "clean up" this work, to give it dignity and poignancy.

Burns Mantle included the work in his *The Best Plays of 1929–1930*. An interesting note was made by Mr. Mantle in his comments on this play: "Possibly no other people could accept this naïve retelling of the story of the Old Testament, as a colored preacher in Louisiana might relate it to his Sunday School class, as the American people have accepted and will accept it.

"It demands, first, something of the background a majority of the American people experienced in living with their puritan and essentially religious forbears. It demands, second, a knowledge of and a kindly sympathy for the Southern Negro and his trusting and child-like religious faith, to give it its best values as a recital in dramatic form."

The play catapulted Richard B. Harrison to stardom. Mr. Harrison had been a dramatic reader and teacher for many years. He played the role of De Lawd with dignity and moving sincerity. After the New York run of 557 performances, he toured with the show. And both he and Wesley Hill died while the show was on the road. The New York *Daily News* carried in its midsection a number of pictures and, above these, was the line: "De Lawd Moves on to Greener Pastures."

Gertrude McBrown, actress-director-writer, once vividly described Richard B. Harrison's torment when he appeared at a Washington reception with bodyguards, hired by the producers. Mr. Harrison told the reception guests of his dreams that someday the Negro would be truthfully portrayed on the American stage. He added: "They waited around till I'm near dead, then offered me this role in this play—and then started serving me on a silver platter!"

Of the play, Sterling Brown once said: "*The Green Pastures* is really Marc Connelly's version of what Roark Bradford said was a Negro preacher's version of religion." If we accept this view, we witness again white people's ignorance of Negro life. A cursory examination of black religion would indicate it is many things to many people. Like other groups, Negroes have cultists, charlatans and great leaders growing out of their religiosity. The failure to understand black religion did not start with Bradford and Connelly. Slavemasters thought their singing slaves had religion while the slaves actually sang out freedom messages. The slavemasters' descendants were equally wrong about the black preacher and his followers.

Nor was black religion chastised exclusively by just one section of white society. In the nineteen-thirties the left wing spoke of it, superciliously, as an "opiate." And the Negro's religion is made a mockery in such plays as *Mighty Wind A-Blowin'*, *Mamba's Daughters* and *They Shall Not Die*. Yet this is the same sensitive religion that prompted the great Sojourner Truth to ask a momentarily discouraged Frederick Douglass: "Frederick, is God dead?"

This same religion with its black preacher has played a historic role in the march toward freedom. Anyone really interested in portraying the truth about the Negro could point out scores of great leaders, past and present, who have made undying contributions to the cause of America. That Connelly and Bradford would malign this group in their work is a monument to the injustices committed in the name of art. Dick Campbell summed it up like this: "I would be a traitor to the religion of my ancestors if I did not decry *The Green Pastures*. And I think that we—as a nation—would not be in foreign or domestic difficulties if Connelly and Bradford's ancestors had produced the crop of ministers that we have!"

After *The Green Pastures* proved to be less than complimentary for the black image, along came *Scarlet Sister Mary* with Ethel Barrymore playing in blackface. In 1931 Paul Green's *The House of Connelly* was produced by the Group Theatre, and it featured Negroes in minor, truthful roles. *Singing the Blues* with Frank Wilson, Isabell Washington, Jack Carter and Dick Campbell also appeared during that era. Then there was *Savage Rhythm* starring Venezuela Jones, Juano Hernandez and Ernest Whitman, as well as DuBose Heyward's *Brass Ankle*.

The year 1932 brought *Black Souls*, a well-intentioned play, but not nearly as fascinating as James R. Millen's *Never No More*. The author of the latter had witnessed a lynching, and his work records this in brutal, devastating, unbearable terms. Rose Mc-Clendon was her usual excellent self in this work. Another play, *Bloodstream*, depicted the brutality accorded black and white convict mine labor.

But the outstanding theatrical event of 1932 did not take place on the theatrical stage. It occurred, rather, on the political stage: Franklin Delano Roosevelt was elected the thirty-second President of the United States. Roosevelt's election was more than political; it was fundamentally revolutionary. Prior to his election the nation had been looking for a return to the "good old days," to the days when there would be two cars in every garage and a chicken in every pot. The nation, in short, looked for what the Negro actors had dreamed of, and it decried Dick Campbell for saying that this was the time to look for "something new."

With Roosevelt's election the country gave up nostalgic dreams and decided to make a complete change. Roosevelt, with his big smile, with his spirit of hope, with his "All we have to fear is fear itself," brought a surge of hope to all America. This bold hope made its way into the theatre. The American stage became a battleground of ideas where old ways were challenged and new dreams daringly dreamt. The so-called propaganda play forged the dreams of black people for freedom and the dreams of white men for a decent living.

One exception was Hall Johnson's poignant, nonpropaganda production *Run, Little Children*, in 1933. Mr. Johnson had, over many years, recorded, arranged and had his choir render the Negro spirituals. It has been said by many people that if Hall Johnson had not appeared on the American scene, many of our spirituals would be unknown today.

Mr. Johnson brought all of his artistry, musical and otherwise, into writing for the theatre. *Run, Little Children* told of a conflict between a pagan cult and a Baptist Church. The music of Hall Johnson's choir flowed from all parts of the theatre, and his wonderfully alive characters were played by such fine actors as Fredi Washington, Austin Burleigh and Edna Thomas. The play was one of the major events of the season; and following its Broadway run, it included Harlem's Lafayette Theatre on its tour.

The year 1934 brought John Wexley's *They Shall Not Die*. This exciting, pulsating dramatic experience dealt with the infamous Scottsboro Case. The "rape frame-up" of nine Negro boys in Alabama revealed Southern injustice and brutality, stirred the national conscience and caused considerable agitation. Mr. Wexley captured all of this in his play, and he was helped immeasurably by such stars as Claude Rains, Ruth Gordon and Frank Wilson.

Two other works involving Negroes deviated from the so-called propaganda play. *Four Saints in Three Acts* by Gertrude Stein and Virgil Thomson had in major roles Edward Matthews, Bruce Howard, Beatrice Robinson-Wayne and John Diggs. The second work was *Kykunko*, an African dance-opera by Asadata Dafora. This adaptation of an African ritual dance was first shown in a small hall on 23rd Street. General acclaim led to its being moved to an uptown house, and the work later became the basis for an African unit of the Federal Theatre project.

Teeth gnashed and people squirmed when Langston Hughes' *Mulatto* opened on Broadway in 1934. Many critics complained that the play was too realistic, too bitter and too hostile. Nevertheless, audiences flocked to it, and the play enjoyed a long run. Rose McClendon played the female lead in this play with all the talent she possessed, which was considerable. Mr. Hughes' work told compellingly of an illicit, interracial relationship in the South and a mulatto son's hatred for his white father. It was later adapted into the opera *The Barrier*, which starred Muriel Rahn and Lawrence Tibbett.

*Stevedore* was another exciting, realistic drama. It opened at

the Civic Repertory Theatre on 14th Street in 1934. This was
the theatre in which Eva LeGalliene had once housed her repertory company. But a group known as the Theatre Union, Inc.,
was interested in another type of drama. It brought a pithy antiwar play called *Peace on Earth* into the old house where the
works of Ibsen and Chekhov had been played. And then it
brought *Stevedore*, which was written by Paul Peters and George
Sklar.

Rex Ingram, Jack Carter, Leigh Whipper, Georgette Harvey
and Edna Thomas were prominent in this tough play, which
was much more than mere propaganda. A militant Negro is
"framed," but the mob is chased at the end by white and black
dockhands. The play was so convincing that it is said tap-dancer
Bill Robinson, while witnessing a performance, became so involved that he jumped to the stage and joined the dockhands in
stoning the mob.

Negroes were shouting and screaming then, in theatre and out,
demanding an end to injustices, demanding fair employment and
fair housing. They recognized, in and out of the theatre, the need
for white support. Anyone who had listened then would have
known the Negro was not going to accept anything less than full
human rights. Nor was he going to accept fully the patchwork,
piecemeal measures that sought to delay his demands. The fact
that these voices of the nineteen-thirties fell on deaf ears is directly related to present-day events in Los Angeles, Chicago and
Springfield.

If the nineteen-thirties brought excitement and social protest
to our theatre, they also saw Paul Green's *Roll, Sweet Chariot*
go down to glorious failure. They saw, too, the advent of the
George Gershwin–Ira Gershwin–DuBose Heyward–Dorothy Heyward folk opera, *Porgy and Bess*, a work generally hailed by whites
and disliked by many Negroes.

I am not equipped to discuss *Porgy and Bess* objectively. When
I saw it as a teen-ager, I found its characters stereotypes and its
music imitative and not nearly as moving as its source. Since
many people insisted the work was great, I saw a revival of it
in the nineteen-forties. But I made a great mistake. My brother,
Melvin, was then eleven years old, and I took him to the theatre
almost weekly. The week before we saw *Porgy and Bess*, we took

standing room to see Paul Robeson in *Othello*. Little Melvin stood through the show and he was enchanted. After the performance I introduced him to Mr. Robeson. The child was deliriously happy, and all through the week he talked about the play and its star. He could hardly wait for the next Saturday, he told his friends, for he was going to see more black actors on stage.

The child practically raced me to the subway, and it didn't run fast enough for him. What must have been ages later for him, we found ourselves sitting in the first row at City Center. Then, the show started. As the characters moved on stage, Melvin began to fidget nervously. He sensed something was going to happen—and it did. One character called another a "nigger." My brother groaned, and when I looked toward him he had slumped in his seat, literally attempting to hide.

When we left the theatre, his head was bowed. He was silent beyond the meaning of the word, and when I finally broke through his silence, he simply said: "I didn't like that."

All that week he was mute, as memories of the play haunted him. When I told my friends what had happened, many of them called me stupid for taking an eleven-year-old to see an opera. My reply was—if he could stand through Shakespeare and enjoy it, he certainly should be able to sit through an opera. I thought then and now that there wasn't anything wrong with either of us, but there was something wrong about *Porgy and Bess*.

The following Saturday I invited Melvin to go with me to see another Broadway play. His answer was: "No, thanks. Somebody might be saying that *word* again."

That was the beginning of a long theatrical silence between my brother and me. When we saw another play together, he was a teen-ager, more than six feet tall, and even then he shuddered when a Negro actor appeared on stage. For he was waiting—waiting to hear "that word."

The nineteen-thirties also saw *The Swing Mikado* develop from the Federal Theatre project. Its success prompted private producers to launch *The Hot Mikado*, produced by Michael Todd and starring Bill Robinson and Eddie Green, a favorite comedian on the Negro circuit.

But the nineteen-thirties brought something else, something

that had its genesis in the Harlem area. They brought a series of glorious attempts to build a permanent Negro theatre and many of the figures involved are prominent in today's theatre.

The first great attempt was made by Rose McClendon and Dick Campbell. Together, in 1935, they laid the foundation for the Negro People's Theatre. They brought to this organization considerable energy, talent and intelligence. Miss McClendon had been a major theatre figure for many years; and at the time their group was organized, she was playing in *Mulatto*. Mr. Campbell, the singer-actor, was a well-prepared, studious man.

The organization presented a Negro version of Clifford Odets' *Waiting for Lefty* to an audience that jammed Rockland Palace. This was the group's only production, for Miss McClendon died, and many of the group members joined what was developing into the Negro Unit of the Federal Theatre.

Local groups offered productions at the YMCA, at St. Martin's Episcopal Church, St. Mark's Church and in other halls and ballrooms. Actor Richard Huey, seen so prominently in *Three Men on a Horse*, had a group known as the Richard Huey Players. He also owned Aunt Dinah's Kitchen, a small shop on 135th Street where theatre people met nightly and exchanged ideas. Actress-director Venezuela Jones also had a group that played numerous local engagements. The Harlem Players, a stock company, reopened the doors to the Lafayette and offered *Sailor, Beware*, with Juano Hernandez, Christola Williams and Canada Lee. This was followed by *The Front Page*. Both ventures were largely unsuccessful; Harlem in the 1930s was hardly interested in a sailor's activities nor in those of newspaper reporters.

The Negro Unit of the Federal Theatre was part of the Works Progress Administration, referred to by many today as the "Granddaddy of the Anti-Poverty Program." Federal funds were poured into various theatre groups, and actors found employment during the difficult depression years. One such group was the Negro Unit, housed at Harlem's Lafayette.

In 1936 this unit presented Frank Wilson's *Walk Together, Children*, a fine folk drama. Like other ventures that followed, it was seen by audiences for as little as twenty-five cents or by showing a card from the Department of Welfare.

A *scene from* Dixie to Broadway (*called* Dover to Dixie *in its successful London run*), *with Florence Mills* (*far left*).

Other productions by the Negro Unit included George Mc-
Entee's courtroom melodrama, *The Case of Philip Lawrence*, J.
Augustus Smith's *Turpentine* (written with Peter Morrell), Ru-
dolph Fisher's hilarious *The Conjure Man Dies*, Shaw's *Androcles and the Lion*, William DuBois' exciting *Haiti* and George
Kelly's *The Show Off*. But the most highly acclaimed production
at the Lafayette was the Orson Welles–John Houseman offering,
*Macbeth*; this opened on April 14, 1936, and actually launched
their careers. Canada Lee was featured in the cast. Jack Carter
was Macbeth and Edna Thomas was Lady Macbeth.

This was an exciting *Macbeth*, set on a West Indian island,
filled with voodoo, intrigue and exotic settings created by Nat
Karson with superb lighting by Abe Feder. Perry Watkins and
Thomas Anderson were there to offer technical assistance for this
Shakespearean work, which was played before people much as
that great author must have originally intended it to be played.
One esthetic critic wanted to elaborate. on the rendering of the
verse, but Harlem couldn't have cared less. It had exciting theatre,
and they took full advantage of it—59,271 patrons saw it.

A note should be made here regarding attendance at the Lafayette. *Walk Together, Children*, which opened February 4, 1936,
was seen by 10,530 people. *The Conjure Man Dies*, also produced
in 1936, drew 11,100 people. When one realizes these plays were
not put on for long runs, one gets an interesting answer to the
oft-quoted cliché about Negroes not supporting theatre.

There were other notable offerings by the Negro Unit. Among
these were *Battle Hymn*, which dealt with John Brown; Andre
Obey's *Noah*; *The Trial of Dr. Beck*; *Natural Man*; *How Long,
Brethren?* and *Sweet Land*.

*Haiti*, which told of that black nation's uprising against the
French, proved to be particularly popular. Rex Ingram played
Henri Christophe and Louis Sharp was Toussaint L'Ouverture.
The setting was exotic, the costumes brilliant. And it was full of
action. It was the first time many Harlemites sat in a theatre and
saw Negroes beating up whites and getting away with it. And
all their deep-seated resentments rushed to the surface. During
the course of the play, you could hear shouts from the audience:

"Hit him again!" "Give him a lick for me!" "Man, that's it! That's it!"

The Negro Unit of the Federal Theatre, and the Federal Theatre itself, so ably directed by Hallie Flanagan, came under Congressional scrutiny. Congressmen declared too many of the productions were critical of America and seemed Communistic, just as governmental forces in the nineteen-sixties would attack HARYOU-ACT and other Anti-Poverty Programs. The attack on HARYOU-ACT Executive Director Livingston L. Wingate and playwright LeRoi Jones' Black Arts Theatre by Sargent Shriver, director of the Office of Economic Opportunity, sounded like several pages torn from the Congressional attacks on the Federal Theatre.

The Federal Theatre was killed by an Act of Congress—just as the Anti-Poverty Program will be killed unless it conforms. By killing the Federal Theatre, powerful American forces took the drama away from the masses and lodged it firmly in the bosom of the aristocratic and middle-class groups. That the Federal Theatre offered employment, experience and training to many present-day theatre artists is obvious. That it offered exciting, low-cost theatre to large segments of the population is undeniable. That all of this was taken away from the people is one of the great tragedies of the American theatre.

While the Federal Theatre dominated the Harlem area, other groups were at work. In 1938 Langston Hughes, Hilary Phillips and others laid the groundwork for the Harlem Suitcase Theatre. This group produced plays in a loft on West 125th Street. Its first production was Mr. Hughes' experimental play, *Don't You Want to Be Free?* It was a rousing, exciting production, played on what can only be described as a bare, improvised stage. Three platforms were built for the occasion. And above the setting hung a rope.

The play, which is actually a forerunner to Mr. Hughes' *Jericho Jimcrow*, utilized every aspect of the theatre. Mr. Hughes' poetry was interspersed with his commentary. A Young Man—first played by Earl Jones, now known as Robert Earl Jones, father of actor James Earl Jones—walked across the hall with a suitcase on his shoulder. On this suitcase was the theatre group's name, lighted. The Young Man placed the suitcase at the edge of the stage and said, in effect, that his theatre was going to put on a play about being colored in America. And as the play unfolded, we saw the first slaves landing in America. We saw Negroes work-ing in the fields. We saw Negro women being abused and then we saw the Young Man going north, singing: "Going down the road, Lord, 'way, 'way down the road. These Mississippi towns ain't a-fitting for a hopping toad!"

This particular song introduced what came to be known as the Blues Sequence of the play. The Young Man sat on the edge of the stage and declared he had the blues. Colored folks made up the blues, he said, and now everybody's singing them. He described the types of blues—the "Left-Lonesome Blues" and oth-ers—and there were examples of these. One man sang out:

> Goin' down to the railroad and lay my head on the track,
> Goin' down to the railroad and lay my head on the track,
> But, if I see a train a-comin', I'm gonna yank it back!

Then, there were the "Morning After Blues" where the husband sang:

> I was so drunk last night, I almost lost my mind,
> I was so drunk last night, I almost lost my mind,
> Seems I drunk some bad liquor that almost made me
>     blind.

In arguing with his wife, he sang:

> I had a dream last night, I dreamt I was in hell,
> I had a dream last night, I dreamt I was in hell.
> I woke up and looked around me, babe, your mouth was
>     open like a well!
> I said: Baby, baby, please don't snore so loud.
> I said: Baby, baby, please don't snore so loud.
> You just a little bit a woman, but you sound like a great
>     big crowd!

While this went on, pianist Carroll Tate rocked the piano in the old-fashioned blues tradition. And the audience swayed with it, laughing, crying, and pounding its feet rhythmically. Director Hilary Phillips had in his cast such extremely talented performers as Moody Scrivens, Emma Jones, Mary Savage, Jay Loftlin and Albert Grant, who later succeeded Earl Jones in the lead. Mr. Grant is at present Deputy License Commissioner for New York City.

*Don't You Want to be Free?* played on weekends for a year. The Suitcase Theatre then lost the loft and moved into the basement of the 135th Street Library. Paul Robeson gave a scholarship to Thomas Richardson, a veteran of numerous theatrical ventures, and Mr. Richardson supervised the group's activities. Playwright Owen Dodson joined and led a verse choir there. And Canada Lee gave dramatic recitals to assist the organization. Plans were under way to present Powell Lindsay's play, *Young Man of Harlem*. It did not come off. The Suitcase members all had outside jobs, and theatre is a full-time occupation. In 1939 the group disbanded.

During the latter part of the nineteen-thirties Dick Campbell and his late wife, singer-actress Muriel Rahn, organized the Rose McClendon Players. They created an organization dedicated to building a community theatre, and they did so on a subscription basis. This group today has members of its alumni in prominent theatrical circles, among them Frederick O'Neal, Ossie Davis, Ruby Dee, Jane White and countless others. Few Negroes in the modern theatre escaped the influence of the Rose McClendon Players.

The Rose McClendon Players were an ambitious organization, aimed at building a strong base for actors, playwrights, directors and technicians. Profits from productions paid for the teaching services of Theodore Komisarjevsky of the Moscow Art Theatre. The group reflected the philosophy Mr. Campbell had expounded at the beginning of the nineteen-thirties—namely, that the Broadway stage was going to do nothing except repeat the tired clichés about Negro life. He declared he had had his share of the mistreatment accorded black actors in the downtown area.

For that reason he went to work for the City of New York Department of Welfare, which was, for him, drudgery. He turned to a series of radio ventures, working as a singer and master of ceremonies for various affairs, then plunged into the building of the type of theatre he wanted to see in the Harlem area.

He drew around him such people as Milton Quander, now a physician in Harlem; Helma Dungee Behagen, a social work supervisor; James Mason, a real estate broker, and a number of other intellectuals. On a night in 1938 the group presented the comedy, *Goodbye Again,* at the YWCA in Harlem. Local critics liked this production and, later that year, the Players presented Arthur Kober's *Having Wonderful Time* to an audience that packed the Public School 136 Auditorium. It was an audience that glittered in terms of achievement and recognition. I know, because I was in the cast.

*Having Wonderful Time* played a number of successive weekends, and then *Goodbye Again* was revived. This revival was an acting vehicle, designed as such, and it delighted audiences. But there were objections from a local critic who wanted to see plays more closely related to Negro life. In fairness it must be reported that on its program the Rose McClendon Players noted: "The plays which have been chosen for the Fall season, while meritorious from a standpoint of good theatre and universal appeal, are by no means indicative of the vehicles we anticipate in the future; for it is our desire to stimulate and encourage Negro playwrights to fashion their unborn creations along the vein of contemporary Negro life. If this pattern is followed, we hope in the near future to present Negro plays of high artistic appeal for the consumption of Metropolitan audiences."

After *Goodbye Again* closed, Mr. Campbell met librarians Carolyn G. Thorpe and Jean Blackwell—now Jean Blackwell Hutson, Curator of the Schomburg Collection. He was invited to use the auditorium of the 124th Street Library and to build there the Rose McClendon Workshop Theatre. To this workshop came such artists as Canada Lee, Dooley Wilson, Christola Williams, Horace Carter, Austin Briggs-Hall, Ed Cambridge, Frederick Carter, George Norford, Maxwell Glanville, Perry Watkins, Marjorie Strickland Greene, Jane White and Carol Wilson.

They met in that theatre north of Mt. Morris Park and painted scenery, acted in skits from various plays, took theatrical courses and argued and fought over any and every thing, sometimes with Mr. Campbell. He was a stormy-tempered man, but he saw all of these arguments as a healthy sign, and he insisted someday they would bear fruit.

The Rose McClendon Players officially opened its doors in 1939. The group presented a short play by the Reverend Sheldon Hale Bishop, then Rector of St. Philip's Episcopal Church, one by Dr. Alain Locke, professor at Howard University and noted author, and one by Guthrie McClintic, producer-director. A one-act play by Warren Coleman rounded out the bill. In the audience sat NAACP Executive Secretary Walter White beside Judge Myles Paige and other prominent community figures.

The first full-length play presented at the workshop was Ferdinand Voteur's drawing-room comedy, *A Right Angle Triangle*. Frederick Carter, Carol Wilson and Marjorie Strickland Greene were prominently featured. The productions which followed were remarkable in the excitement they created in Harlem. One such was George Norford's *Joy Exceeding Glory* wherein Father Divine invaded the serenity of a Lenox Avenue home. This play, incidentally, was later optioned by the Theatre Guild, renamed *The Head of the Family*, and shown at the Westport County Playhouse. In 1965 it was being considered for a television series.

Another robust venture was Abram Hill's *On Strivers' Row*. This comedy showed director Campbell and playwright Hill at their finest. The Van Strivens of Harlem's Strivers' Row are pretentious, more middle class than middle class itself. In the midst of one of their swanky affairs appears one Joe Smothers, a jive-talking, swinging Harlem hipster. As played by Frederick Carter, the Harlem stage depicted a known community figure hitherto ignored by white theatre writers.

A particularly noteworthy production by the Rose McClendon Players was William Ashley's *Booker T. Washington*. For the title role Mr. Campbell called on Dooley Wilson, who had captivated audiences as Androcles in the Federal Theatre's production *Androcles and the Lion*. With Add Bates, P. Jay Sidney and an excellent cast, Mr. Wilson had dispersed notions that Negroes were amateur thespians. He did this again in *Booker T. Washington.* Ethel Waters was so impressed with his performance that she recommended him for the part of Little Joe in *Cabin in the Sky.* His performance as Little Joe was widely acclaimed. On the strength of it he went on to Hollywood and played Sam in the Humphrey Bogart–Ingrid Bergman film *Casablanca.* Anyone who saw that film readily remembers Mr. Wilson's rendition of the song "As Time Goes By."

*Booker T. Washington* enjoyed a long Harlem run. It was taken to the 1939 World's Fair where it was again successful. The Rose McClendon Players thrived until the beginning of World War II, when Mr. Campbell was offered the position of United Services Organization Director. The Players group disbanded for the duration of the war. It never started up again. Time and events laid the group to rest, but it did not die. Any Negro theatrical venture in modern times has a representative, a veteran, of that group. And this long association, the working together over a period of time, brought the type of ensemble acting so prevalent in Negro shows.

During the latter part of the nineteen-thirties optimism prevailed in Negro theatrical circles. Ethel Waters, Willie Bryant, Georgette Harvey, Fredi Washington, Anne Wiggins Brown, José Ferrer and a cast of veterans brought dynamic performances to *Mamba's Daughters.* Their acting was superior to the play. When the play opened, that great critic from *The New York Times*, Mr. Brooks Atkinson, was suffering from a bout with influenza. In reviewing the play Mr. Atkinson found neither Miss Waters' nor Mr. DuBose Heyward's work noteworthy. The day after his review appeared, a number of theatre luminaries took out an advertisement in the *Times* without the knowledge of the management of *Mamba's Daughters.* They felt the play deserved to run. Mr. Atkinson is a fair man, honest and straightforward—not a frustrated writer, actor or director who has turned to reviewing as a last resort. Everyone in theatre knew he would do exactly what he did in the case of *Mamba's Daughters*—return and rereview the play. He wrote in his Sunday column that he had been ill, that

Miss Waters' performance was beautiful, but that he still had reservations about the play.

Actually, Mr. Atkinson was more charitable toward *Mamba's Daughters* than many people thought he should have been. The play was clumsily written and filled with stereotypes. The light-skinned villain, wonderfully played by Willie Bryant, had become a cliché by then. And the solicitous, ever-loving Mamba had seen other days. There was also the "usual Negro church scene" with everyone shouting and waving hands. In the midst of this, the preacher began shouting: "Confess your sins!" He pulled out his handkerchief and started to wipe his face. As he did, a pint of liquor fell from his pocket. The congregation began to snicker, but the preacher rose to the occasion. He said: "I told you all to confess your sins. And I just confessed mine! I put my liquor on the floor!"

The importance of *Mamba's Daughters*—beyond giving Negro actors work—was that it introduced Ethel Waters to the popular theatre. This fine artist had previously recorded songs, appeared in nightclubs, and on Broadway she had been "spotted." By spotted I mean she had appeared in *As Thousands Cheer* and *At Home Abroad* as a solo performer, apart from the rest of the company. This, indeed, was the pattern then, as it was with Bert Williams during his early days with the *Follies*. And as it was with Lena Horne during her early film career.

But these were the nineteen-thirties, and anything that brought hope was welcomed. And Negroes were full of hope. Katherine Dunham had won the hearts of New Yorkers, and now everyone spoke of the forthcoming *Cabin in the Sky* in which she and her dance troupe were to appear with Ethel Waters, Dooley Wilson, Dick Campbell, Todd Duncan, Rex Ingram and J. Rosamond Johnson. A musical version of *A Midsummer Night's Dream*, known as *Swingin' the Dream*, was scheduled. Louis Armstrong, Maxine Sullivan, Oscar Polk, Juano Hernandez and Butterfly McQueen were in that short-lived production. Richard Wright's powerful and magnificent novel *Native Son* was published, and there was talk of making it into a Broadway play. There was talk, too, of the building of a Negro Playwrights' Company. Abram Hill, Austin Briggs-Hall and Frederick O'Neal met to organize the American Negro Theatre. This was, indeed, a time when dreams seemed to be close to fulfillment.

But the world was about to go up in flames in 1939. Hitler's armies invaded Poland, and England and France declared war on Nazi Germany. Alarming stories spread about Jewish people being killed in gas chambers. Rumors circulated, too, about a possible Selective Service draft in America for young men over twenty-one. And this nation, which had been mired in a terrible depression, which had seen such antiwar plays as *What Price Glory?*, *Peace on Earth*, *Bury the Dead*, *Johnny Johnson* and *Idiot's Delight*, now found war inevitable. Consciously and subconsciously, America prepared to take its stand in the coming holocaust.

The nineteen-thirties came to an end. It was a decade in which people at first reached back to the nineteen-twenties, seeking the "good old days." Suddenly, they decided to strike out on a new course. Out of the debris of despair and disillusionment emerged a fighting spirit, and a part of that spirit was an instrument known as the Harlem theatre movement—an instrument that made it possible for Negro actors to work together, to bring ensemble playing to the modern star-studded, misguided theatre! This ensemble playing, this group identification and expression, this collective action would later transfer itself into the black nationalism that scared hell out of America's powers as well as the Negro's former allies—scared the latter to the point where they attempted to vitiate black nationalism, dilute it, and unconsciously sought to thwart its development.

# Chapter IX

## *Fear and War: The Nineteen-Forties*

Harlem shuddered, then laughed nervously. And all America trembled. The war clouds over Europe burst open and torrents of fire poured on that continent's cities and people. Winston Churchill urged for "the new world to come to the rescue of the old." And President Roosevelt, who had pledged peace, sought Lend-Lease aid to Britain, and instructed American ships to fire on the Nazis if attacked. Roosevelt and Churchill met somewhere at sea to map the destruction of Nazi Germany. And the Russians, who had been our enemies, were suddenly our friends, even though we disapproved of their government.

America that had steadfastly seen "no more war" now saw a war. And its theatre, the staunch supporter of antiwar dramas, reversed its field and urged support for the coming holocaust. Maxwell Anderson and Robert E. Sherwood, known respectively for *What Price Glory?* and *Idiot's Delight,* would later jump on the bandwagon, Anderson with *Candle in the Wind* and *The Eve of St. Mark* and Sherwood with *There Shall Be No Night.*

In Harlem people talked about the war in tones of disbelief. Everyone knew it was on the way, yet few could understand American intervention for democracy abroad while no such thing existed at home. Harlem and its people were once again caught— caught in the dilemma created by America's changeable ideas of equality, with eternal promises and eternal failures to live up to them for black people. Up and down the streets young men met on corners, talking, talking.

"This is what I put down on my draft board," one said. "I told them folks I had to support my mother *and* my father. And do you know what them cats did? They drafted my father!"

"You ain't seen nothing," another man said. "I been trying for years to get my wife to go to work. Don't you know that no sooner than I went down there and got a deferment because I'm supporting her, that chick went out and got herself a slave? Man,

I hit the ceiling! I told her she'd better get down there first thing in the morning and put that job down. In other words, quit fast!"

The draft became a reality and then there were comments like these:

"This draft is giving me a *cold!*"

"Man, for years I been trying to get a government job and now I'm gonna get the very one I don't want!"

"Did you hear that Negroes are jumping off closets in their bare feet, trying to get flatfooted so they can be deferred?"

"They have taken that word deferred out of the dictionary. I know a cat who has no arms. They inducted him last week. He asked: Just what am I supposed to do? The Man told him: You see that man over there drawing a bucket of water? Well, he's blind. You show him what to do with the water!"

Grown men sang out in the streets: "Uncle Sam ain't no woman, but he sure can take your man!" In more serious tones, irritated black people argued that when colored Ethiopia was attacked, Uncle Sam hadn't raced to her defense, but when white Europe was in trouble, Uncle was right there. Others declared openly they were not going to fight for colonial England, colonial France and jimcrow America.

But, in the last analysis—despite all the objections—Harlem and Negroes generally did exactly what black people had done since the seventeenth century. The young men went off to fight the war.

And the streets lay empty, lay empty and alone. Heavy clouds of loneliness settled over them, dimming their bright lights to a single, shadowy glow, a glow that seemed eternally dim. The seemingly never-ending clouds devoured the laughter and the song of the streets. It was all gone now—gone off to war with the young men, gone off possibly never to return.

The streets were tear-stained, empty. Suddenly, it was possible to walk from 116th Street to 125th Street in five minutes instead of the usual one hour and a half. Familiar faces that once stopped you every half block were now missing, and those that you did know were neither physically nor spiritually present. Their hearts and minds were with loved ones who were far, far away from home.

No one knew it then—or at least no one said it—but something was happening to that land known as Harlem. Its children that had been boxed in there, who had learned to live there and to love it, were torn away from it and sent to other parts of the world. Some of them were to return physically, but never completely. Some who returned did so only momentarily, then fled to suburbia. The streets probably knew this before anyone else and so they lay crying, lay crying alone, for their children had been taken from them.

Their children had gone off to fight the war, and the dream continued—the dream of achieving freedom, human decency and recognition. Negroes set out again to prove themselves worthy of common human rights, just as they had before the nation was founded. What they established once again is that American Negroes are as American as any other group and, in the last analysis, react accordingly, even when the group's best interest has been castigated and reduced to a mockery. This remains the paradox of this nation, and possibly one of the reasons black people are not as heavily involved as whites in the anti-Viet Nam movements, although their children fight there in disproportionate numbers.

One of the dreams that continued to flow through the community was the building of a theatre. There came into existence in 1940 a group known as the American Negro Theatre, familiarly known as ANT or the "Ants." Playwright-director Abram Hill, Austin Briggs-Hall, Frederick O'Neal, Hattie King-Reeves and a number of former Rose McClendon Players organized this group.

ANT moved into the basement of the 135th Street Library, the former home of the Harlem Suitcase Theatre. Its first production was a revival of Abram Hill's *On Strivers' Row*. The group went on to produce Theodore Browne's fine play about John Brown, *Natural Man*, Owen Dodson's beautifully poetic *The Garden of Time*, Abram Hill's fiery *Walk Hard* and the play that brought it renown and failure—*Anna Lucasta*. There shall be more said about *Anna Lucasta* in a later section.

While ANT was in the formative stage, a group consisting of Theodore Ward, Powell Lindsay, George Norford, Theodore

Browne and Owen Dodson organized the Negro Playwrights Company. The first production was Theodore Ward's *The Big White Fog*, directed by Powell Lindsay.

*The Big White Fog* had been produced by the Federal Theatre in Chicago, and it met there with a measure of success. Mr. Ward proved to be a realistic writer, a craftsman, poetically inclined, and his work glowed with theatricality. He told of a Negro family and its travails in "the big white fog." The play opened at the Lincoln Theatre on 135th Street—the scene of so much earlier Negro theatrical history. Canada Lee was in the cast, and the play introduced Frank Silvera to New Yorkers. Virgil Richardson would later play a prominent role in this work. Despite the work's overriding power, the expenses involved in keeping a professional show going in Harlem—or any other place at that time—were devastating. This was the Negro Playwrights' first and only production.

In the meantime, there was excitement and expectation about the forthcoming *Native Son*. Paul Green had joined Richard Wright in adapting his novel for the stage. Orson Welles was going to direct it. And Canada Lee was going to play the lead!

Any one of the names mentioned would have caused a furor. Paul Green had gone from his early plays of Negro life on to write *Johnny Johnson*, one of the fine antiwar plays of the nineteen-thirties. The Group Theatre had produced it with a cast headed by Russell Collins in the leading role. And Morris Carnovsky, Phoebe Brand, John Garfield, Luther Adler, Lee J. Cobb and other Group Theatre veterans had played in it. In addition, Kurt Weill had composed original music for it. This was Mr. Weill's second American show, his first being Max Reinhardt's *The Eternal Road*.

Richard Wright was a Mississippi-born Negro of little formal education. In his youth, he left his native state for the big city so that he might, in his own words, "justify my existence here under the stars." He educated himself; then in 1938 he wrote a volume of short stories known as *Uncle Tom's Children*. These were powerfully written, angry stories, and they made America sit up and take notice. Then he wrote *Native Son*.

*Native Son* has been described in various quarters as "one of the finest novels ever written by an American," "the finest novel ever written by a Negro," "an American version of *Crime and Punishment*" and "a disgrace to Negroes because it labels them killers" or "sheer Communist propaganda." It has been praised and it has been cursed, but it has always commanded respect. And no one has doubted the words of one critic: "This man can write!"

For he could—with shocking brutality, with insight, with a vivid language, and strong characterization. In his narrative, while his hero sits in the death house, waiting for his execution, Wright states: "There was no day for him now and there was no night. There was but a long stretch of time that was very short, and then, the end." Not too long after the dramatic adaptation of *Native Son* opened, Mr. Wright moved to Paris, where he wrote several other works, among them *The Outsider, The Long Dream* and *Listen Here, White Man.* Wright died at a relatively young age, on alien soil. He was a literary giant in a field too often peopled by dwarfs.

The third figure involved with *Native Son* was Orson Welles. After his Negro version of *Macbeth*, Mr. Welles staged a number of other shows for the Federal Theatre, but one particular work put him in the middle of a controversy. Composer Marc Blitzstein wrote what can only be described as an American opera, known as *The Cradle Will Rock.* It was a work, a cartoon really, filled with social significance. If one really looks at that work, he can readily see what attracted Mr. Blitzstein in later years to *The Three Penny Opera*, and why his contributions to it are notable.

*The Cradle Will Rock* is about Steeltown, U.S.A. There are such characters as the Moll singing, "If you wonder why a guy no doubt turns out a rotten bastard and the other way about, it's because he's got that nickel under the foot." And there is Mr. Mister, the capitalist, and Reverend Salvation and Editor Daily, tools of Mr. Mister. And there is our hero, Larry Foreman, declaring this cradle will rock!

Mr. Welles was enthusiastic about Mr. Blitzstein's work, but the Federal Theatre was then being hounded by Congressional inquiry. And *The Cradle Will Rock* was "too hot." Orders were given that the play was not to be done. And that proved to be the play's *doing*.

Not too long ago when actor John Randolph of the original cast of *The Cradle Will Rock* appeared in one of my plays, he reminded me of the following:

The company had been rehearsing *The Cradle Will Rock* while anxiously awaiting news of what Washington thought of the play and what that city planned to do about it. The company arrived at the scheduled theatre, ready to put on the show, but learned that Washington was not going along with *that* show's being put on the stage. An irate group of actors rose to the occasion, and the flamboyant Mr. Welles was one of the ringleaders. They invited the audience that attended opening night to follow them. "No one knew where we were going," said Mr. Randolph, "but we all took off down the street, marching together. As we marched, groups of other theatre and nontheatre people joined in the sidewalk parade. We walked and walked until we found an empty theatre. And we walked right into the place.

"There was a law that we could not get up on the stage. We would have been thrown out of Actors Equity, called this-and-that. But there was no law against the composer, Blitzstein, sitting at the piano and playing—which he did. And the actors sat in the audience, and as Blitzstein played, we got up and sang our roles. Not one of us got on that stage, but the effect was electrifying. And the audience raved."

I was in that audience, and we did rave. And *The Cradle Will Rock* opened *outside* the Federal Theatre. I saw it again and again, sometimes for free, and other times for thirty cents. And it once caused me considerable embarrassment. I had one whole dollar and I invited a lovely Harlem damsel to visit the show with me, expecting to pay thirty cents for each ticket. When we arrived at the theatre, the show was a smash hit and the price had jumped to fifty-five cents per ticket! If I hadn't known Howard DaSilva—who played the lead—and John Randolph, that young lady and I might still be walking back to Harlem at this moment!

There was a fourth figure that rounded out the quartet responsible for *Native Son:* Canada Lee. Mr. Lee was a Harlem boy of West Indian ancestry, named James Lionel Canegata. In his youth he studied the violin and became proficient in playing it. But the young man was multitalented. At one time he achieved a measure of success as a jockey. He also knew how to box, and this led him to follow a career in the ring. It was in the ring that he earned his stage name. The story is told that, during a fight, a radio announcer had difficulty referring to the young man as Lee Canegata. He

invariably called him "Lee Canada," then "Canada Lee." It was
also during this same fight that Mr. Lee sustained an eye injury.
And so he left the ring that night with a new name and a new
career.

He took his violin and went into show business. For a time he
played a number of local engagements; then, in the nineteen-thirties, he was booked into the Lafayette Theatre. He conducted his
own orchestra and played the violin. By the time he was booked
there again, he was also announcing the numbers his orchestra
would play, and later serving as the master of ceremonies for the
entire show. He next learned the acting profession, and when the
Harlem Players organized a stock company at the Lafayette, Mr.
Lee was in the group.

From the Harlem Players, he went into the Federal Theatre.
He was seen as Banquo in Orson Welles and John Houseman's
production of *Macbeth*. He was also in *Haiti*, and he had had
minor roles in such shows as *Stevedore*. He played special engagements for the Harlem Suitcase Theatre, worked with the Rose
McClendon Players and the Negro Playwrights Company, and
when the role of Bigger Thomas beckoned, he was well prepared
for it.

And play the leading role Canada Lee most assuredly did. He
brought to it all the anger, fury, resentment and frustration known
to a Negro youth. The script by Messrs. Green and Wright was
less cohesive than the novel and much less comprehensive, but it
was gripping drama throughout. And Mr. Welles' imaginative
staging underscored the work most effectively. Actually, it was a
distasteful drama for a war-weary, escapist America, but it was
such a powerful drama, so artistic that no one could ignore it
without suffering pangs of guilt in later years.

*Cabin in the Sky* continued to run, with Ethel Waters singing
"Happiness Is a Thing Called Joe." Other Negro shows of the
nineteen-forties were *Jump for Joy, Harlem Cavalcade* and *Memphis Bound,* which had relatively short runs.

Paul Robeson's *Othello,* directed by Margaret Webster, reached
Broadway in 1943. It was instantaneously successful. Mr. Robeson
had performed this role in England with notable success. He repeated it in America, supported by such excellent actors as José

Ferrer and Uta Hagen. The play ran for 296 performances—a record run—and Mr. Robeson was justifiably acclaimed the outstanding actor of the year. When José Ferrer also won an award, Mr. Robeson said, "I'm glad he won a prize, for my conscience was beginning to bother me. He certainly deserved one."

*Othello* was the second Negro venture in which José Ferrer appeared on his way toward stardom. His first was with Ethel Waters in *Mamba's Daughters*. He would later direct *Strange Fruit*. Mr. Ferrer is one of the many prominent personalities who have benefited from working with black artists. Eddie Cantor, Leon Errol, Orson Welles, Florenz Ziegfeld, John Houseman, Howard DaSilva, Will Geer, Humphrey Bogart, Tallulah Bankhead, Morris Carnovsky, Oscar Hammerstein II, Jerome Kern, Richard Rodgers, Hoagy Carmichael, Claude Rains, Ruth Gordon, Garson Kanin, Johnny Mercer, Phil Harris, Lawrence Tibbett, Benny Goodman, Ira and George Gershwin, Artie Shaw, Glenn Miller, Glen Gray, Jimmy and Tommy Dorsey, Gene Krupa, Harry James, Stan Goetz, Skitch Henderson, Rudy Vallee, Bob and Bing Crosby, Helen Morgan, Mel Ferrer, Fred Astaire, Ginger Rogers and Elvis Presley are only a few of the names that might have been in artistic trouble if there had been no black artists on this continent. And all of those musicians and disc jockeys that crowded Harlem's Savoy Ballroom in the nineteen-twenties and nineteen-thirties might have found life a little less profitable if they had not done so.

The production of *Othello* had an interesting sidelight. When it opened amidst acclaim, the New York *Daily News'* columnist Ed Sullivan wrote a laudatory column about Mr. Robeson's work, urging him to be cautious in terms of political activities. Mr. Sullivan's devotion to America is without question. His devotion to fact is less durable than his Americanism, for during the nineteen-fifties when Paul Robeson's name was chastised in political circles, Mr. Sullivan wrote that the Robeson Othello was not really a great piece of work.

But Mr. Sullivan is America—at least one phase of it. He is mediocre America, in which the untalented develop a "gimmick"—a gimmick that permits the writers who cannot write to develop into columnists simply because they are on a given scene. They should thank their God because in a tasteful, sophisticated society the Sullivans, the Winchells, the Leonard Lyonses and Hedda

*Ethel Waters made a brief solo appearance in* As Thousands Cheer.
Brown Brothers

Hoppers would be applying for charity, and if eligibility require-
ments depended upon talent, they would be in the poorhouse.

This, incidentally, is no "white only" province. It is rampant in
the Negro press as well.

During the Christmas season of 1943 Billy Rose produced Oscar
Hammerstein II's adaptation of Bizet's opera *Carmen*, known as
*Carmen Jones*. Mr. Hammerstein wrote new lyrics to Bizet's score,
and he moved the setting to the United States. Hazzard Short
directed and Muriel Smith and Muriel Rahn alternated in the
leading role. The show actually started offstage when Dick Campbell—acting as his wife's representative—openly fought Billy Rose
about the salary scales he paid Negro actors. The result of the
fight was that Muriel Rahn was the only cast member who earned
as much as two hundred dollars weekly.

*Carmen Jones* captivated New York audiences. Many of its well-
wishers claimed it was closer to Bizet's real work than those versions
presented in opera form. The work certainly proved to be durable.
As late as 1953 Dick Campbell and Muriel Rahn toured with the
show. It should be noted here that the original cast of *Carmen
Jones* included Luther Saxon, Napoleon Reed, Carlotta Franzell,
Elton Warren, Glenn Bryant and drummer Cozy Cole.

For all of its success and acclaim, *Carmen Jones* troubles me.
Actually, it seems that in the adaptation, the Negro stereotype is
*sought*. I feel this is more insidious than many other works that
perpetuated the stereotype. *The Green Pastures*, *Porgy* and *Porgy
and Bess* seem to me to be works created by people who didn't
know anything about Negroes. *Carmen Jones* seems to be a work
that deliberately used the stereotype to assure a measure of success.

The nineteen-forties brought another popular musical, *Early to
Bed*. It had music by Thomas "Fats" Waller, known for his "Ain't
Misbehavin'," "Honeysuckle Rose" and his rendition of "I'm
Gonna Sit Right Down and Write Myself A Letter." George
Marion provided the book and lyrics for this show, which was
"integrated." Richard Kollmar played the leading role magnifi-
cently, and Bob Howard and Jeni LeGon were prominently fea-
tured. And when the latter two took off on "Hi-De-Ho-High in
Harlem," the audience's feet pounded rhythmically. And Mr.
Howard's rendition of "I'll Be So Happy When the Nylons Bloom
Again" was particularly delightful.

*Memphis Bound* starred Bill Robinson, Avon Long and Frank Wilson, but it was a commercial failure. Something new, however, was happening, and this became evident when *On the Town* opened with a "mixed chorus." *Bloomer Girl* then brought Dooley Wilson back from Hollywood, and his singing of "The Eagle and Me" was a show-stopper. And so was Richard Huey's "I Got A Song" in the same production. Another highlight in Negro ventures was James A. Cross and William Wyckoff's singing "What the Well Dressed Man in Harlem Will Wear" in Irving Berlin's *This Is the Army*.

Negroes were singing then. They were singing on juke boxes "Sweet slumber till dawn, turn the lights down low. I will hold you in my arms again tonight." They were singing, happily, hopefully, offstage and on. They sang of a foreseeable Double Victory—a victory over fascism abroad and jimcrow at home. The millennium was dimly seen!

No one was cynical about this optimism. A. Philip Randolph had organized his March on Washington Movement, had gone to Washington and told President Roosevelt that if he didn't do something about discrimination in war plants, there would be ten thousand Negroes sitting on the White House steps the following week. The story is told that the President looked up and asked Mr. Randolph: "Where do you think you'll get that many, Phil?"

And Mr. Randolph is said to have answered: "From among those who are being jimcrowed out of jobs!"

Well, the thought of ten thousand people on *any* doorstep is sobering in the first place. And the thought of ten thousand Negroes would scare any American silly. He could be the most progressive-minded liberal without one iota of prejudice and he would still be scared. For that matter, he could be a Negro and be scared. The thought runs through many minds that those ten thousand Negroes would be sitting out there, drinking a little corn, raising pure hell and rocking America's boat. Mr. Roosevelt was an intelligent man as well as a fair man. He simply didn't have time to deal with *that* many people, so he promptly issued Executive Order 8802, which was to become known as the Fair Employment Practices Commission or FEPC.

National defense, and later war jobs, brought greater income to Negroes. And Negro servicemen distinguished themselves on foreign fields. Men like Dorie Miller and those of the 99th Pursuit

Squadron and the 369th Regiment brought pride to black people. The newspaper *PM* sent journalist Roi Ottley abroad to report on the activities of Negro troops, and he wrote glowing accounts. Excitement raced through black America's veins. The long dream was coming to an end and there would be brightness—and freedom!

It was during this period of optimism that *Anna Lucasta* reached the American stage. This play, written by Philip Yordan, was originally about a Polish family. Claire Leonard, Mr. Yordan's agent, was also Abram Hill's representative. She suggested to Mr. Hill that he try out the work at his American Negro Theatre. Mr. Hill studied the play, then set about to adapt it for a Negro family. He rewrote it and made it Negroid in speech and tempo. He then invited the Broadway director Harry Wagstaff Gribble to come to Harlem and stage the play. Mr. Gribble added some rewrite because the author had given him *carte blanche* for changes. Mr. Gribble saw a Broadway future for this work, and he saw correctly.

The opening cast included Hilda Simms, Frederick O'Neal, Alice Childress, Alvin Childress, Earle Hyman and Herbert Henry. When the play opened in the basement of the 135th Street Library, this company's ensemble acting lifted a mediocre play above the shoulders of many downtown ventures. And the critics sang.

*Anna Lucasta* was then moved to a Broadway house, where it settled down for a long run. The great Negro actors who moved in and out of its cast are listed here, although some surely have been omitted through error. These actors included Canada Lee, Ossie Davis, Ruby Dee, Isabelle Cooley, Sidney Poitier, Maxwell Glanville, Duke Williams, Frank Silvera, John Proctor, Doris Block and Monte Hawley. They were a happy crew. You could see them leaving the theatre after a performance, patting each other on the back, stopping for coffee and planning their next venture. Some were writing plays; some were going into directing; some into other acting ventures. All were committed to the theatre and all expected brighter things for the Negro artist.

*Anna Lucasta*, for all its trailblazing, is a mediocre play that could never have "made it" as a "white play." It is, first of all, a poor imitation of Eugene O'Neill's *Anna Christie*, which is not a very good play itself. And *Anna Lucasta* actually represents something vicious in terms of the double standard—namely, it suggests that the remedy for a bad play is to make it Negroid and it will succeed. And this time it worked. But the day that white audiences begin to see Negroes as *people*, this gimmick is going to be in trouble. And plays like *Anna Lucasta* and the musical adaptation of *Golden Boy* will not grace our stages.

While *Anna Lucasta* enjoyed commercial success, Abram Hill and the American Negro Theatre readied a new show. This was Mr. Hill's adaptation of Len Zinberg's novel, *Walk Hard—Talk Loud*. Mr. Hill called his play *Walk Hard*, and it followed *Anna Lucasta* into the 135th Street Library Auditorium. It was the story of a Negro boxer and the prejudices he faced. The leading role was played by Roy Allen, now an assistant director for CBS-TV. After the war *Walk Hard* moved to the Chanin Auditorium in the downtown area, where Maxwell Glanville played the lead. It was met unkindly by the critics.

World War II had barely ended when James Gow and Arnaud d'Usseau, authors of *Tomorrow the World*, brought in *Deep Are the Roots*. As directed by Elia Kazan, this play had a cast that included Lloyd Gough, Carol Goodner, Barbara Bel Geddes, Harold Vermilyea, Charles Waldron and Helen Martin, Gordon Heath and Evelyn Ellis—the latter three well known to Harlem theatregoers. Miss Martin had distinguished herself in the maid's role in *On Strivers' Row*. Mr. Heath had performed on radio and won considerable respect for his *Hamlet*, directed by Owen Dodson for Hampton Institute's Theatre Arts Festival from July 23 through July 28, 1945. He had been supported by such talented actors as William Greaves, Henry B. Scott, Roy Allen, Austin Briggs-Hall, Dorothy Ateca, Marion Douglas, Hazel Thomas, John Hall, Edward Alford and Frank Harriott. Alternating with this was *Outward Bound* with the same company, plus Vinie Burrows. Evelyn Ellis was a theatre veteran, known to the old Lafayette Theatre and to countless Broadway productions. With the cast of white veterans, these three brought this sincere, entertaining and sometimes mechanical effort to the stage in a captivating manner.

Gordon Heath played the Negro lieutenant who returns to his home in the Southern United States, where his mother has long worked as a domestic for a Southern Congressman. The Negro wants to become a teacher in the Negro school in his hometown. The Congressman's oldest daughter, who has been the Negro's "adviser," has other ideas. And she turns out to be not as "liberal" as she thinks she is. There is a devastating scene at the end where this older sister realizes she is prejudiced, that she really thought the Negro was inferior. But the play ends with a note of hope that understanding is on the horizon.

"We didn't write that play for Negroes," co-author Arnaud d'Usseau told me when I met him in the nineteen-fifties. "We were talking to whites who *think* they are progressive, liberal, or whatever they want to call themselves. We were saying: Take a look at yourself and tell yourself just how little prejudice you *really* have!"

Tolerant theatre audiences supported *Deep Are the Roots* during a long run. The play eventually was taken to London, and then it returned here for a tour. By that time all of the actors—with the exception of the Negroes in the cast—had Hollywood offers. It was this stint in London that made Gordon Heath take another look at the Statue of Liberty and at the plight of the Negro theatre artist in America; he packed his bags, went back to Europe and settled in Paris, where he still lives. He is co-owner of the café "L'Abbaye," and he works in European films and stage shows. He recently directed *In White America* for continental audiences.

Twenty years were to elapse between the time I saw Gordon Heath in *Deep Are the Roots* and our next meting, in early 1966. While I sat waiting for him, I remembered that James Edwards had taken his role in the touring company of *Deep Are the Roots.* While on the West Coast, Mr. Edwards was invited to star in the film version of *Home of the Brave*—an invitation that might have been extended to Mr. Heath had he toured with the show. And many roles later played by James Edwards and Sidney Poitier might have belonged to Mr. Heath.

When I saw him, I saw, too, that time had whitened his hair, but his face remained youthful. He was in his fifties, his mind still alert, his theatrical taste still sharp. He declared, in answer to my question, that he had no regrets about moving to Paris and that he would do it again. He had taken one look at the 1965–1966 theatrical season and he declared he had "had it." He walked out on the first act of most of the season's hits, and he charged that the American theatre was going no place at a remarkable pace.

We sat in New York in my favorite restaurant, La Famille, along with actors Jess Smith, Lee Payant and research specialist Horace Carter. We all laughed at Mr. Heath's statement, and then a sudden silence fell across the table. Mr. Carter mentioned that once there was a powerful force that pulled him into the theatre, that there one could hear great ideas exchanged, but now the theatre has been palpably silent on such issues as Viet Nam, Harlem, Los Angeles, Selma and Mississippi.

"When you get more drama on television, in books or in newspapers, a culture is in trouble," said Mr. Heath. He flew back to Paris the very next day. And with him flew many dreams that could have made a great contribution to black drama and to the American theatre.

Immediately after World War II, Robert Ardrey's *Jeb* caused a considerable stir. Herman Shumlin produced this work about a returning Southern Negro serviceman who wanted to practice a trade he had learned in the army. The Southern townspeople would not hear of this, and a conflict ensued that compelled the hero to flee from the Southland.

Dick Campbell read *Jeb*, then promptly called Herman Shumlin's office and suggested Ossie Davis for the leading role. Mr. Davis, prominently featured in the Rose McClendon Players' prewar productions of *On Strivers' Row* and *Joy Exceeding Glory*, had been away at war and had returned to his home in Waycross, Georgia. Mr. Campbell sent for Mr. Davis, who fulfilled all the promise he had shown before his wartime service. But despite his remarkable performance, *Jeb* folded all too quickly.

Another postwar disaster was Lillian Smith's dramatization of her popular novel, *Strange Fruit*. With the assistance of her sister, Esther, Miss Smith made her novel into a panoramic view of the Georgia of her day. It was not successful dramaturgy, but it was a totally sincere effort. Miss Smith was surrounded by theatre workers with notable backgrounds. José Ferrer was her director and his cast included Mel Ferrer, Jane White, Juano Hernandez, Dorothy Ateca Carter, Ken Renard, Herbert Junior, Earl Jones, Alonzo Bosan and a host of brilliant performers.

Miss Smith's work told of Nonnie, a Southern Negro woman, who is in love with Tracy, a white man. The two cannot marry because of conditions in the South. In the course of the play Tracy is killed by Nonnie's brother, and Tracy's servant, Henry, is lynched.

If white critics decried the dramaturgy of the play, they had to take a backseat in terms of what many Negroes said about it. Dan Burley, the late Negro newspaper columnist, chastised the work in no uncertain terms. He said Nonnie was nothing but a "slopjar" for Tracy and he thought the work was disgraceful. Abram Hill took the play to task, and many Negroes simply refused to see it. One college student summed it up like this: "I know everything that's in *Strange Fruit* and I'm not about to pay my good money to see that trash!"

When I met Miss Esther Smith she mentioned that her sister was sincerely hurt. She said that her sister believed she had dealt with a delicate subject in a fair manner, with sincerity and complete honesty. I agreed with Miss Esther Smith that this had been done, but when I reported this to several Negroes, I heard this answer: "What she wrote has nothing to do with the price of pork chops in Harlem. If these white folks think Negroes are going to pay to see themselves insulted, then they don't really know colored folks—no matter how close they've been to them."

*Strange Fruit* is that type of work so often turned out by well-intentioned white writers who deal sincerely and sympathetically with Negro characters. They bring to the stage or to literary pages pasteboard characters who are devoid of all human experience. It is almost incredible for a woman of Nonnie's background to become involved with a Tracy—unless there happened to be something in it for her. Nonnie and her type of Southern Negro woman with any degree of intelligence long ago gave up "loving white folks"—if they ever did. Indeed, the Southern Negro woman is a pragmatic human being, forced to be so, and driven toward a matriarchal structure she neither wants nor advocates. She has little time to waste with the drifters she often marries, and she is not about to get herself involved in an interracial situation that is going no place. That there are exceptions to this goes without saying. But one of the problems white writers often face when dealing with Negroes is the use of the exceptions rather than the rule.

A play that seemingly dealt with the rule was Maxine Wood's *On Whitman Avenue*, directed by Margo Jones. This was an angry play with biting dialogue and long devastating speeches. It told of

a Negro veteran who rents the upstairs section of a two-story building in an area where he and his family are unwanted. Canada Lee
starred in the play and co-produced it.

The play offered interesting insights into the thoughts of Negro
children. At one point the Negro child asks a white youngster:
"You ever hear of Joe Louis?" When this line was delivered, black
and white members of the audience gasped. For the first time on
any stage the meaning of Joe Louis was defined. He was the Negro
hero—the Superman, the Home Run Hitter, the Cowboy, the
Father of the Black Country. And as a side thought here, it should
be noted that the white press has not allowed another Negro hero
to escape unscathed. Paul Robeson was too far left of center, Jackie
Robinson too explosive and loud-mouthed, Floyd Patterson too
frightened and neurotic, Sonny Liston too shady a character, Bill
Russell too black-conscious, Wilt Chamberlain too difficult, Willie
Mays too easily fatigued and Jimmy Brown too standoffish. And
Adam Clayton Powell is too flamboyant, James Baldwin and LeRoi
Jones and John Killens too angry, William Branch and Alice
Childress too arrogant, and so on and so forth—all of which means
that Negroes can be anything but human beings in this society.

In *On Whitman Avenue* Negroes were projected as human beings. In one scene when the Negro family has been forced out of
its home, Canada Lee cried out: "This is the Mississippi lynch mob
moved north!" There were other glaring truths—such as when Will
Geer told his family: "I don't know how you can tell a man to
fight for his country then not be able to live in it."

Such truths drew cheers from sympathetic Negro and white
audiences. And the play brought Harlem's newspaper, the *People's
Voice*, into direct conflict with Louis Kronenberger, then drama
critic for the liberal *PM*. The *Voice* editorialized that there was a
Broadway lynching going on, aided and abetted by *PM*. Mr.
Kronenberger attempted to answer with the rationalization that a
bad play about a good cause is detrimental to the cause. The
answer heard in Negro circles was: "When are these folks going to
learn that we're not a *good* cause nor a *bad* cause? We are human
beings who want our rights!"

From *On Whitman Avenue* Canada Lee went into the cast of
*The Duchess of Malfi*, which starred Elisabeth Bergner. He appeared in this play in "whiteface"—a feat that caused considerable

comment. But neither this trick nor Miss Bergner's considerable talents could evoke a long run.

A Negro version of *Lysistrata* failed on Broadway despite a fine cast. John Marriott was featured in Eugene O'Neill's *The Iceman Cometh*, and he distinguished himself in it. Perry Watkins, the Negro set designer, co-produced Duke Ellington's *Beggar's Holiday*, which was based on *The Beggar's Opera*. This completely integrated venture starred Alfred Drake, Mildred Joanne Smith and Avon Long. There followed the musical version of Elmer Rice's play *Street Scene*, with Langston Hughes' lyrics being set to music by Kurt Weill.

A popular hit, introduced during 1946, was *St. Louis Woman*, written by Countee Cullen and Arna Bontemps, with music by Vernon Duke and lyrics by Johnny Mercer. From this show came the hit song, "Come Rain or Come Shine." And in its cast were such performers as Ruby Hill and Harold Nicholas, plus a spirited singer named Pearl Bailey.

*St. Louis Woman* was based on Arna Bontemps' novel, *God Sends Sunday*. Mr. Bontemps, who is today Chief Librarian at Fisk University, was one of the pioneering writers of the Black Renaissance. His lyrical poetry brought favorable remarks from outstanding critics, as well as numerous prizes. He was, in later years, to define the Black Renaissance for another generation, to write numerous anthologies and collect materials of Negro authorship that would have been otherwise lost. For *St. Louis Woman* he was fortunate in drawing for his collaborator a writer of Countee Cullen's caliber.

Mr. Cullen was the son of a Harlem minister. He attended the New York Public Schools, then entered DeWitt Clinton High School. While still a student there he wrote a poem that won a prize and brought him considerable fame—"I Have a Rendezvous with Life." During the period known as the Negro Renaissance Mr. Cullen and Langston Hughes were outstanding poets, great friends, yet with distinctive styles. Despite his radical statements, Mr. Cullen was a lyric poet, a classicist.

Mr. Cullen went on to write many other poems. He became a teacher in Frederick Douglass Junior High School, or P.S. 139, and later he turned to the drama. His adaptation of *The Medea* is a particularly noteworthy work, but it is seldom if ever produced. His collaboration with Arna Bontemps on *St. Louis Woman* proved to be particularly inspiring, and Negro theatre writers believed a new day was about to dawn for the black theatre worker. These two created a work that was entertaining, and they managed to earn a healthy run. But they never collaborated again. Mr. Cullen died not long after, and another great theatrical promise was lost.

*St. Louis Woman* was followed by *Finian's Rainbow*, a play with book and lyrics by E. Y. Harburg and music by Burton Lane. This work, labeled by many as "Broadway at its best," was integrated, and it had a cast headed by David Wayne, Ella Logan and William Greaves. And it caused all America to sing "How Are Things in Glocca Moora?" *Finian's Rainbow* took a serious matter and lampooned it without compromise. In a land called Missitucky appears the Irish Finian. He has stolen a rare vase and the Leprechaun wants it back. In the course of the play a Southern white political leader is turned into a black man. And he gets a dose of what it means to be black in America. In the end he undergoes some profound changes.

One of the high spots of the show was the part where a Negro college student had gone to work for the politician. This politician insisted that the Negro learn to "shuffle," to act "like a colored man." The politician suddenly has an attack of gastritis and calls for the Negro servant. At this point the Negro servant "shuffles in" with the politician's bicarbonate of soda, saying: "Yassuh, boss. Yassuh!"

Everyone laughed at this scene, but the well-intentioned, very sincere authors didn't know what they were unleashing on the American public. From the most progressive-liberal sources, and even from psychoanalysts, came this remark: "That one scene says more in terms of the American Negro than all the plays that can be written!"

The answer to this was obvious but never heard: "Do you think when Bert Williams appeared as a solo act in the *Follies*, when Ethel Waters soloed in *As Thousands Cheer* or as Lena Horne has been spotted in pictures, that this really does anything for the mass of black people?"

"But that scene doesn't do any preaching," was the answer from white lips.

Where in hell is the preaching, many Negroes asked—except in your white point of view? What you're really saying is that I'm controversial. Put me in any play and I'm just that—until you folks straighten up and fly right. Put me as the central role in *The Passion Play*—or let me play Judas. Or put me in *Dead End*, *Winterset*—even *Marat/DeSade*. Immediately these become problem plays, or propaganda vehicles. The real issue here is that you American whites have a color syndrome that you're going to have to swallow. And I hope that when you swallow it, you don't throw up and mess up the whole world.

The one thing *Finian's Rainbow* did was to take a serious American topical matter and make it "palatable" to white audiences. This was, in itself, a laudatory venture, but it was to backfire later, because the one thing that has been documented by most Negro theatre work since then is that it is not particularly interested in presenting work that is palatable to white audiences. This is evident in the writing of James Baldwin, LeRoi Jones, William Branch, Alice Childress, Adrienne Kennedy and a score of Negro playwrights. This explains why whites can still write plays about black people and collect on them. Besides, it gives the white public an interesting rationale: "You folks are *inside* the problem. You need to get *outside* so you can really see it and write about it." Well, if Shakespeare was *outside* of England, O'Casey *outside* of Ireland, O'Neill *outside* of America, Sholom Aleichem *outside* Jewish life, then the word *outside* needs to be redefined.

All that such silly rationales happen to do is to offer white America an opportunity to rearrange her prejudices. And, in this rearrangement, the theatre loses much of its vitality, daring, truthfulness and meaning and it becomes a symbol of nontruth, of trying to say something while really saying nothing.

But in the nineteen-forties, the Negro was still trying to captivate white audiences. Miss Katherine Dunham and her dance group made several spectacular appearances. Her *Bal Negre* and *Carib Song* were particularly noteworthy. And Kenneth Spencer and Pearl Primus appeared to advantage in a revival of *Show Boat*, which was already showing its age despite a remarkable performance by Jan Clayton. During the same period *Mr. Pebbles and Mr. Hooker* and *Another Part of the Forest* also used Negro actors.

*Mr. Pebbles and Mr. Hooker* may be discounted, for it was a minor work, geared toward entertaining audiences. But *Another Part of the Forest* cannot be ignored, for it was the work of Lillian Hellman, a major playwright in America's rating system. Miss

Hellman had "stubbed her toe," in terms of Negro life, with *The Little Foxes*. She created in that exciting play a maid, played by Abbie Mitchell, who was totally false. I do not care whether or not Miss Hellman can show me sixty maids of that type that she knew. For every one she can show, I can produce for her three times that number that would never sit in the Giddens home and put up with the kind of nonsense *her* maid took. The type of maid I know would have been on the "first thing smoking" or "forty going north," as Southern Negroes used to call whatever was leaving the South immediately.

In *Another Part of the Forest* Miss Hellman used the same type of Negro servants; they were there, they commented, but they were never realized as human beings. Anyone who sees this as a dramatic mistake, as a course in development, is invited to look at her *My Father, My Mother and Me* in which she has her Negro maid referring to getting a "nigger-kike"—a remark, incidentally, that caused actress Lynn Hamilton to lose her job because she could not stomach it.

Off-Broadway activities mushroomed in the postwar world. A talented professional group known as New Stages produced Barrie Stavis' fine play, *Lamp at Midnight*, which opened on December 21, 1947. At the American Negro Theatre, *Rain* was shown on December 26, 1947. Randolph Goodman's adaptation of *The Lower Depths* with a Negro cast—known as *A Long Way from Home*—was produced by the Experimental Theatre on February 4, 1948. On February 9, 1948, New Stages brought to its Greenwich Village theatre Jean Paul Sartre's *The Respectful Prostitute* starring Meg Mundy and John Marriott. It was a hit and it later moved to Broadway.

The American Negro Theatre offered *The Washington Years* on March 12, 1948, *Sojourner Truth* on April 20, 1948, and Harry Wagstaff Gribble's *Almost Faithful* on June 2, 1948. And at the 115th Street People's Theatre James C. Morris' *State Line* was produced under the direction of Richard Fisher. As author Earl Conrad noted: "Everybody and his brother is doing theatre."

Another casualty reached Broadway in 1948. This was Dorothy Heyward's *Set My People Free*, which starred Canada Lee, Juano Hernandez and Mildred Joanne Smith. In the huge cast were William Warfield and William Marshall, and Thomas Anderson was production stage manager.

This moving, pulsating drama told of slave insurrectionist Denmark Vesey's attempt to free his people. It was an extraordinary attempt—ahead of its time—but it had dramaturgical problems. It hit a peak at the end of its first act—a peak that simply could not be maintained. And so it closed all too soon.

There was considerable drama offstage as well as onstage during the nineteen-forties. The hot war ended in 1945, but the cold war began, and it was anything but cold. This became obvious at San Francisco when the United Nations was founded. The United States and Britain viewed the Soviet Union with suspicious eyes, and the Soviet Union was equally suspicious. Distrust reigned over the United Nations. American and British money had been poured into Adolph Hitler's armies for an attack on Russia, to destroy communism. The Russians had proved to be foxes, and they signed a nonaggression pact with Hitler to give them time to prepare to fight him. Hitler doublecrossed his British and American allies, invaded Austria, Czechoslovakia, then Poland and forced a war. He also forced Britain and America to fight on the side of the Soviet Union. With the war's end, the Russians felt America and Britain were looking for an excuse to attack them again. The Americans and Britains saw Russian communism as a menace to their capitalistic structures. And so, like little children, they snarled at each other, these big, big nations, and they called each other names. And they brought considerable alarm to all the world— alarm that helped maintain the status quo in *all* the nations involved.

Tom C. Clark was then the United States Attorney General. With the help of J. Edgar Hoover's Federal Bureau of Investigation, he issued a list of organizations considered subversive. Numerous groups that had been active in the field of civil rights were called "Communist fronts." And Federal employees were given loyalty oaths to sign, noting whether or not they had ever belonged to those "fronts." Furthermore, the Federal Bureau of Investigation scrutinized the records of those employees in a thorough manner. An FBI agent took up one hour of my time investigating a war veteran who became an orderly in a United States hospital. Not only did the agent want to know if the man proclaimed loyalty; he wanted to know if I knew of any *positive acts* of the man's loyalty. In short, had the man done any red-baiting? Fortunately, I recalled a time when the man denounced Russia, and when I told the agent this, the latter's face beamed. The orderly subsequently passed his loyalty test and he was allowed to continue emptying bedpans.

Hysteria reigned. And it usurped the fight Negroes had waged for freedom. The logic was thus: Since Negro organizations have been listed as subversive and therefore pro-Communist, to rally to the Negro cause was to be suspected of being disloyal. People began to flee from some very respectable groups, including the NAACP, which had to declare itself absolutely pure. This fleeing directly affected not only the Negro cause but Negro lives. In Trenton, New Jersey, six black men were arrested in what became known as a "modern Scottsboro case." In Martinsville, Virginia, seven black men were arrested and later executed in a bizarre case. In Mississippi a man named Willie McGee was executed because it was declared that he had had sexual relations with a white woman.

This comedy of errors was rapidly taking on tragic proportions. Eleven leaders of the American Communist Party were arrested and brought to trial for "conspiracy to teach and to advocate the overthrow of the American government by force and violence." A parade of disenchanted ex-Communists helped the government to seal the fate of these men. Along with ten Hollywood writers, a group of professional people were imprisoned because they belonged to the Joint Anti-Fascist Refugee Committee—a group that refused to give the government a list of those who supported the fall of Spain's dictator, Franco. And Alger Hiss went to jail, and later Ethel and Julius Rosenberg were to be electrocuted in a highly questionable case.

Somehow that fabulous invalid known as the theatre hobbled along, seemingly unaware of the offstage drama. Yet the theatre and its audiences were then defining current taste in terms of the Negro and the drama. Theodore Ward, who had attracted considerable attention for his *The Big White Fog* with the Negro Playwrights Company, had his new play, *Our Lan'*, presented at the Henry Street Settlement. *Our Lan'* was a play about Negroes during the Reconstruction Era, told in moving and dramatic terms. When it opened, the critics sang its praises. Then a strange thing happened: the Theatre Guild decided to bring the work to Broadway. It is hindsight to state this in the nineteen-sixties, but anyone who could *see* and *understand* Mr. Ward's play and still believe that Broadway would welcome it at any time must have been suffering from naïveté—or expecting to create income tax exemptions.

But *Our Lan'* did move to Broadway. And that capable theatre artist Eddie Dowling directed it. In the process, he created enemies in the cast. That very fine actor and writer Charles Griffin tells this story in his own words:

"I was in the cast, guy, and we were all optimistic. We knew we had a hit. Then—one day when we were in rehearsal—I was sitting out in the audience behind Dowling. Something went wrong onstage and his assistant told him about it. The assistant repeated the criticism. Dowling jumped up and said: 'Leave them alone! Aren't they beautiful? So simple! Just like children!' "

Eddie Dowling ushered in Mr. Ward's play "just like children." He took a play that had a revolutionary theme and he tried to make it into *The Green Pastures* all over again. And the Negro spirituals he used were far from revolutionary in presentation. Mr. Ward was justifiably upset and angered over what was done to his play. The result was a commercial failure, one that was to be pointed to again and again as evidence that Negro drama does fail—but no one added that it fails when polluted and misinterpreted.

That hysterical era almost effectively silenced social criticism in the theatre. The most notable work of the time was Arthur Miller's *Death of a Salesman*, a particularly fine dramatic piece. But it was a product of its times. It took on the attitude that today permeates the American theatre and much of our thinking. The fault, it said, is also within us, not totally in our social, economic and political structure. Mr. Miller's leading character, Willy Loman, appealed to bank presidents as well as to the common man. What Miller launched with dramatic force was an age of introspection, of putting on stage imperfect, small men who even under the most ideal social circumstances would be doomed to failure.

This was the era when the stage went overboard in degrading its heroes. They didn't have Achilles' heels. They had clay feet, mired in manure and mud. They repelled audiences and kept them at a distance; no one wanted to jump onstage and help *them* out of a struggle.

Negroes began to find themselves with fewer and fewer white allies. This, then, began the era that eventually produced James

Baldwin, LeRoi Jones and scores of black writers—the era of chastising the white liberal. It started long before, when whites ran off to the suburbs, to Hollywood, or withdrew within themselves and left black people behind to starve or struggle alone.

Severe rumblings were heard in Negro circles when theatre artists began to concentrate on self-promotion. The American Negro Theatre found itself in the unique position of defending itself, of declaring it did not willfully promote segregation. Its critics pointed out in sharp terms that Broadway was rapidly engaging in desegregation, that the "big money" was down there and ANT could be only a "training ground" for the big street. A series of desperate dramatic wars were waged. Cliques formed and some wanted to start a new theatre. And the eternal answer offered by a Negro theatre worker when his work was questioned was this: "Hell, I work on Broadway more often than you do!"

In effect, the omnipotence of Broadway had been established. The success of *Anna Lucasta* as a Broadway entry had opened new doors to Negroes, but—like the Provincetown Players and later New Stages—the group had been destroyed by Broadway. People came to Harlem, no longer to witness vital theatre, but to look for something that would "sell downtown." And critics judged ANT's offerings and other Harlem groups on the basis of Broadway entries.

This proved to be unfortunate. When ANT produced *Home Is the Hunter,* the downtown critics reviewed it sharply and devastatingly. In 1946—over the objections of playwright-director Abram Hill—the group voted to revive its favorite comedy, *On Strivers' Row.* Kronenberger declared in *PM* that the "two brands of satire do not mix well." He lamented that Mr. Hill did not grasp the opportunity to sharpen and polish his work. Despite Mr. Kronenberger's objections, *On Strivers' Row* drew large audiences from the community, and the play enjoyed a successful run.

An interesting note about that production was the fact that a touring company was organized under the direction of actress-director Osceola Archer. Her cast consisted of Norma Wallen, Geneva Fitch, Joe Purviance, Lettita Toole, Oliver Pitcher, Jay Powell, Cecil Scott, Doris Allen, Patrick Steele, Audrey Beatrize, Lula Hurston, Chickie Evans, Maurice Thompson, Eva Mooney, James Trotman and a newcomer to the theatre listed as Harold Belafonte.

At about the same time, the 115th Street People's Theatre presented Oliver Pitcher's play, *Spring Beginning*, which was produced and directed by Leslie Jones. Maxwell Glanville, Ruby Dee, Austin Briggs-Hall, Clarice Taylor, Theodore Grant and Doris Block played major roles in Mr. Pitcher's poetic drama. And Virgil Richardson saw his play produced at the Harlem Boys Club. There were numerous other offerings, sometimes with fratricidal overtones, but Harlem drama was playing according to Broadway standards. The criterion became not what the drama said to the people of the community, but whether or not it had anything that would interest the commercial theatre. Everyone knew more than everyone else in those days; and as a result, the focus of the Negro community theatre was lost.

Abram Hill resigned from the American Negro Theatre. He subsequently adapted and directed a version of *The Power of Darkness*, which played very well and to good audiences. Mr. Hill then went on to Lincoln University where he taught for a while, then joined the New York City school system. Today, regrettably, he remains away from the theatre. How many, one wonders, how many talented actors, writers, directors and producers remain outside the theatre while the mediocre dominate it?

While hysteria was driving people to become introspective, a group named People's Drama came into existence. It revived John Wexley's *They Shall Not Die*, but this time there were six boys, not nine. These six were to symbolize the Trenton Six case. The play was shown at a hall on 41st Street, and it drew large audiences. It was also during this period that the Harlem Showcase presented my *Shame of a Nation*, also about the Trenton Six. The latter work starred Albert Grant, Helen Marsh, Dorothy and John Tarrant, Melvin Mitchell, Altman Fisher, Larney Rutledge, Martin Corbin, Leslie Slote and Doris Huggins.

Other Negroes began to have plays produced. At the 115th Street People's Theatre Harold Holifield's *Cow in the Apartment* was seen. Gertrude Jeannette had her *This Day Forward* produced at the Elks Community Theatre.

The offstage drama shifted into high gear. Henry Wallace and Harry Truman split openly, and Wallace declared himself a candidate on a third-party ticket. Truman continued a get-tough-with-Russia policy. And all the work that had been done to cement relations with Russia was suddenly being undone. As one Negro said then: "If Uncle Sam can make us love the Russians, then

The Rose McClendon Players were founded in 1939 by Dick
Campbell. Members of the group, seen in 1940, include (left
to right) Sidney Easton, Billy King, Jr., Rosamond Johnson,
Dorothy Paul, Dick Campbell, J. Homer Tutt, Christola Williams, Leigh Whipper, Viola Dean, P. Jay Sidney.

M. Smith

hate them all in one decade, nobody needs to tell me we can't get justice in twenty minutes if Uncle really wants us to have it. You just let the day come when Uncle declares it's unpatriotic and disloyal to be anti-Negro!"

Later, Paul Robeson made a speech abroad and said that he found it unthinkable that the American Negro would wage an aggressive war against the Soviet Union, which had abolished all racial discrimination within one generation. When Mr. Robeson's words reached America, they were reconstructed and he was quoted as having said: "The Negro won't fight for America."

Roy Wilkins of the NAACP and Adam Clayton Powell hastened to decry Mr. Robeson and declare that Negroes *would* fight for America, although—since neither happened to be clairvoyant—how they knew this remains somewhat mystifying.

Since every Negro celebrity is, according to white America, an authority on race relations, that great baseball player Jackie Robinson was promptly called to Washington to refute Robeson's alleged statement. Many people wondered silently why Joe DiMaggio had not been called to discuss Italian-American relations during World War II, but no one said this out loud, for this would have been suspect.

More followed. During the summer of 1949 Mr. Robeson was invited to sing at Peekskill, New York. His first concert was prevented by a group of hoodlums. Another was scheduled and actually took place. But it shouldn't have. On the way home, concert-goers were viciously attacked by rockthrowers who lined the highways. Pictures exist of New York State Troopers who stood along the highways permitting these attacks to be made on the concert-goers. And after thousands of people had been injured, Governor Thomas E. Dewey ordered an investigation, not into *who* was *responsible* for the violence but to find out whether or not the Communists had used New York State to try out their organizational tactics.

The Peekskill riots, more than anything else, sealed the fate of the Negro and his white allies. This is reported here with a measure of understanding. Whites could not only lose their jobs for being pro-Negro; they could be physically assaulted. And they were.

With all the violence, the running and the backtracking, it was relatively easy for the American power structure to involve the nation in the Korean War the very next year.

The decade of the nineteen-forties began to move to a close. In the process it brought two efforts that involved Negro actors in "white" plays. Powell Lindsay organized the Negro Drama Group, and he took a group of professional actors on Southern tours. Some of the plays he produced were *Murder Without Crime* and *Night Must Fall*. Later Milton Wood and the American Negro Repertory Players went South with *Angel Street* and *Blithe Spirit*. These ventures—unrelated as they were to the Negro experience—draw large enthusiastic audiences, and they proved what should have been known long ago: that Negro audiences are hungry for theatrical enterprises, and they will sometimes buy what they really do not care to see.

As the decade came to an end, the internecine struggle that racked white and white, and white and black, crept into the relationship between black and black. The American Negro Theatre faced total dissention and eventually closed its doors. The 115th Street People's Theatre had a series of arguments leading to a mass exodus which resulted in the founding of the Harlem Showcase. These fights made interesting theatrical copy, but what they did in effect was to leave the Negro theatre worker at the mercy of downtown producers.

No one complained at first. The Playwrights Company presented the Maxwell Anderson–Kurt Weill adaptation of Alan Paton's *Cry, the Beloved Country*. This novel of South African life was called *Lost in the Stars* in its musical form. It opened at the Music Box on October 30, 1949. Todd Duncan played the lead and was ably supported by Leslie Banks, Gertrude Jeannette, Julian Mayfield, Warren Coleman and Sheila Guyse. It was a work of good intentions, moralistic in tone. It told of an African priest journeying to Johannesburg to locate his son. The son, in the meantime, has become involved with the seamy side of city life. He kills a white liberal and is later executed. The white liberal's prejudiced father undergoes a change in terms of human relations. Mr. Weill's music seemed more Germanic than African. Mr. Anderson's book was the work of a benevolent white man, condescending in terms of character, particularly black character. But it was no more condescending than Mr. Paton's sincerely well-intentioned, well-written book. Mr. Paton seemed to be saying in his book that the white man had taken from the African his "simple tribal life" and failed to replace it with "something of value." This, despite Mr. Paton's devout religiosity and sincerity in terms of brotherhood, is sheer white-supremacy ignorance. Had he studied tribal Africa, had he known the real history of the Zulus and other South African black people, he might have written a more truthful novel. But he fell into the trap of so many sincere whites. He accepted the "white standard," attacked it and failed to realize there is also a "black standard." And Mr. Anderson followed suit in his play. But Mr. Anderson had already documented his "whiteness" when he adapted the Medea legend into what he called *The Wingless Victory*. In that play, after his Medea—known as Oparre, a nonwhite—has been victimized by her Jason, ostracized by a puritanical society, Anderson had the audacity to have her on her deathbed asking Jason to give her his hand that she might kiss it!

The day after the *Lost in the Stars* premiere saw Marc Blitzstein's musical version of *The Little Foxes* open at the 46th Street Theatre. He called it *Regina* and featured were Lillyn Brown, formerly of the Lincoln Players, and William Warfield. *Regina* did not enjoy the success of *Lost in the Stars*. *Regina* was actually an opera, and why it was presented in the commercial theatre is a question someone else will have to answer.

The decade which began with the nation trembling ended with it trembling again. The cold war continued to look as though it might become hot at any moment. Known progressives and liberals became less and less willing to lift their voices, and the American Negro found himself a controversial character without support. The way was steadily being paved for Joseph McCarthy to wreck human lives by smear, innuendo and blatant lies. The coming era was to silence the theatre still further as a living instrument, to make it no longer a place where ideas flourished. It made a mockery of free speech and showed brave Americans to be really gutless, whining, selfish creatures, self-centered to the point where sacrifice and sacraments are ornamental things to be worshiped at a shrine but not in reality. This deceit made America once again betray the Negro. And all the hopes and dreams that had been spawned during the nineteen-forties became nightmares that linger with us in the nineteen-sixties.

# Part Three

## TODAY

*The wasted years return to haunt me—*
*The wasted years return to taunt me.*
*I dream of things that quickly passed,*
*Of a song, a love that did not last,*
*And as I think about these things,*
*Something within me awakes and sings:*
*"Those days you spend amidst toil and tears*
*Will only add to your wasted years."*

# Chapter X

## *The Nineteen-Fifties and the Millennium*

The fearful fifties found America in flight—a flight from others, from self, into self. Days and nights collided into streams of selfishness. To no one in the world did we owe commitment; we knew only self-gratification. People who once stood firm and shouted militantly of brotherhood and human rights now shifted their feet, nervously, restlessly, then turned quickly and ran. Americans left their ideals, their beliefs and their cities and raced toward the suburbs, cringing with fear lest they be labeled and thereby lose their middle-class status. It was "to hell with you, I've got to look out for me."

And "look out for me" we did. The cities of America were allowed to deteriorate as the nation sought suburbia. Into the cities came those people who had been displaced by the mechanization of the farms. They settled in what had been fine apartments, now sliced up into furnished rooms. In New York this pattern flowed through Harlem, Bedford-Stuyvesant, West Side Manhattan and the Lower East Side. Few people argued as buildings deteriorated. To fight with landlords over poor service was to be labeled a Communist or Communist-sympathizer.

The devil claimed America's soul, starting with the late nineteen-forties, and this claim was staked into the nineteen-fifties. Ex-Communists became authorities who "belonged" and who did not. People pointed their fingers at very close friends. When actor J. Edward Bromberg died after a series of houndings, playwright Clifford Odets wrote a glowing statement, ending with "Goodbye, sweet friend." Not too long afterward Odets was called before the House Un-American Activities Committee, and he accused Bromberg of being a Communist and of luring him into the Party. Director Elia Kazan also confessed his sins before that committee and named many a former friend as being a Communist.

Between the late nineteen-forties and -fifties, labor unions joined in the act. The National Congress of Industrial Organizations expelled a group of unions for "slavish adherence to the Communist

Party line." The New York City CIO Council came under fire and was labeled Communist-dominated because it had not supported the demands of Michael Quill's Transport Workers Union for a ten-cent subway fare so that transit workers could get higher wages. It was, indeed, a time of "to hell with you, I've got to look out for me."

This age of madness saw some weird alliances; it also saw long-standing friendships collapse.

One afternoon I stopped off to see a lawyer I had known for many years. We attended the same playwriting class at City College. We became good friends. He was very kind to me. We double-dated frequently, saw numerous shows and spent long hours in endless discussions. When I went away to college he gave me a sealed envelope that I later found to be full of bills.

When I stopped at his office, he rushed out and greeted me warmly. We reviewed old times. He had served heroically in the Navy, returned home, married and had become a parent. We talked about the theatre, and he revealed that his law practice had become voluminous and he had no time to do any writing. The hours slipped by; then I told him I had to leave.

He approached me with a strange look on his face.

"I've got to tell you something," he said. "My wife and I are friends of yours, always. Believe me. But I don't get up to see the shows you're doing in Harlem like I used to. And we don't invite you out to the house because—because of the times. Because of what might be said."

I stared at him. Politically he was at worst, a liberal, had always been one, and there was nothing in his background that suggested otherwise. He repeated: "You know what might be said."

"Yeah," I said. "Thanks, Herman. Be seeing you around."

Be seeing you around. It was the biggest lie I ever told. I walked out of his office, knowing that I was never going to see him again if I could avoid it.

If human beings didn't want to get involved in controversial things, neither did the theatre. The plays offered during the early nineteen-fifties were bland, noncommitted efforts. Ethel Waters played the leading role in Carson McCullers' *The Member of the Wedding*, which opened at the Empire on January 5, 1950. She received star billing over Julie Harris and Brandon de Wilde. Although she claimed she brought God into the play, she really only brought her name to what was not particularly good theatre. She was at most a "glorified mammy" in what became a hit.

Joshua Logan's *The Wisteria Trees* was in the same category. He adapted this from Chekhov's *The Cherry Orchard*, and all he proved was that anything Logan could do, Chekhov could do better. The play opened at the Martin Beck Theatre on March 29, 1950. Helen Hayes headed a cast that included Vinie Burrows, Ossie Davis, Georgia Burke, Alonzo Bosan and Maurice Ellis. On April 19 of that same year Katherine Dunham and her dance troupe opened at the Broadway Theatre.

That was all. Negro actors began to sit around in Harlem bars, wondering what had happened. Negroes were working on Broadway when there was work, but there was little work. True, a group of Negroes, led by Frank Silvera, appeared in Sidney Bernstein's production of *Nat Turner*, written by Paul Peters, at People's Drama in Lower Manhattan. This sprawling, interesting play had a good run. James Edwards later replaced Frank Silvera when the latter went to Hollywood. And the play moved from the Lower East Side to Harlem, to the Elks Community Theatre on 126th Street, where it attracted large audiences.

But generally there was little happening. Negroes sat, talking about what used to be and what ought to be. One night actor-writer Charles Griffin came uptown with some news that annoyed black theatre workers. Mr. Griffin had gathered some statistics that were devastating. He showed us figures indicating that more Negro actors worked regularly during the depression than at the present time.

Ellsworth Wright, then an actor-producer and now an Actors Equity official, jumped into the air and knocked over three cups of coffee. He screamed: "Haven't I been telling you folks that?"

Actor-director Maxwell Glanville roared: "You know one thing? We've been given the business!"

This incident led to a series of meetings that gave birth to the Council on the Harlem Theatre. There existed in the Harlem area what remained of four drama groups—the Harlem Showcase, the Committee for the Negro in the Arts, the Elks Community Theatre and the Penthouse Players. It dawned on members of these groups that some Negroes were working in theatre, but the majority were not. The Council on the Harlem Theatre was made up of representatives of the four local drama groups. The Council's aims, outlined by Maxwell Glanville, Alice Childress, Ruth Jett, Sylvester Leaks and William Coleman, were: (1) to support mutually local drama groups by using actors, scenery, mailing lists and audiences, (2) to create a calendar that would prevent a conflict in terms of production scheduling, (3) to agitate and press for the production of plays that would reflect the Negro culture in its true light.

Several productions benefited from the Council's efforts. Gertrude Jeanette's sensitive *Bolt from the Blue*, Harold Holifield's fantasy *J. Toth* and my play *The Cellar* were among the beneficiaries of this mutual cooperation. And so was *Just a Little Simple*.

*Just a Little Simple* was, for lack of a better word, Alice Childress' adaptation of Langston Hughes' *Simple Speaks His Mind*. Mr. Hughes had contributed columns to the *Chicago Defender* over a period of time. While doing so, he met a Harlem character and named him Jesse B. Simple, or Jess Semple, then "Simple." Negroes immediately saw this folk character as an indication that Mr. Hughes was telling off middle-class colored folks, reminding them to "just be simple." And Mr. Hughes' character grew into a very believable human being—so believable, in fact, that when Mr. Hughes wrote that Simple liked possum, an avid reader immediately packed some possum in ice and shipped it to the newspaper office. (I was there when all of this happened. And everyone laughed. However, neither Mr. Hughes nor any friends has revealed what happened to the possum. But, you can't get any kind of bet in Harlem that the possum was returned to its sender.)

When the loquatious, beer-drinking, wizened Simple came out in book form, he split white liberal-progressives and Negroes further apart. A lot of well-intentioned whites saw Simple as a stereotype. They said he was always drinking beer, hanging around bars and talking improper English. He had a broken marriage, a troubled love-life, and he was a disgrace to Negroes. They were ready to hand Mr. Hughes his head.

But a very important thing happened. Negroes in Harlem read *Simple Speaks His Mind* and they loved it. They laughed and cried at the same time. At party after party you would hear Simple quoted: Inadvertently, someone would get out the book and start reading parts of it. From the very first sketch to the last there was laughter, then tears, then anger.

"If you want to know my age, don't look at my face, look at my feet," says Simple. "These feet have stood on the Rock of the Ages.

These feet have worn out thousands of pairs of sox, sneakers and shoes. These feet have had one hundred corns, ten bunions and has run from white folks."

Simple is devastating when he discusses Harlem landladies, and he enjoys the speech at a banquet more than he does the food—at least, at one particular banquet. A group of Harlem society ladies have given an affair in honor of Dr. So-and-So, who seemed remarkably a combination of W. C. Handy, W. E. B. DuBois and Langston Hughes. Anyway, old Dr. So-and-So was called a genius by *The New York Times*. At the banquet in his honor, he jumps to his feet and declares he is not honored. He charges the society ladies with waiting around till he's half-dead, then recognizing him after the *Times* does. He tells them they have given a big dinner so they could eat, but are they raising funds to send Negro artists to school? Did they buy his books or his paintings when he needed them to do so? The old man shouts: "I ain't honored." Simple's comment is: "As for me, I'd buy that old man a beer anytime."

Simple has much to say about being away from his native Southland. "If I was down home, I would just fish and dream, dream and fish—if I had not had to leave home due to white folks. White folks sure have caused a lot of inconvenience in my life."

Simple works for the "mop and broom" squad—the maintenance group. When his boss tells him he doesn't work as hard as he used to, Simple retorts: "A dollar doesn't buy me as much as it used to, either."

He has wonderful imaginary flights and in one of them he sees himself before the House Un-American Activities Committee, charged with wanting to "tear this country down." He replies: "Not all of it—just from Virginia on down to Texas." When called Red, Simple blandly asks the Committee: "When I ride the railroad next time, do I get in the black car or the red?"

Alice Childress, hitherto known primarily as an actress, had written a one-act play, *Florence*, which was produced at the American Negro Theatre. She undertook the task of adapting *Simple Speaks His Mind* for the stage. In a highly skillful manner she used Jess Semple as the master-of-ceremonies in a Harlem variety show. She wove several of Mr. Hughes' sketches into her adaptation and she included her play, *Florence*, as well as Les Pine's one-act drama about voting rights. John Proctor directed and Ellsworth Wright produced the work for the Committee for the Negro in the Arts.

*Just a Little Simple* had veteran actor Kenneth Mannigault in the leading role. And it was ideal casting. When the play opened at Club Baron, 132nd Street and Lenox Avenue, in September, 1950, it was obvious to all that Harlem had another hit show.

Life got interesting in Harlem. A number of downtown producers discussed moving *Just a Little Simple* to a Broadway house. The producers promptly rejected this offer. They said the purpose of doing the show uptown was to build a Negro theatre, not to hold a series of tryouts for Broadway. The producers remembered that *Anna Lucasta* had indirectly led to the death of the American Negro Theatre, and *The Respectful Prostitute* had similarly contributed to the breakup of New Stages.

There were other interesting notes: James Edwards had played the lead in Hollywood's *Home of the Brave*. Sidney Poitier, Ossie Davis, Ruby Dee, Dotts Johnson and a number of fine actors were called west to make *No Way Out*. And there was joy, admiration and gratitude that Mr. Poitier was going to play the leading role in a film.

Many Negro theatre artists remembered the Sidney Poitier who came to New York from Florida with a West Indian accent "so thick you could cut it with a knife." The young man went to the American Negro Theatre and wanted to learn to act. Several people told him, bluntly but sincerely, to give up and go into another branch of theatre. Mr. Poitier did not give up. He bought himself a radio and he listened to it, hour after hour. And on the streets he stopped friends, listened to them talk. And bit by bit his West Indian accent slipped away.

He made his way into such shows as *Anna Lucasta* and *Lysistrata*, and he was a candidate for a role in *Lost in the Stars* when he took the screen test that won him the leading role in *No Way Out*. And he had trouble believing his own good fortune.

"Imagine!" he told Duke Williams over a ten-cent beer. "Imagine *me* walking around town waiting for Richard Widmark to return so we can go to Hollywood and make a movie!"

That movie was the first of many to be made by the tall, thin young man. With its completion, he went to South Africa with Canada Lee and Charles McRae to make *Cry, the Beloved Country*. When he returned home, he said: "Don't say a word about race prejudice here, man. That South Africa is heading for hell in a hurry. Canada Lee was sick when we got there, and I swear to you he got sicker."

He elaborated on black life in South Africa—a life now too well known to be discussed fully here. He told, too, how the American Negro actors had to be admitted to the Union as Director Zoltan Korda's bonded servants. They lived in a farmhouse on the outskirts of Johannesburg. One night Sidney Poitier went for a walk. He saw the hills of sand that frame Johannesburg. He thought to himself: This is October and here I am thousands of miles from home. It's probably getting ready to snow back there. He walked to the white-sand mountains and lifted some of the grains. He let these trickle through his fingers and, for a moment, he was back home, picking up snow flakes. Suddenly, the screech of car brakes pierced the air. Shouting voices assailed his ears and beams of light searched his face. The South African police raced toward him, shouting at him, demanding to know what he was doing outside the township, asking for his pass, insulting him. It took a considerable amount of time for the young man to convince the police that he was an American actor in South Africa to make a movie, nothing more.

When *Cry, the Beloved Country* was completed, Mr. Poitier came home to America, to fame, to little fortune, and less work. He married, moved into a Queens apartment and went to work on a construction job.

In the summer of 1951 the Apollo Theatre decided to offer two plays—*Detective Story* and *Rain*. Mr. Poitier was invited to play the lead in the former and he was surrounded by a sturdy cast. Despite this, the show was hastily mounted, poorly directed and Harlem was less than enthusiastic about it. Police brutality was too long a problem in Harlem for the people there to show any empathy toward law enforcement officers. The play went on to Brooklyn, then to Washington's Howard Theatre.

After that Mr. Poitier and ex-barber Johnny Newton opened a barbecue shop on Seventh Avenue between 130th and 131st Streets. They called it "Ribs in the Ruff" and the place attracted numerous theatre people. Mr. Poitier worked the midnight shift and Mr. Newton handled the day shift. They worked hard, too, and they had difficult times. Theatrical work for Sidney Poitier was not always forthcoming. Sometimes he appeared on television in walk-on roles. Sometimes he was an extra in a quick movie. And anyone who stopped off at his shop could see that he was hurt because he was being consistently overlooked by the movie medium. Once he told a friend: "I'm a restaurant owner who acts as a sideline."

If the pitfalls of an acting career hurt Poitier, they took second place to the usual Negro theatrical tragedy known to each decade. An ill, almost penniless Canada Lee returned from abroad amidst acclaim and glowing newspaper accounts of his work in *Cry, the Beloved Country*. Lee had everything but work. He had been listed as a supporter of "left-wing activities," and this listing made acting jobs difficult to obtain. While newspaper critics sang praises about his acting, he hoped for work. He threatened at one time to take his notices, get a shoeshine box and stand on Broadway and reveal his true plight.

Canada Lee, like Bert Williams and so many fine artists, was a sensitive man. In the words of Adam Clayton Powell, spoken at Canada's funeral, "the real subversives of America broke his heart." All too soon the newspapers headlined that Canada Lee was ill, that he was in a coma.

I was walking up Seventh Avenue with actor Richard Ward, talking about Canada Lee's illness, when we decided to stop off at Sidney's and have some barbecue. When we crossed 127th Street I had a strange, forboding feeling and knots formed in the pit of my stomach. I was relieved when a passerby yelled at me and I stopped to talk to him. Richard Ward moved on up the street, toward Sidney Poitier, who stood in front of his shop, leaning against the awning. Ward turned and shouted to me: "My God! My God! Sidney just told me—Canada's dead!"

The night exploded with tears, endless tears. They beat upon the streets in an unrelenting flood that drowned out the car noises and the laughter so familiar to Seventh Avenue. And silence came to Harlem—a silence that was welcomed by none.

That night Sidney Poitier faced hundreds of friends who made their way to his shop to offer condolences, to weep with him. The pain-wracked young actor was almost numb. He knew what we all knew—that something had been taken from us which nothing could replace.

Sidney Poitier was in pain for many days. Not only had he lost a beloved friend, but his own career was wavering. It was a long time before life began to straighten itself out for this young man. But it did. Eventually, he was called to Hollywood to make *The Blackboard Jungle*. He appeared, too, in the television play *A Man Is*

*Ten Feet Tall*, later filmed as *The Edge of the City*. And there followed *Something of Value, The Defiant Ones, Lilies of the Field* and the Academy Award.

He remained a Harlem boy, genial, always ready to laugh at himself, never status-conscious. About a month after he won the Academy Award he was seen wandering around Pennsylvania Station with two bags under his arm. He was on his way to Philadelphia, and he appeared surprised because people kept stopping him, asking for autographs. And he almost missed his train.

Two weeks after that he stood in a swanky Harlem restaurant, discussing the "have and have-not nations." An old friend approached him and congratulated him on his award.

"Thanks," Sidney said. "It didn't mean a thing to my kids, though. Man, I took them to see that film and they went to sleep. I started shaking them. I told them, 'It's bad enough to go to sleep on your old man's work. But, to go to sleep when your old man's paid your way in to see him is just too much!' "

The conversation went on, then he said: "Let's step outside and get some air. We can talk some."

Only Sidney Poitier would have done that. He walked out onto 125th Street without sunglasses or any of the paraphernalia used by stars. He stood there as though he were at home, and he talked on and on about the state of the theatre, the state of the world and what was going to happen next. A crowd gathered around him. A young man walked up to him and held out his hand.

"Excuse me," he said. "I just wanta shake your hand. You sure did us proud when you won that award."

"Thank you," said Sidney. "That was for all of us."

Old men and young men, old ladies and young ladies, and streams of children flocked around Sidney Poitier. They held out paper bags for him to sign, notebooks, and some shared pieces of paper with others. They echoed the theme: You did us proud, and he repeated: That was for all of us. And he thanked them as he signed autographs.

I stood there, watching, beaming proudly. Suddenly, my vision blurred, for tears filled my eyes. Through my tears I saw the tall young man, talking pleasantly to the people on 125th Street, signing his name again and again. I remembered that this was Sidney Poitier, who had had a thick West Indian accent and had been told to give up theatre. This was Sidney Poitier who had stubbornly clung to his aim, had been mistreated in South Africa and denied many roles at home. This was Sidney Poitier who had worked the midnight shift in a barbecue shop, always hoping, reading and studying for the day when he could make an artistic contribution. And now he stood there on 125th Street, an immortal figure, loved by those very people he loved so very much for so long a time.

After Mr. Poitier was seen in *Detective Story* during the summer of 1951, Somerset Maugham's *Rain* was scheduled for a showing. This play brought Nina Mae McKinney back to Harlem. Miss McKinney was a long-time favorite, and she had distinguished herself in a number of films, notably *Hallelujah* and *Sanders of the River*.

*Rain* had Maxwell Glanville, Emory Richardson, Roman Henderson, Milroy Ingram, William Robinson, William Hairston and another group of fine actors who were prisoners of their material, inadequate direction and a dated play. Harlem Negroes couldn't have cared less about the problems of Sadie Thompson in the South Seas.

The Apollo management—meaning Mr. Frank Schiffman—charged that Harlem wasn't interested in serious drama. This was a curious charge from Mr. Schiffman, who had taken over the Lafayette years ago and systematically ushered in vaudeville, motion pictures, then closed its doors. He had, in addition, seen to it that the Harlem Opera House—which once housed Negro performers—had gone out of business. The Apollo, therefore, remained the only house in Harlem that offered "live" shows—a factor that assured Mr. Schiffman he would never have to apply for relief.

Well, Mr. Schiffman opened his mouth at the wrong time and at the wrong place when he said Harlem wasn't interested in serious drama, for the Council on the Harlem Theatre held a meeting and said something about Mr. Schiffman that could not be considered laudatory. Part of the statement read: "The owner of the Apollo has insulted the Negro people by bringing to this community two inferior pieces of little meaning to our lives. Ridiculous prices were charged and when we exercised the buyer's right, we were accused of lacking taste."

The argument with the Apollo served as a catalytic agent. Productions by Negro authors followed in astounding succession. The Committee for the Negro in the Arts produced William Branch's first play. This was the pithy, exciting long one-act drama entitled *A Medal for Willie*. It opened at the Club Baron on October 15, 1951. Elwood Smith directed a cast that included Clarice Taylor, Julian Mayfield, Kenneth Mannigault, set designer Roger Furman, Jeanette Conliffe, Helen Owens, Helen Martin, Charles Griffin, Eli Rill and later an actor who was to earn quite a reputation. His name was Eli Wallach.

Mr. Branch's play told of a Southern town that turns out to award a medal to Willie posthumously. Willie has died a hero's death in the war. But, Willie—before he went to war—had had his troubles in the town. Much goes on in the Southern town as preparations are made for the big day. But on the big day Willie's mother, when she steps forward to accept the medal, tells the Southland in direct terms that Willie should have "come down here with his machine gun and shot up some white folks." She flings the medal in the townspeople's faces and walks off the stage.

Mr. Branch's play didn't only shock white people. It shocked Negroes. Many pseudo-academicians argued that the mother wouldn't have done that, that she would have cherished the medal and cried over it. Besides, they added, we don't want to show white folks how angry we really are.

There were other troubles. Some brainwashed Negroes believed that black people are always just beginners, eternal students, promising. They wanted to change some of Mr. Branch's lines. He and director Elwood Smith resisted this. Then, there was another matter: Branch had in his play a scene where a Negro woman was straightening her mother's hair. Pandemonium raged, followed by paranoia. Cliques huddled, quickly, declaring Negroes should not be putting things like that onstage. This was an "inside thing" and we would be following the stereotype if we did this. And so on and so forth.

Branch and Smith refused to relent. The scene remained in the play. After endless meetings people finally understood what the author kept telling them: Every black woman who saw the show knew that many Negro women do straighten their hair. And every white woman who saw it knew that white women have their hair done. But this is all indicative of how silly the color bar is in this country.

*A Medal for Willie* opened to glowing notices, and the very next day Mr. Branch was inducted into the United States Army. His play ran until the Christmas holidays, when Harry Wagstaff Gribble, director of *Anna Lucasta*, brought to the Club Baron a vehicle known as *Ride the Right Bus*.

*Ride the Right Bus* was based on a story idea suggested by John Proctor, director of *Just a Little Simple*. It was originally titled *The Feast of St. James* and Messrs. Gribble and Proctor presented the work to the Harlem Showcase, suggesting sponsorship. What actually happened is that Mr. Gribble and his partner, A. Raymond Gallo, had tried to produce the work in the Greenwich Village area. The theatrical unions were not willing to go along with this venture. They saw it as an inexpensive way of holding a Broadway tryout. Which it was.

Messrs. Gribble and Gallo offered the Harlem Showcase a considerable amount of money to lend its name to the production. Despite all the idealism that surrounded the Harlem theatre movement, no one was turning down money. And so the Showcase went along with lending its name.

That was the beginning. Several members of the Board of Directors had a number of criticisms of the play. There were matters to be explained. Mr. Gribble added scene after scene to explain various actions. As these were put into the play, many actors began to get that eerie feeling. And my son Melvin, then a baby, attended one rehearsal and started yelling out: "No! No!"

Out of the mouths of babes. But no one listened to Melvin and rehearsals continued. And things got worse. The cast of *A Medal for Willie* felt the Showcase had stolen its theatre, the Club Baron. And there were loud shouts. The Showcase members were angry, too, for what had happened was that Mr. Gallo had rented the hall without the Showcase's knowledge.

By the time the show opened in December, 1951, no one thought anything else could happen. Well, it did. It was the coldest night of the year and the boiler broke. There was therefore no heat in the Club Baron. Actor Richard Ward stepped out on stage before curtain. He had his hat on, his overcoat turned up at the collar. He made a short speech, apologizing for the broken broiler, and invited the audience to warm up by ordering a few drinks.

The curtain went up on schedule—at 8:30 P.M. And the play went on and on. The final curtain fell at 1:20 A.M. On his way out of the door, Ray Gallo told one of the Showcase members: "Tell Harry Gribble the play is too damned long."

"If he doesn't know that by now, he'll never know it," was the answer.

Something even more incredible happened the next day. People began to call the Harlem Showcase office for tickets. Every Showcase member was disgusted, ashamed and embarrassed. The switchboard operator told callers the show was "highly horrible" and recommended that they stay away from it. Several callers became belligerent and insisted upon having tickets. And for several nights the show drew good houses.

Suddenly, people began to believe the Showcase's switchboard operator when she said the play was terrible. Fewer and fewer people showed up, and this led Ray Gallo to run around out front and try to give passersby tickets. The passersby reasoned that any show where people gave out free tickets just had to be bad. They told Mr. Gallo: "No, thank you."

All of this is reported here in a light vein, but *Ride the Right Bus* was actually a theatrical tragedy. Mr. Gribble has for years been called one of the great American directors. But desperation can cause tragedy in the theatre. He wanted another *Anna Lucasta*, wanted it very badly, and this led to a resounding defeat. After the Christmas season, *Ride the Right Bus* closed and *A Medal for Willie* reopened for a good run.

An interesting sidelight to the Showcase's greed was the fact that the extra income from *Ride the Right Bus* put the group's members in a higher income tax bracket, and they all had to pay the government.

*Ride the Right Bus* may have seemed a comedy of errors, but it offered an intriguing lesson to Harlem theatre workers. It made them increasingly suspicious of the most sincere white efforts to "help" Negro theatre. And it made workers turn again to their own efforts.

Alice Childress' second play, *Gold Through the Trees*, followed *A Medal For Willie* into the Club Baron. This work, beautifully mounted, offered glimpses of Negro history over many centuries. It, too, enjoyed a good run and pleased audiences.

A wild thing happened during the summer of 1952. Roger Furman, set designer and actor, organized the Negro Art Players for the specific purpose of bringing summer stock to Harlem. He had next to no money, and people shook their heads kindly or laughed at him openly. While they were doing this Mr. Furman attracted such actors as Luther James, Jack Stackhouse, Bertha Scott, Richard Fisher, Isabell Sanford and Esther James. He then negotiated with the Elks Community Theatre to bring a bill of one-acters there in July. And staged in the round were: Tennessee Williams' *Mooney's Kid Don't Cry*, Mr. Furman's *The Quiet Laughter* and Charles Griffin's *The Oklahoma Bearcat*. And when local audiences began to leave their apartments and their furnished rooms nightly to see his work, Mr. Furman had the "last laugh."

The summer of 1952 hummed with excitement. Maxwell Glanville and Julian Mayfield formed a production company and planned to offer three one-act plays under the collective name *Alice in Wonder*. Both men were by now theatre veterans. Mr. Glanville had appeared in leading roles at the Rose McClendon Players, at the American Negro Theatre and in the Broadway theatre. Mr. Mayfield had been seen prominently as the son in *Lost in the Stars*, and when plans for *Alice in Wonder* were being laid, he was playing a leading role in Stanley Greene's off-Broadway show *Wedding in Japan*.

Mr. Mayfield's two one-acters, *A World Full of Men* and *The Other Foot*, were combined with Ossie Davis' first play, *Alice in Wonder*, to round out the bill. The two producers drew a cast of veterans. Roy Allen was their stage manager and Leon Bibb their set designer. The cast included Howard Augusta, Geri Bryant, Jack Stackhouse, Bertha Scott, Maurice Thompson and Ed Cambridge, and the star was Miss Ruby Dee. They arranged to open at the Elks Community Theatre in September, 1952.

Actor William Marshall, star of the film *Lydia Bailey*, contributed one hundred dollars to launch the venture. Sidney Poitier, along with Johnny Newton, had opened his Seventh Avenue barbecue restaurant, Ribs in the Ruff. They agreed that tickets for the show could be sold there. Everyone saw great things ahead for Harlem and its theatre.

Publicity gimmicks flooded the community. In newspaper ads and columns, on subway steps and building walls, one question was prominent: "Why is Alice in Wonder?" At first the publicity staff did this posting, then other theatre workers joined in. Soon Negro teen-agers were writing the question on street corners—all unbeknownst to the management. The next bit of writing saw the answer to the question: "You'll find out when you see Miss Ruby Dee in *Alice in Wonder*."

Opening night brought celebrities and local audiences. The first play, *A World Full of Men*, was a realistic piece, set beneath the train stop at 125th Street and Park Avenue. The scene was set with a masterful bit of pantomime by Howard Augusta, playing a derelict. Then, we saw the travails of a Southern girl (Geri Bryant), tortured by a "sharp cat" (Maurice Thompson).

The second play, *The Other Foot*, was set in the Harlem apartment of Sammy, played by the wonderfully comic Kenneth Manigault. Sammy is a backslapping, supercilious postal worker who fancies himself an authority on the woman question. Sammy's co-worker, Drew (Ed Cambridge) is worried because he believes his wife is "bedding with another man," J. C. (Jack Stackhouse), referred to as a "regular sixty-minute bed artist." Sammy is abusive, reminding Drew to be modern, broadminded, because women have sex drives, too. Eventually, Sammy learns that his own wife (Toni Griffith) once went with J. C. Although it was before their marriage, Sammy is suddenly not quite as broadminded and benevolent as he verbalized. He creates a scene. That night J. C., Drew, Drew's wife (Bertha Scott) and J. C.'s girl friend (Geri Bryant) visit Sammy. All is well with Drew and his wife, but J. C.'s girl friend reveals that she used to go with Sammy before he was married. The shoe is now on the other foot. Sammy sits in despair as Drew tells of how much he has learned. He begins to slap Sammy on the back, telling him how great it is to be broadminded.

The third play was set in upper Harlem, or "Cadillac Country" as author Ossie Davis described it. Alice (Ruby Dee) has seen her husband, Jay (Maxwell Glanville), offered a big television contract by a national network. Alice's brother (Ed Cambridge) has been involved in political activities to restore the passport of a militant Negro singer. Things move into high gear when the network director asks Jay to go to Washington, testify before a committee and denounce the militant Negro singer. There are further complications because Alice begins to see that Jay is "selling out." She cannot compromise on principles. She packs her bags and leaves Jay.

The three plays won fine reviews from local and daily critics. They ran for several weeks and delighted audiences. Economically, however, they faced problems. The Actors Equity off-Broadway salary schedule was then twenty-five dollars weekly. The stage-

*Canada Lee in the dramatization of* Native Son, *adapted by Paul Green and Richard Wright, and directed by Orson Welles.*

Culver

hands insisted upon placing a union man with this show at the rate of sixteen dollars nightly—which was just enough to plunge the show into financial difficulties. But the venture was not in vain. Producer Stanley Greene of New Playwrights, Inc., saw _Alice in Wonder_ as an effort that deserved repeating. He optioned the play, had Mr. Davis expand it into a full-length piece and retitle it _The Big Deal_. _The Big Deal_ opened at New Playwrights' Theatre in 1953 and enjoyed a good run.

The next Harlem entry was my play _The Cellar_. Motion picture cameraman Don Tatum and Raphael Lowman, a local businessman, leased a loft on the corner of 125th Street and Lenox Avenue, at 290 Lenox Avenue. They built a theatre in that loft— a well-equipped one. The Harlem Showcase had optioned _The Cellar_ from me in September and Messrs. Tatum and Lowman invited the group to produce it in their loft.

_The Cellar's_ cast had Richard Ward, Helen Marsh, Jack Stackhouse, Larney Rutledge, Willard Bartley, Freddie Simpson and William Coleman in it. The play was a melodrama about a Negro blues singer who befriends a fugitive from Southern injustice. The singer's fiancé is a brutal detective, anxious to rid Harlem of those elements that give it a bad name. He hounds the fugitive to the point of destruction.

The work was scheduled for three weekends. But something exciting happened. Audience members grabbed leaflets, programs and tickets and went about the city, imploring people to see the show, and the demand for tickets took on positive form. _The Cellar_ continued from November, 1952, until late April, 1953.

In 1952 the Greenwich Mews Theatre, housed on West 13th Street in the basement of the Village Presbyterian Church and Brotherhood Synagogue, began a series of "integrated" offerings. Robert Graham Brown was seen in Shaw's _Widowers' Houses_. This was followed by Les Pine's _Monday's Heroes_, directed by Michael Lewin, with Hilda Haynes playing the mother in a Jewish family, Terry Carter and Bill Gunn alternating as one of the sons, and with Bea Roth, Salem Ludwig and Bernard Kates prominently featured. The Mews insisted that its policy was to cast without regard for color unless the play specifically called for Negro and white characters.

It was a policy that created a lot of "pros" and "cons." The pros declared this was part of the battle—of a people working at a given craft without racial barriers. Actors, they argued, should not be kept from playing roles because of color. Jewish actors play Italian roles and Irish actors play Germans. Why then exclude the Negro actor from this opportunity?

The cons were equally pointed. This, they said, was not the question at all. What was being done was denying Negroes their identity. They were being falsely integrated, and the result of this would be deculturization and dehumanization of Negroes. The answer, they claimed, was to put on more plays by and about black people. And another thing the cons claimed was that this was reverse chauvinism, that had a Jewish woman played a Negro mother in a Negro play, there would have been screaming and yelling. After all, Broadway had cast a white woman in *My Darlin' Aida* and even the NAACP squawked.

The argument continued then and it continues today.

While this argument raged, William Marshall organized a company that produced *Othello* at Mothers Zion A.M.E. Church in Harlem. Therese Hayden directed Mr. Marshall, Lloyd Richards, Henry B. Scott, Helen Marsh and Joan Copeland. It was a successful production and it played several out-of-town engagements. Then Mr. Marshall was called back to Hollywood to make *Demetrius and the Gladiators*.

At Harlem's YMCA Ed Cambridge directed *Nuts to You,* a musical, then followed with a musical version of *The Egg and I.* The latter proved to be particularly rewarding. Downtown producers urged Mr. Cambridge to usher his work into the Jan Hus House after it completed its Harlem run. Mr. Cambridge did, and one of his cast members was a young lady named Diana Sands. Miss Sands won the Off-Broadway Award for her performance.

The last professional show to be seen in Harlem during the nineteen-fifties was Sidney Easton's *Miss Trudie Fair.* Comment here is admittedly subjective because I worked with this production as Associate Producer and Director of Public Relations. Mr. Easton wrote a flavorful period-piece, and it dealt with a woman known as Miss Trudie who operated a theatrical boardinghouse. Characters roamed in and out of the boardinghouse—small-time producers, classical actors, agents and two-for-a-nickel hustlers. The church-going, sentimental Miss Trudie was a former theatre worker, and whether the actors paid their rent or not, never worried her. Miss Trudie became involved with a two-for-a-nickel hustler who married her, took control of her boardinghouse and brought disaster to a happy home. Fortunately, by the end of the third act, all ended well.

Author Sidney Easton was then in his sixties. He had started off in minstrels, tent shows and carnivals in his native Southland. In the early 1900s he came to New York City, and Bert Williams and George Walker made him something of a protégé of theirs. He followed them around, learned many of their techniques, then later went out on his own. He won a large following on the vaudeville circuits, made a number of early movies with Claudette Colbert and Gary Cooper, then wrote with Ethel Waters a popular hit, *Go Back Where You Stayed Last Night*.

Mr. Easton then wrote an original screenplay entitled *Lifeboat 13*. He gave a copy of this to a friend, Leigh Whipper, who was going off to Hollywood to make a film, *Mission to Moscow*. Mr. Whipper was to present this screenplay to Twentieth Century-Fox productions, and he did. Nothing happened. Then, years later, Mr. Easton and his wife, Harriett, were sitting in a theatre where a film known as *Lifeboat*—starring Tallulah Bankhead, William Bendix, John Hodiak, Henry Hull and Canada Lee— was being shown. Mrs. Easton turned to her husband and said: "Honey, all of this sounds just like your screen play."

Mr. Easton told her to shut up and watch the film. But then it all sounded familiar to him, too, and after the showing the couple went home and looked into the family files. There were a number of similarities, and the next thing the Eastons did was to call a lawyer.

There followed litigation, and when Twentieth Century-Fox saw Mr. Easton's original script, it decided to settle out of court. This it did—and it cast a jaundiced eye at Leigh Whipper. But Mr. Whipper disclaimed any connection with the entire venture. All he knew was that he had taken Mr. Easton's original work to Hollywood, had left it with someone of alleged influence, then heard nothing more about it. It could have all been very innocuous. Some clerk might have stuck this script in the files; then when Fox asked John Steinbeck to fashion a script about a lifeboat, someone might well have pulled out Mr. Easton's script and said: "Here. We own this. If it suggests anything to you, use it."

This is admittedly speculation, based on the fact that I have seen it done more often than I care to record. But for Fox to settle out of court indicated that Mr. Easton had a lot of facts on his side.

Mr. Easton continued to write plays, and somehow he met Stanley Greene, formerly of the American Negro Theatre, Broadway, and executive producer for New Playwrights, Inc. Mr. Greene immediately optioned Mr. Easton's *Miss Trudie Fair*.

The play introduced Juanita Bethea to theatre audiences. Other veterans included Ted Butler, Mary and Freddie Simpson, Frank Cottrell, Howard Augusta, Service Bell, Javotte Sutton, Grace Kemp and Harold Cruse. And the work became a personal crusade for radio's Hal Jackson. It was almost impossible to hear his broadcast without mention of *Miss Trudie Fair*.

The play opened for a run in White Plains, New York, then moved on to the St. Albans area of Queens. There it played an exciting engagement and finally moved into 290 Lenox Avenue—the former home of the Harlem Showcase. Audiences flocked to it, loved it and came again and again.

Trouble came, too. Actors had worked for minimum salaries, and now they wondered about real compensation. Were we, they asked, moving to Broadway? If not, why not? They said enough people liked the show. Then, they asked another question—this one because producer Stanley Greene had been invited to play the lead in the Hedgerow Theatre's Philadelphia production, *The Emperor Jones*. Actors wondered why he couldn't use his influence to get *that* kind of recognition for a play he had produced.

By this time tempers flared. Stanley Greene was a genial, accommodating man—too much so, in fact. He had taken abuse, first, from white people who refused to underwrite this venture, and now he was taking it from his cast. Like too many Negroes, he did not fight those who had made him mad. He turned and cursed at me. When I cursed back, he turned on the author. Well, Mr. Easton may have played a number of comic, blackface roles in his day, but he was no Uncle Tom. He told Mr. Greene in direct, unequivocal terms exactly what he thought of his producing ability, his directorial ability and his management qualifications. Suddenly, Mrs. Greene and Mrs. Easton were not speaking. Besides, stage manager Harold Cruse and actor Ted Butler got into an argument that made backstage life miserable.

This started innocently enough. Ted Butler has a speech pattern that can only be described as Southern—which is understandable because he is Southern, and, in fact, the reason he came North was that he got caught in labor strife. This strife made it necessary for Mr. Butler to hide in a coffin and be shipped out of his native Southland to keep from being *buried* in a coffin and stuck in the ground.

Mr. Cruse had some questions about Mr. Butler's pronunciation of certain words, particularly since the actor was playing a New England insurance broker. Butler naïvely asked Cruse to list the words he pronounced incorrectly. Cruse obliged, and when Mr. Butler walked offstage and reached for the list, he found that Cruse had a looseleaf notebook filled with words.

Other words were exchanged, these expertly pronounced by both parties. What they called each other with the adjective "black" involved cannot be recorded here. But it took the whole stage-managing crew to keep them from exchanging punches.

By this time the cast had divided into cliques, and no one knew who was speaking to whom. Sometimes the cliques overlapped, and there were further problems. In addition, the local Harlem paper declared the entire production represented a backward step for the community's theatre movement, and the whole cast bristled. The landlord did more than bristle when he did not get his rent. He asked *Miss Trudie Fair* out of his theatre.

*Miss Trudie Fair* closed. There was talk of its being done elsewhere, but by this time Stanley Greene was deeply involved with *The Emperor Jones*, and other cast members were looking elsewhere for other work.

The next offering at 290 Lenox Avenue was Ruth Jett's production of Sally Howard's imaginative play *The Jackal*. The play opened for a limited engagement and sparked a furor. Harold Cruse was then editing a publication for the Acme Theatre group. Mr. Cruse happened not to like Miss Howard's play and he said so in vitriolic terms. And what the producers and actors said about Mr. Cruse, his writing ability and his theatrical knowledge was equally vitriolic. *The Jackal* closed after its limited engagement.

And that was all. Harlem lay quiet. Many long-time residents began to move away, to buy homes in St. Albans, Hollis, Mt. Vernon and New Jersey. The children of community drama had forsaken her, had moved away from the land of their birth, to downtown and outlying theatres. The community that had brought so much to the American theatre found itself without a theatre group. And it was to remain without a major professional group for the next thirteen years—the longest time in the community's history that it spawned no vital theatrical endeavor.

Throughout 1953 theatre talk had centered around a young man named Louis Peterson. Mr. Peterson was an accomplished pianist from New England who had studied at Morehouse College. After school he went into the theatre and appeared in minor roles in a number of shows. One was a production at the Blackfriars known as *A Young American*. Beyond establishing a measure of sincerity and musical ability, neither Mr. Peterson nor the rest of the cast helped the play, and the play certainly did not help them. The work created its greatest interest when it was rumored that Canada Lee was planning to move it to Broadway and take over Mr. Peterson's leading role.

Mr. Peterson was more interested in writing for the theatre than in acting. He joined a playwrights' group headed by Clifford Odets, and during that time he wrote *Take a Giant Step*. He found a group of young producers interested in his work and they optioned it for Broadway. Frederick O'Neal, Pauline Myers, Jane White, Helen Martin, Maxwell Glanville, Frank Wilson, Estelle Hemsley, Estelle Evans and a high-school basketball player named Louis Gossett rounded out the cast. The show opened in Philadelphia, and the news soon reached New York: "It's a winner!"

It was just that and more. It came at a time when Negroes were doing next to nothing in the theatre. They had gone through the wave of uptown optimism, then looked toward downtown and found, to use the vernacular, that "there was nothing happening." The most significant event prior to the opening of *Take a Giant Step* was the Howard DaSilva–Arnold Perl production of *The World of Sholom Aleichem* at the Barbizon Plaza. Mr. Perl had dramatized the works of the noted Jewish writer Sholom Aleichem and added to it a gem known as *Bontche Schweig*, written by Isaac Peretz. Mr. DaSilva served as narrator and director, and a wonderful cast surrounded this production— notably, Morris Carnovsky, Ruby Dee, Gilbert Green, Sarah Cunningham, Will Lee, Phoebe Brand, Marjorie Nelson, Jack Guilford and Vincent Gardenia.

This bill of one-acters represented an absolutely delightful evening. They reached the theatre the "hard way." Many of the actors had been "blacklisted" for pseudo-political reasons. They were an angry group, about as dangerous to the American status quo as a mosquito flying around the nation's capital. These people got out and began to hold a series of readings for backers, and they raised the needed money to launch their show.

They brought Ruby Dee to the cast. And it was exactly at this point that I got into trouble with them, for I was assigned to review the plays for a Harlem newspaper. And in my review I echoed the sentiments of many Negroes who saw *The World of Sholom Aleichem*. They pointed out that each actor in the company appeared in two of the three plays offered—with the exception of Ruby Dee. The feeling echoed by Negroes was that she had been "stuck there to further the cause of integration." And so I put this in my review.

You would have thought I attacked *The World of Sholom Aleichem*. Author Arnold Perl jumped up and down and insisted that I should have built up the *positive* aspects of the venture. He went on to state that it was wonderful to see the way Jewish people accepted Miss Dee in the leading role of one of their plays. Finally, when I could bear his holier-than-thou comments no longer, I said: "Does it mean anything to you that while Jewish people may accept all this, Negroes find it patronizing?"

He didn't answer. He sought out Ruby Dee and insisted that she write me a letter, wishing I had played up the "positive" aspects of the show. We had been friends for too many years for me to answer her letter.

Those were my salad days, when I was green in judgment, young in spirit. I had prepared a series of articles for Harlem's *New York Age*, and Frank Silvera called me up. He suggested that we get into a controversy over the Harlem theatre movement. Publicity, he said, is publicity. I told him that I would hand him his head if he attacked me in the press. After all, I said, I cut my eye teeth in the Harlem theatre and he didn't know a thing about it. Mr. Silvera suggested it was all for the cause and there would be no ill-feelings.

Well, he wrote a very interesting article, pointing up the need for a Harlem theatre, and he went into considerable detail. And I answered with an article, suggesting that he knew little or nothing about the entire Harlem theatre, that he had worked very little in the area and that he was therefore in the position of an outsider advising the community of its needs.

I wish I hadn't written it, for Mr. Silvera didn't bother to answer me in print. He got me on the telephone and accused me of accusing him of "passing." I told him this was not the case. He went on to declare that just because he had performed non-Negro roles in films like *Viva Zapata* and *The Miracle of the Bells* was no indication that he was "passing." He pointed out that he had made it clear to all concerned that he was a Negro. I told him this was not an item of discussion. I had not accused him of trying to "pass." All I had said was that he knew very little about the Harlem theatre movement; and the more he talked, the more convinced I was that I told the truth. He became increasingly angry, and finally I refused to argue about the whole thing.

On many levels it was a tragic argument, for Frank Silvera is one of the truly gifted performing artists on this continent. It is true he is often a little too opinionated and that sometimes his own talent gets in his way. He is a man with remarkable gifts— gifts that sometimes lead him to overacting and posturing when he should not. He is also a victim of an artistic form that recognizes the character actor last. The actor who achieves total recognition is the young actor, the one who gets the girl at the end— or loses her. Mr. Silvera is therefore doomed in this society to playing roles that are secondary among those written for his age group. And so the youngsters he has befriended—the Poitiers, the Edwardses, the Belafontes and the Louis Gossetts—will, in this society, outstrip him and bring him untold frustration.

The hassle with Frank Silvera proved interesting from one angle: Alvin "Chick" Webb of the *Amsterdam News* and Edward "Sonny" Murrain of the *New York Age* both called me and asked me to review the opening of *Take a Giant Step*. I told them no in direct and unequivocal terms. I had read Louis Peterson's play and I liked it. And I was not going to get into another hassle with theatre people, especially black ones.

At any rate, *Take a Giant Step* opened on Broadway on September 24, 1953. The critics liked it, with the exception of the New York *Daily News*. That critic found it "too long," but he hoped that Mr. Peterson would remain in the theatre.

Mr. Peterson, in a sense, is to "blame" for much of what happened to him. For one thing, he put Negro characters on the stage without apology, and his theme was far more than that of being a Negro in America. He saw adolescence as a painful step, a giant step. For the Negro youth, he saw an extra dimension. Sometimes his play was faulty in dramaturgical terms and sometimes his skill as a writer bailed him out of difficult situations. But he was always humorous and poignant, helped considerably by young Louis Gossett, who seemed to sense every word the playwright was saying. He gave a performance that was an indication of things to come—of things he did in A *Raisin in the Sun*, *The Blacks* and *The Zulu and the Zayda*.

Despite favorable reviews, *Take a Giant Step* turned out to be financially unsuccessful. The play closed after a short run, and Mr. Peterson turned his attention to television. He wrote three fine television scripts, the first of which starred James Dean. His second was a play that utilized a white cast, although it was obviously a sequel to the *Take a Giant Step* boy who had college difficulties. His third television show was *Joey*, which starred Anthony Perkins and Kim Stanley. This sold to Hollywood for an enormous sum but, as of this date, it has not been filmed.

Mr. Peterson apparently grew tired of the nonsense a Negro writer faces in the drama. He went off to Hollywood and, for a time, he wrote screenplays. One very fine play of his about the tobacco farms of Connecticut never reached the stage. His last play, *Entertain a Ghost*, was presented off-Broadway for a short engagement.

On many levels Mr. Peterson symbolizes what has happened to the Negro writer in the legitimate theatre. Fame is offered to him. He is *the* Negro dramatist—whether he wants to be or not. He can appear publicly to great acclaim, but a real appreciation of his work, of its intent, and rewards for it are not often forthcoming. And so the writer wanders off to television, radio, the movies or essay writing where the rewards are greater than those offered by the theatre. It has happened to too many black dramatists for it to be an accident—and to too many white dramatists, which leads one to suspect the function of the theatre as it now exists is to dissipate and frustrate creative forces!

*Mrs. Patterson*, written by Charles Sebree and Greer Johnston, opened on Broadway during the 1950's. Miss Eartha Kitt starred in this vehicle and captivated audiences. The play was originally the work of Mr. Sebree, a brilliant artist and set designer. Mr. Johnston, his collaborator, had written numerous plays previously. One, *The Crow's Nest*, was produced in Harlem during the 1940's by the New York Players Guild, and it starred Ruth Attaway and Earle Hyman.

*Mrs. Patterson* showed in poignant terms the influence of a well-to-do white woman on a Negro child. The work had a great deal of symbolism. It created, too, a group of staunch supporters and detractors. Its run was a limited one.

In 1954 William Branch returned from military service. While stationed in Germany he began writing a play that came to be known as *In Splendid Error*. He brought the finished script back to civilian life, and the Greenwich Mews Theatre promptly optioned it.

This play dealt with Frederick Douglass and John Brown in eloquent terms. Film actor William Marshall was engaged to play Douglass, and Alfred Sandor was a brilliant John Brown. Clarice Taylor, Kenneth Mannigault, Maxwell Glanville, Albert Ottenheimer, Howard Weirum and Austin Briggs-Hall were among the veterans who played the Branch work.

The play started off with problems—ideological and otherwise. Since everyone knows more about playwriting than the playwright, there were those who declared the work was too long, too talky, that John Brown's role was better written than Douglass' and that the author was using this historical drama to make a contemporary point. In addition to all of this, there were personality clashes, fistfights and threatened lawsuits. Despite all of this, *In Splendid Error* played for many months, then was seen at a number of tributary theatres.

After *In Splendid Error* Mr. Branch turned to television writing. For the Columbia Broadcasting System and the National Broadcasting System he prepared a number of scripts. His most notable work was the story of Mary McLeod Bethune, known as *Light in the Southern Sky*. For this NBC production Mr. Branch won the Robert E. Sherwood Award, presented to him by Mrs. Eleanor Roosevelt.

That award proved to be the worst thing that could have happened to William Branch, for he never got another assignment from NBC. Or CBS. As a matter of fact, he called at NBC one day about an assignment and he was offered a job as a porter.

Branch turned then to working with Jackie Robinson in preparing a series of columns for the *New York Post*. This ended when Branch won a Guggenheim Award, and he turned to adapting Peter Abrahams' novel *A Wreath for Udomo*. This novel was a timely study of the rise of Kwame Nkrumah and the liberation of Ghana. But it went beyond the revolution. It projected Udomo, the prime minister, trying to run a modern state. And it discussed in bold terms the deals and counterdeals made by modern statesmen, even at the expense of very dear friends.

What attracted Branch to the material was obviously the fact that it reflected his basic theme—a complicated choice of morals. Udomo is a troubled man. After he has rid his country of white colonialism, he finds himself at loggerheads with tribalism—the worship of ancestry so exemplified in the so-called modern states by the First Families. Udomo has other problems, too. A white supremacist state has made him the best offer in terms of industrialization at a terrible price. That price is for Udomo to lead the white supremacist state officials to Mhendi, a revolutionist, who happens to be Udomo's best friend.

Mr. Branch's play is superior to Mr. Abrahams' novel in terms of characterization, perception and dramatic effect. The play was produced at Cleveland's Karamu Theatre in 1959. The critics acclaimed the work, and it was optioned for Broadway. Philip Burton, father of actor Richard Burton, was signed to direct the play, and the usual effort followed—the search for a star. The two ranking Negro stars had availability problems. It is a tribute to their imagination that Richard Burton threatened to don blackface and play what he called one of the most magnificent acting roles created by a black dramatist.

At any rate, *A Wreath for Udomo* opened to a hostile London audience. The English at that time had been bragging that they had no Little Rocks, no Montgomerys and the like. Mr. Branch reminded them they had colonial problems. England was hardly the place to present *A Wreath for Udomo*, and the British critics attempted to bury it as quickly as possible.

After Mr. Branch's *In Splendid Error*, Alice Childress' *Trouble in Mind* found its way into the Greenwich Mews Theatre. This was a charming comedy about a group of Negro actors going into rehearsal for a forthcoming production, and it made some acidic comments about white attitudes toward the Negro in the theatre. When a young Negro actor is applying for a job, he admits to an elderly actress that he has no experience. The elderly actress promptly replies: "Just tell the Man you were in *The Green Pastures* or *Anna Lucasta*. All Negro actors were in those shows."

This was Miss Childress' first major written work to be seen outside the Harlem area. She had earned considerable respect for her acting in *Anna Lucasta*, in Barnard Rubin's *The Candy Story* and George Tabori's *The Emperor's Clothes*. Her one-acter, *Florence*, had successfully played People's Drama for a weekend in 1949. But now the professional theatre saw her outside her native Harlem, writing with her swift stabs of humor, her perception and her consummate dramatic gifts. The always excellent cast included Clarice Taylor, Hilda Haynes, Stephanie Elliott, Charles Bettis, Howard Augusta and James McMahon. *Trouble in Mind* was subsequently optioned for Broadway, but the demands for changes to meet the taste of an expense-account audience forced Miss Childress to withdraw her play.

Since *Trouble in Mind* Miss Childress has prepared a book, *Like One of the Family*, a series of sketches about a Negro domestic. In addition, she has written two other plays—*A Man Bearing a Pitcher* and *Wedding Band*, which have had a lot of trouble getting produced. Miss Childress represents a figure that is not unknown to students of the American drama—a major talent that is rarely produced. It would be easy to blame this on race relations if the cold truth were not that Barrie Stavis, author of *Lamp at Midnight* and Robert Ardrey, author of *Jeb*, fall into the same category. Obviously, the American theatre is trying to "have its cake and eat it, too." And in so doing, its finest playwrights are denied a hearing.

In the nineteen-fifties actor Luther James turned to producing and directing. He organized Comet Productions and engaged me to adapt John Steinbeck's *Of Mice and Men* for a Negro cast. Mr. James produced this play in a Greenwich Village cabaret and his reviews were glowing. This was the first New York appearance for Clayton Corbin, who recently starred in *The Royal Hunt of the Sun*. Other outstanding performers included Howard Augusta, Chuck Gordone and Bill Gunn.

Another product of the decade was Norman Rosten's *Mr.*

*Johnson*, adapted from the novel by Joyce Cary. Earle Hyman played the leading role in memorable fashion, and Robert Lewis directed. Playwright Rosten dealt with a Till Eulenspeigel-type African who spoke of the King of England as his "friend." This genial, naïve African constantly got himself into difficulties, and in the end, his good white friend had to kill him—because he didn't want anyone else to do it. The author had good intentions, but the "mark of the handkerchief" was on *Mr. Johnson's* head and Negroes did not like it. An interesting commentary was the fact that director Robert Lewis never understood why they didn't. He lamented that Negro groups had not booked theatre parties for the show.

Sammy Davis, then starring in *Mr. Wonderful*, joined other Broadway celebrities in urging people to flock to *Mr. Johnson*, citing Mr. Hyman's performance. Mr. Hyman is a brilliant actor. He first came to public attention in *Anna Lucasta*. Since then he has performed in films, on television, played a fine *Othello* off-Broadway, and appeared in a number of classics. In the nineteen-sixties he journeyed to Sweden and Norway, learned their languages and played Shakespearean roles there.

Mr. Hyman's fine performance kept *Mr. Johnson* going for a while, but then the closing notice was posted.

The years 1956–1957 were remarkable for the Negro in the theatre, and once again people started talking about the millennium. Three Negro-authored shows had professional engagements during that period—*Take a Giant Step*, *A Land Beyond the River* and *Simply Heavenly*. The first to open was the revival of *Take a Giant Step* at the Jan Hus House. This time the critics wrote even more glowing notices about Mr. Peterson's work. And this time the audience response was far greater than the play had known on Broadway. Outstanding performances by Bill Gunn, Frances Foster, Juanita Bethea and Godfrey Cambridge assisted Mr. Peterson's play immeasurably.

*A Land Beyond the River* was developed from one of the cases that exploded into the decision by the United States Supreme Court on May 17, 1954, that segregation in the public schools of America is unconstitutional. The case involved a rural area called Clarendon County, South Carolina. A group of farming folks, led by the Reverend Dr. Joseph A. DeLaine, agitated for bus transportation for Negro children to rural schools. The NAACP, then being pushed by its rank and file to justify its existence, rallied to the cause of the people of Clarendon County. Solicitor General of the United States Thurgood Marshall was head of the NAACP's Legal Division. And Mr. Marshall had been waiting for this moment. Since 1935 he had been steadily crawling up on the "separate but equal doctrine" that grew out of the Court's *Plessy vs. Ferguson* decision in 1896. Those who yell out that the 1954 decision came "suddenly" and that we should proceed cautiously should have looked at Mr. Marshall's record a long time ago.

In 1935 Mr. Marshall won the Donald Gaines Murray case, and a Maryland court ordered Mr. Murray admitted to the University of Maryland. In 1938 Mr. Marshall assisted the late Charles H. Houston in winning the *Gaines vs. Canada* case against the University of Missouri. He hit at segregation again when he won equalization of Negro teachers' salaries with those of whites. Again he was hitting when he fought exclusion of Negroes from jury service and convictions extracted by torture. He was involved, too, in voting and registration cases and won a remarkable victory in the white primary decision of 1944. He continued the crusade in the housing covenant cases which ended in victory in 1949.

The education cases became his personal vendetta. In 1948 he scored two victories—first when the University of Oklahoma law school was ordered to admit Ada Lois Sipuel, and then the University was told it could not segregate a Negro student in the cafeteria or in class once that student was enrolled. In 1950, there came the decisive university case, *Sweatt vs. Painter*, at the University of Texas, which opened the doors to all tax-supported colleges and universities.

The Clarendon County case was a "natural" for Mr. Marshall, and he urged the people there to "go for broke." They changed their petition from a fight for bus service to one for "separate but equal schools." When the case reached the United States District Court in Charleston, Judge Waites Waring asked the plaintiffs if they weren't attacking segregation. It turned out that the Negroes were doing just that, and they changed their petition to a demand for equal schooling.

The South Carolina Supreme Court shuddered, then declared that "separate but equal schools" happened to be constitutional, but the state would have to make the Negro schools "equal."

Judge Waring dissented and said, in effect, that the time for equal rights for Negroes was *now*. And the NAACP appealed to the United States Supreme Court.

By now there were four other cases—one in Virginia, one in Topeka, Kansas, one in Washington, D.C., and one in Delaware. The combined cases came to be known as *Brown vs. Board of Education of Topeka, Kansas*. And the United States Supreme Court unanimously outlawed segregation in the public schools of America. It said:

"In *Sweatt vs. Painter*, supra, in finding that a segregated law school for Negroes could not provide them with equal educational opportunities, this Court relied in large part on 'those qualities which are incapable of objective measurement but which make for greatness in a law school.' In *McLaurin vs. Oklahoma State Regents*, supra, the Court, in requiring that a Negro admitted to a white graduate school be treated like all other students, again resorted to tangible considerations . . . 'his ability to study, to engage in discussions and exchange views with other students and, in general, to learn his profession.' Such considerations apply with added force to children in grade and high schools. To separate them from others of similar age and qualifications solely because of their race generates a feeling of inferiority as to their status in the community that may affect their hearts and minds in a way unlikely to ever be undone . . ."

Negroes shouted and laughed over the decision. All kinds of jokes circulated—about Mr. Charlie looking around one day and seeing Negroes on school picnics with barbecue sandwiches. Someone suggested the Court's decision might lead to wholesale suicide among Southern whites. It was all very amusing, then—

Economic reprisals were used against the Negro citizens of Clarendon County. When I was last there in 1959, the White Citizens Council was a potent force. Storeowners proudly displayed signs, announcing membership in this organization. Negro farmers found it virtually impossible to obtain loans from banks. They could not purchase seed, fertilizer and other needed crop materials. The Citizens Council dominated the local agricultural board, and Negro allotments for tobacco and cotton were given on a jimcrow basis. Farms owned by Negroes were burned to the ground. And black farmers were unable to use local harvesting combines for their crops.

There was also discrimination in issuing public assistance—even that reimbursed by Federal grants. A Negro widow with a number of children was denied Aid to Dependent Children and told to go to work. And despite the fact that I documented all of this in a detailed report which Edward Gray of the United Auto Workers placed in the hands of so-called liberal politicians, it was not until 1964 that the Agriculture Department showed any awareness of the problem.

Life was tough in Clarendon County in 1959, but it was worse in the forties and fifties. This rural area lies outside Orangeburg, county capital. Racial struggles there have never had the exposure received by other Southern areas. For one thing, it is reported that the Associated Press correspondent for the area, Mrs. Luther B. Wheeler, is a member of the White Citizens Council and that she refuses to report racial strife in the county. And the county's radio station was, in 1959, equally unsympathetic to Negroes.

Joseph Armstrong DeLaine—known among his friends as J. A.— has deep roots in the soil of Clarendon County. This large, reddish-brown-skinned, very serious man came from a prominent family in the area. The son of a country preacher, he was educated at Allen University; then he returned home, became pastor of an African Methodist Episcopal Church, a schoolteacher and a farmer. For a time he taught in the Santee River section and, in his own words, "It broke my heart to see the little Negro children walking through mud and dirt to get to school. Sometimes we had to scrub them off before starting class. And on their way back and forth white kids would pass them, riding buses, and shouting and throwing things at them."

Dr. DeLaine set out to petition for school buses for Negro children. He trudged the country roads late at night, talking to people, urging them to join him. He had two willing allies in an elderly minister, the Reverend Mr. J. W. Seals, and farmer Bill Ragin. Those rural farming folk listened. And they huddled together to form a force that was to shake the state's capital and the United States Supreme Court.

Thurgood Marshall saw this as an excellent opportunity to attack the "separate but equal" doctrine. The Negroes agreed to change their petition and argue that their school was "separate all right, but it sure ain't equal." Glenn Ragin was one of the youngsters involved in the test case. And this test was to be changed in Charleston to an attack on segregation in the public schools.

After the Supreme Court's decision, tragedy struck again and again. Economic sanctions were used against the petitioners. Dr. DeLaine's home was set on fire. The Fire Department raced to the scene, noted that the house was a few feet outside the city limits and let the building burn to the ground!

Dr. DeLaine then moved to Lake City, and again his home was a target. Nightly mysterious riders drove by his home and fired shots at it. Dr. DeLaine called on the local sheriff for help, and the sheriff blandly suggested that Dr. DeLaine shoot at one of the cars "to mark it so it can be identified." The minister saw this was going to be a long night, so he had his family stay with relatives. This is the way he phrased the remainder of the story:

"I crawled into bed with my clothes on. I was tired, but I wasn't fixing to undress. Later that night I heard the cars pulling up in front of my house. A barrage of shots was fired. I jumped out of bed and I forgot my religion. I stuck my rifle out the window and I fired it. I pray to God that I fired to mark the car. One sure thing, though—that mob got away from my house in a hurry. They broke all kinds of speed records.

"I knew they'd be back. I jumped into my car and drove it as far as it would go. I left it at a gas station, then I hitched a ride with a Southern white truck driver. By then the news was out: The law wanted me. My conscience was bothering me, too, so I told the truck driver I wanted to go back and turn myself in. The truck driver told me: 'Reverend, you got to be kidding. I'm taking you to the state line and you get yourself a lift from there going north.'

"The truck driver did the right thing, for by the time he dropped me off, South Carolina had a price on my head. And when I made it on to New York there was still a price, plus extradition papers. But Bishop Ward Nichols fought my extradition and we won the case."

Dr. DeLaine told me all of this in 1956 in a Harlem restaurant. He looked up at me and there were tears in his eyes. "Maybe we didn't win it," he said. "I still get letters from my parishioners, asking for money. They're suffering all kinds of reprisals and they ask me for help and I can't help them."

He pulled from his pocket six letters and invited me to read

The great Paul Robeson, with Uta Hagen, in the production of
Othello *that played on Broadway in 1943.*

them. They were from six different people, yet they all said the same thing: Reverend, I cooperated with you in the fight and I'm really having it hard now. I can't get credit to buy supplies. Can you help me out. Yours in Christ.

Tears filled my eyes, too, for several reasons. The thought of families deprived of the basic things in life because of a just cause seemed intolerable. The hunger, the pain and the anguish they knew in a land where things grew abundantly was outright cruel and inhuman. This was the new lynch mob, this economic reprisal. There was no need now for ropes, firearms or gas chambers. This new lynch mob could frustrate and starve a people into fratricide.

Another reason I cried was my own ignorance. For most of my life I had walked about the city, making fiery speeches, writing essays and plays filled with advice for my black brethren below the Mason-Dixon Line. I sent plenty of money down there, too. But I stayed in the North. Now, the Southern Negro had taken steps to liberate himself and *me*. Guilt gnawed at my insides.

When I mentioned this to Dr. DeLaine, he smiled, benignly. "Something's been happening down there a long time," he said. "All my life I've heard ministers complaining about jimcrow. Negroes didn't just start raising sand in 1954. They started in 1619. But they didn't have television and newspapers and radio.

"When I started organizing the bus case, I sensed something that may take on political significance down the line. Neither black folks nor white folks are as stupid as the Know-It-Alls would have you think. Many a white woman and white man told me, silently: 'I'm on your side.' If all of this ever gets going on a political level, a lot of bigots in this country will be in real trouble."

Trouble for bigots was a long time coming. Autherine Lucy entered the University of Alabama and was terrorized. The Montgomery bus boycott claimed headlines and brought added indignities. The Black Revolution was a reality to white America. And the White Citizens Council intended to contain that Revolution.

Dr. DeLaine invited me to join him in fund-raising and public relations efforts to assist the stricken soldiers of the Revolution. I dared not refuse. We raised some funds, particularly through the help of the National Committee for Rural Schools and the United Automobile Workers. Then, one Saturday morning Dr. DeLaine and I were invited to the office of A. Philip Randolph, the acknowledged dean of the civil rights movement.

A meeting was held to plan a civil rights rally at Madison Square Garden. We drafted a proposal which was sent out to numerous groups, calling for their support. At this same meeting Dr. DeLaine called the committee's attention to the stricken Freedom Fighters who faced reprisals. Mr. Randolph said emphatically that some of the funds raised at the rally would definitely go to those brave Negroes who were—and still are—on the firing line. We did not dare let anyone think we would forsake those who challenged jimcrow.

As plans for the rally got under way, Dr. DeLaine called to say we had to prepare a speech for him. We did so; then on the evening of the rally, we arrived at the Garden. We were both shown to seats on the dais and I began to tremble. I had attended these rallies all my life, first as an usher, then as a script-writer. I always sympathized with those who sat on the dais, for they had to remain through long, never-ending speeches. An usher or a writer could always sneak out during the speechmaking.

I have often thought that if America's bigots were compelled to sit through all of the rally speeches, they would tire of prejudice and grant Negroes their rights. That, of course, is a simplification, but they would assuredly get tired.

This meeting proceeded as usual. Mr. Randolph spoke eloquently and called for real action. He said that, because Negroes cannot bear the brunt of being black and red, we reject the support of Communist groups. Later Adam Clayton Powell spoke and called for another March on Washington if race relations continued to deteriorate. Mrs. Eleanor Roosevelt interviewed Autherine Lucy about her future plans. Novelist Fannie Hurst spoke. Labor leader David Dubinsky spoke. NAACP leader Roy Wilkins spoke. Actress Jayne Mansfield, who had been a guest at both the Democratic and Republican conventions, spoke. Actress Judy Tyler spoke. Cab Calloway sang "Minnie the Moocher" and spoke. Then, Judge Waites Waring and his wife were introduced and applauded for the Judge's courageous dissent. But Dr. De-Laine's name was not mentioned once.

He sat throughout the long program, his face saddened.

Mrs. Eleanor Roosevelt brightened the evening for Dr. DeLaine. She was having some magazine pictures taken, and she called to the minister and asked him to pose with her. He did. And that was the only recognition he received that night.

That very night I saw what was happening to the Black Revolution in the North. I saw why it had taken a bunch of country folks to stir the nation. The black and white Northern leadership had lost itself in high-sounding phrases while becoming very, very middle class. This leadership had no direct relationship to the ordinary Negro or white person. The Northern leadership thus followed the pattern of the bourgeoisie when the latter married the aristocracy. It was this pattern, this marriage, that made the Northern leadership scream, shudder and denounce Malcolm X when he drew a large personal following from Harlem.

The disappointed Dr. DeLaine wanted desperately to tell his parishioners' story. He thought perhaps he ought to call a rally of his own and have me write a script as I had for other rallies. I agreed, then began to dramatize the experiences of the people of Clarendon County. In the midst of my work, Dr. DeLaine was assigned to a parish in Buffalo and he left the city.

One coincidence followed another. Playwright David Timmons and I met frequently to discuss our work. One particular night when we were to meet at Timmons' home, I declared it was too cold in his place. Being a New Englander, Timmons hated steam heat, and he had removed all radiators from his apartment. So we decided to meet at the home of Stella Holt and Fran Drucker, business managers of the Greenwich Mews Theatre.

I read the work I was doing and Stella Holt asked me to leave the script there. She said she was going to have the Greenwich Mews produce it. It was all I could do to keep from laughing at her. After the things I had said and written about the Mews group, I knew its directors wouldn't look twice at one of my plays. Both Stella Holt and Fran Drucker insisted they would, so, with considerable help from Timmons, Austin Briggs-Hall and John Killens, I completed the play and sent it off.

The Mews' Board of Directors haggled, quibbled and fumbled. I shrugged and asked for my script back. But Stella Holt and Fran Drucker are veteran theatre workers with enviable records. They told me in no uncertain terms to keep my mouth shut. Then they charged the Mews' Board of Directors with not knowing how to read the Negro speech and rhythm. They called for a reading of the play before the Board, then obtained the services of Richard Ward, Austin Briggs-Hall, Robert Graham Brown, Howard Weirum, Helen Marsh, Helen Martin and Jacqueline Barnes, who read the play one Monday night before the Board. Those actors read with such humor, fire and dramatic sense that the Board of Directors laughed, cried, then cheered. And they wanted to put the play on immediately.

There was only one thing wrong: I didn't like the play myself and I wanted to do some rewriting. Stella and Fran, lovingly known as "The Special Delivery Girls," began to wear out my telephone. In addition, Michael Howard was assigned to direct the play. We had a number of conferences while Stella shouted that we were "dotting every 'i' and crossing every 't'."

The play, remarkably directed by Mr. Howard, opened on March 28, 1957. The ensemble-acting cast included Robert Graham Brown, representing Dr. DeLaine, Helen Martin, Richard Ward, Jacqueline Barnes, Fran Bennett, Clayton Corbin, Donald Julian, Diana Sands, Ted Butler, Albert Grant, Peggy Devello, Charles Griffin, Howard Weirum, Lionel Habas, George Lucas and Eric Richmond. Replacements for cast members included Ivan Dixon, Fred Grossinger, Harold Scott, Douglas Turner, Lynn Hamilton, Helen Marsh, Roscoe Lee Browne, Isabell Sanford, James Alpe, Billy Read and Will Lowrey, Jr.

Those names are listed not only out of respect and gratitude, but also because they indicate the present makeup of the professional Negro theatre worker. In that listing you find veterans from the Rose McClendon Players, the Harlem Suitcase, the American Negro Theatre, the Harlem Showcase, the Committee for the Negro in the Arts and various drama schools. And in all the professional shows being done today those institutions will be prominently represented.

*A Land Beyond the River* was scheduled for a ten-week run, but the public supported it, and, with the exception of a hot-weather break, the play continued throughout the year. The most satisfactory thing about it was the fact that the United Automobile Workers used it for theatre party purposes and, in this way, funds were raised to buy a harvesting combine for the people of Clarendon County.

Through United Automobile Workers officials Andrew Dabbakkian and Edward F. Grey, *A Land Beyond the River* was taken to New Haven where it was sponsored by Mitchell Svirdorf, presently director of the City of New York's Human Resources Division. Later it played Great Neck; then Stanley Greene and Maxwell Glanville produced it in Brooklyn for a limited engagement, then in Newark, New Jersey.

A *Land Beyond the River* is, in many ways, a strange play. It is far from the well-made play and sometimes the dramaturgy is coarse. This is, in a sense, deliberate, for the emphasis of the work is on character illumination—an emphasis I feel that is necessary when one is dealing with well-known historical facts. But, most of all, in this play, I was happy to be able to bring to the stage a group of "simple" human beings I had met through the years.

The next year brought *The Man Who Never Died*. This was the first work by Barrie Stavis to be seen in New York City since the nineteen-forties. Mr. Stavis was one of the moving forces of a brilliant group known as New Stages. His play *Lamp at Midnight* dealt with Galileo, and it is acknowledged by many as one of the finest plays written for the American stage.

In *The Man Who Never Died* Mr. Stavis told the story of labor leader Joe Hill, who met a firing squad on a number of deliberately false charges. Joe Hill was remarkably well played by Mark Gordon, and Richard Ward was prominently cast as a Negro co-worker. The reviewers had trouble with Mr. Stavis' work. They wanted to chain it to a propaganda realm. But Mr. Stavis' play was anything but propaganda. He was dealing with a man who was ahead of his time, which seems to be the playwright's recurrent theme. He did the same thing in *Lamp at Midnight* and in his latest play, *John Brown*.

The reviewers could not kill the play. Mr. Stavis went out on a number of speaking engagements, and theatre parties came to the house. Many union members found, too, great identification with the play, and they supported it. The play continued at the Jan Hus House for a good run.

Meanwhile, another offstage drama was being played. Lorraine Hansberry, a Chicagoan, had written poetry and reviewed plays for *Freedom*, an uptown journal. She had started working on a number of plays, but never completed any. One night she sat working on a family play; then she became annoyed with it, flung the pages into the air, and they scattered over the floor. Her husband, Robert Nemiroff, got on his hands and knees and picked up page after page. He carefully arranged these and placed them on a desk. Miss Hansberry later said that was a turning point in her career. She sat down and completed the play.

That play was *A Raisin in the Sun*. She drew the title from Langston Hughes' book of poetry, *Montage of a Dream Deferred*:

> *What happens to a dream deferred?*
> *Does it dry up like a raisin in the sun?*
> *Does it fester like an old sore and run,*
> *Or, does it explode?*

One night the Nemiroffs entertained music publisher Philip Rose and his actress-wife, Doris Belack. They talked about Lorraine's writing, and as the evening progressed, she read her play. The Roses were impressed. The next morning Philip called Lorraine and told her he wanted to option her play.

Lorraine laughed when she told the story. She said: "I told Phil I'd take his money and keep it."

Mr. Rose wasn't laughing. They drew up legal documents and he had an option on *A Raisin in the Sun*. Then he really went to work. He contacted Sidney Poitier, who agreed to star in the play. He went out and signed Lloyd Richards to serve as director, then began a series of backers' auditions.

Everybody everyplace had criticisms of the work. Mr. Rose tried to get co-producers, but he was turned down. Finally, David Cogan, an accountant, agreed to join Mr. Rose. Money began to come in, never in any great amounts. Mr. Rose wasn't discouraged. He put his company into rehearsals without knowing where he would open the show. He held some runthroughs in New York City, then got a house in Boston.

Off the show went to Boston, where it opened to good reviews. The company went on to Philadelphia, where more good reviews followed. The Shuberts remembered they had told Mr. Rose they would arrange a New York house for him if he did well on the road. Mr. Rose took the show on to Chicago, where its success was repeated. And then New York saw it on March 11, 1959, and the critics sang.

*A Raisin in the Sun* not only won the Critics Circle Award; it made money. And it projected its cast members beautifully. Sidney Poitier—and later Ossie Davis—Ruby Dee, Claudia McNeil, Diana Sands, Ivan Dixon, Louis Gossett, Lonne Elder III, Douglas

Turner and director Lloyd Richards made notable contributions to this moving family drama.

*A Raisin in the Sun* created controversy offstage, too. Negroes got tired of hearing whites say: "Even though I'm of such-and-such background, I could identify with that Negro family." And some Negroes answered, bluntly: "Yes, I could also identify with the Nazi victims and the victims of the potato-famine." Then— someone accused the play of being too much like O'Casey's *Juno and the Paycock*. Right behind that accusation came another— that it was really a Jewish play with a Negro cast and that is why it did so well. And there were Negroes who became angry because critics said the play really said nothing about the Negro plight, that it was not an angry play, and they lauded the playwright for showing "balance" in her writing.

Then there were Negro intellectuals who felt whites had "patronized" the play. They declared no urban Negro would do what Miss Hansberry's hero did—give thousands of dollars at one time to a man whose address he didn't know. Those intellectuals claimed that, had this been a "white" play, the critics would have questioned that fact. But since it was a Negro hero, it was overlooked.

*A Raisin in the Sun* crystallized the era Negro playwrights began to call the "nots." The critics said *In Splendid Error* was *not* a message play, *Trouble in Mind* was *not* vindictive, *Take a Giant Step* was *not* just about Negroes, *Simply Heavenly* was *not* an angry play, *A Land Beyond the River* was *not* a propaganda play, and *A Raisin in the Sun* was *not* a Negro play. In other words, black playwrights were being praised for *not* making white people uncomfortable in the theatre. Black playwrights began to worry about their work.

But they were being produced and Negro actors were working. They worked, too, in integrated hits such as Sammy Davis' *Mr. Wonderful* and in Lena Horne's *Jamaica*. Everyone saw great things in store for black artists. The American Society of African Culture held a writers' conference at the Henry Hudson Hotel in 1959, and in looking back over the decade, everyone admitted that the decade which began as the fearful fifties had developed into one of optimism and output.

The millennium was here! Loudly proclaimed was the Second Black Renaissance.

# Chapter XI

## *The Nineteen-Sixties: Broadway Reconsidered*

In 1945 the United States embarked upon a policy of integrating its jimcrow Navy. We Negroes who served at the Great Lakes Naval Training Station were assigned to Camp Robert Small. Many outstanding professionals served there—schoolteachers, musicians, lawyers, ministers, writers and professional athletes. Among the latter were football players Buddy Young, Paul Patterson and Marion Motley and baseball player Larry Doby. When the news circulated about the Navy integrating, we shook our heads.

We had a notion we were going to get the worst of this integration. While being in the Navy was no holiday, we did have Chicago nearby and liberty every night and every weekend. In fact, many Army men referred to Camp Robert Small as "The Playhouse." We laughed at this, but we didn't laugh for very long.

Washington tore down that Playhouse. And we did get the worst of it. A draft list was promulgated with two hundred names on it. We Negroes were told to lash our gear in seagoing fashion, and replacements poured in for all of us. There were Negroes among our replacements, but the majority were white.

We stood there, watching our replacements arrive. I nudged a friend and pointed: "Look! Look at that cat over there, crying like a baby!" I said.

"Who the hell can see?" asked my friend. "I'm crying, too."

I would have done some crying, too, but my stomach was doing headstands. When another rumor circulated that we were going to be made into amphibian units and fleet marines, my teeth clattered so loudly that I could hear no other rumors.

One of my shipmates was particularly caustic about what he called doublecrossing Negroes who went around making speeches and writing stuff about black servicemen *wanting* to get to the front lines so they'd have an arguing point in the postwar world. The man continued his tirade, then, when still more white replacements appeared, he shouted: "This isn't integration! It's dis-integration!"

This memory is brought back to me now as I review the state

of the Negro in the American theatre during the nineteen-sixties. For a time the optimism from the nineteen-fifties reigned. There was continued civil rights activity, and the tired soldier who had replaced the little man with the big, big hat in the big, big house in Washington was himself replaced by a younger man. The replacement was a man who could at least use the English language, and though he said more than he performed, he did say it well.

Black people became central figures in American life. Television appearances by prominent Negroes became more frequent, even though a large number of them were called to refute the views of Malcolm X. There was dramatic excitement in Negro life, and the mass media started capitalizing on it, but not dramatizing it.

The theatre was involved with such trivia as Ketti Frings' adaptation of Richard Wright's novel, *The Long Dream*. Lloyd Richards directed a cast that was superior to the material. More fascinating than the play is the story James Baldwin tells about its creation. Baldwin says he heard it like this from a Negro playwright: "She [Ketti Frings] was sitting by this swimming pool, see, and reading this book and she thought: 'This would make a perfectly *darling* play.'

"So she wrote the first few scenes and called out her Negro butler, chauffeur and maid, and read it to them and asked: 'Now, isn't that the way you poor, downtrodden colored people feel about things?' 'Why, yes, Miss Frings,' they answered; and, 'I thought so,' says the playwright—and so we go on. And on and on."

Baldwin's anecdote is tragic as well as fascinating. For one who knows Negro life, the whole thing is bizarre and false. The play tells of a Negro businessman in Mississippi who has had to "wheel and deal to make it." He has Uncle-Tommed for a crooked, influential white Southerner. For this service the Negro has had certain advantages. But the Negro's son is less than enamoured of the relationship. He challenges it and the son loses his life in the process. His death is directly traceable to the white Southerner. At the end of the play, the Uncle Tom picks up his dead son, looks into the face of the white man and tells him: "I've been your nigger. I ain't going to be your nigger no more."

No one who knows anything about Negro life—or life—would have the nerve to put a scene like that on a stage. Remember, this Uncle Tom Negro was a gun-carrying double-dealing, ruthless man. There he stood with his dead son in his arms before the white man who was responsible for the son's death. And no one else in sight. It is sheer romanticism to think that sonless father would have delivered a speech, walked out, carrying his son and leaving that white man to Mississippi justice!

In real life that white man would have been as dead as the Negro's son. But Miss Frings had her own notions of Negro life. She had read about how wonderfully nonviolent and moralistic Negroes were, and so she wrote a completely fabricated scene. All of this exceeds poor dramaturgy. It indicates again the naïveté—or sheer arrogance—of many white intellectuals. If they really believe the nonviolent movement is nonviolent, they don't understand black language. Negroes are being nonviolent because they don't have as many guns as white people. And despite this, at the height of their nonviolence in Clarendon County, Montgomery and Birmingham, many a white man went to an early grave because he did not understand what the Negro was saying.

But the theatre generally on this continent is neither life-size nor larger than life. Realities are discounted and fantasies and wish-fulfillment become the mode. We do not really see the American white man on our stages, let alone the black man. Thus, we have such untruthful plays as *The Caine Mutiny Court Martial, Tea and Sympathy* and *A Majority of One*—plays that are bent on making the nontruth into truth. Baldwin notes: "This cannot fail to have a terrible effect on the actor's art, for the depths out of which true inspiration springs are precisely the depths he is forbidden to reach.

"I am convinced that this is one of the reasons for the nerve-wracking *busyness* on our stage—'Keep moving, maybe nobody will notice that nothing's happening'—and the irritating, self-indulgent mannerisms of so many of our actors. In search of a truth which is not in the script, they are reduced to what seem to be psycho-therapeutic exercises."

The point Baldwin makes again and again is that the theatre is perishing for lack of vitality. Vitality, he notes, humanly and artistically speaking, has only one source: Life. The life actually being led in America is not what we pretend it to be. White men are not what they take themselves to be, and Negroes are very different from the popular image of them.

A vivid theatre work showed up at the 41st Street Theatre not too long after *The Long Dream* proved to be a nightmare. This was Robert Glenn's arrangement of Langston Hughes' *Shakespeare in Harlem*. Its theatrical effect was much like that achieved by Mr. Hughes in his *Don't You Want To Be Free?* although the former play lacked the vital blues sequence known to the latter. The curtain raiser was Frederick O'Neal reading James Weldon Johnson's *God's Trombones*. *The New York Times* declared this work was just as good as, if not better than, any American Negro presentation. The producers displayed more artistic sense than business sense. *Shakespeare in Harlem* never attracted the audience it deserved.

During the 1961–1962 season Errol John's *The Moon on the Rainbow Shawl* was produced on Manhattan's Lower East Side. Mr. John, a man of West Indian ancestry, spent a considerable amount of time in London. There his play created considerable interest and he won a prize. It was staged here by the Theatre Guild with a cast of American Negroes. The Guild had obviously begun to believe the oft-quoted bromide that Negro plays do not make money. Therefore, Mr. John's lively, robust, poetic drama was shown off-Broadway. Nevertheless, it attracted appreciative audiences over a period of time.

In May, 1961, producer Sidney Bernstein brought Jean Genet's *The Blacks* to Lynn Michaels' St. Mark's Playhouse on the Lower East Side. This was a searing drama, written—in the words of actor Louis Gossett—"as only an outsider could write of black people." Gene Frankel directed an excellent cast that, at various times, included such actors as Roscoe Lee Browne, Godfrey Cambridge, Helen Martin, Carl Byrd, Ethel Ayler, Cicely Tyson, Mia Angelou, Cynthia Belgrave, Brunetta Barnett, Jay Riley, Raymond St. Jacques, Chuck Gordone, Vinie Burrows, Lynn Hamilton, Peter De Ando, Clebert Ford, Leah Scott, Louis Gossett, Ed Cambridge, Larney Rutledge and Maxwell Glanville.

The play enjoyed a long run and earned considerable money. Whites flocked to see it, for those were the days when American whites seemed to enjoy having Negroes verbally assault them. Guilt complexes were riding the crest of the national wave, and a play that said Negroes would do the same thing in power that whites were doing was particularly welcomed. *The Blacks* actually proved to be more of a freak than a play, written with a sense of abandon and staged with hostility. And audiences loved it.

A number of Negro writers took sharp exception to *The Blacks*.

John Oliver Killens in his book of essays, *Black Man's Burden,* has this to say:

"Behind the avant-garde's beards and dark glasses, they rationalize, apologize, as they strut and posture. The underlying statements of *The Blacks* and *The Balcony* are the same, that all civilization stinks, *period.* 'When the *have-nots* overthrow the *haves,* nothing will really change except the relative positions of the adversaries. It will be the same thing all over again. There is no revolution ever. It's the same merry-go-round, so stop the world, I want to get off.' Well, pardon me, fellows, I don't want to get off. The world never looked so good to me before."

Killens continues: " 'Sure—don't worry how you treat the *blacks.* The blacks will do the same to you when they seize Power.' This is Genet's message as far as I'm concerned. . . . Actually, the so-called avant-garde is really a rear-guard action in disguise. It is neither revolutionary, anti-bourgeois, as it sometimes makes pretensions of being, nor anti-white supremacy; it is not even anti-Establishment. It is essentially anti-people: 'The West is humanity, humanity is the West, we're all sick to the guts, so let's, man, like all of us get into this here Western style pigsty, and have one final everlasting orgy.' "

John Henrik Clarke, editor of *Freedomways Magazine* and editor of the book *Harlem: A Community in Transition,* said Genet never read any history about black people—for the one thing missing in the history of black people is revenge for past misdeeds.

My colleagues have stated it well. The avant-garde theatre is one of tricks, of inventions, showing little or no empathy for human beings. It is, indeed, often more contemptuous of people, mocking them, decrying them, than the theatre is traditionally. No matter how tyrannical Richard II happens to be, we are moved by his lament: "O that I were as great as my grief or lesser than my name." Hamlet's drivel sickens us, but when he goes into action, we go with him. We walk out of the door with Nora in *A Doll's House,* and we cry out with Juno when she asks the Mother of God to take away these hearts of stone and give us hearts of flesh! But we walk out of the theatre after witnessing the work of the avant-garde boys, saying: "Isn't that just like the human animal?" And the first one that jostles us in the crowd is likely to have a punch thrown at him!

Broadway producer Alfred de Liagre got himself involved with a show called *Kwamini*, which proved two things already known: that Brock Peters, Terry Carter and Sally Ann Howes are brilliant performers, and that American whites know next to nothing about black Americans and less than that about Africans. Dick Campbell took an African scholar to see Mr. de Liagre. The producer insisted "Kwamina" meant "born on a Sunday." The African said it meant "born on a Saturday." Mr. de Liagre knew he was right because his writers had said so. Finally, the African persuaded Mr. de Liagre that he *knew* the meaning of "Kwamina," but it took a great deal of persuading. Magnify this to the international level and one can easily see why American foreign policy is more often than not a misguided missile.

The season that brought *The Blacks* also brought a sharp, satiric review known as *Fly, Blackbirds*. Clarence Jackson wrote some of the music for this. It opened at the Mayfair Theatre on West 46th Street and brought to the attention of New Yorkers two talented personalities, namely dancer-actress Thelma Oliver and singer-actress Micki Grant. Both were to win acclaim again and again. Miss Oliver was particularly brilliant in her appearance with Gwen Verdon in *Sweet Charity* and Miss Grant was in *Tambourines to Glory* and *Brecht on Brecht*, and she appeared as Juliet in an interesting television production. *Fly, Blackbirds* had only a modest run at the Mayfair, for few are the plays that break even there.

The years 1961–1962 were noted for another venture. In the words of *The New York Times*, Ossie Davis' satire, *Purlie Victorious*, "romped in." And it won critical acclaim.

Ossie Davis is one of the most talented men in the American theatre. And therein lies his problem. For this tall, intelligent, graying, proud man came into the theatre, interested in writing. Fortunately and unfortunately, it was learned that he is a good actor—a phenomenon rare for a writer, and detrimental as well. Mr. Davis went on to job after job, working regularly as a Negro actor, never quite getting as much writing done as he wanted to do.

Being a good actor wasn't his only problem. He was husband, father, janitor, Sunday School teacher, civil rights worker, friend and human being. All these tied up his time in a devastating manner. He and his wife, Ruby Dee, had lived in their Mt. Vernon home for less than a year when Mr. Davis took one look at the plumbing bill. He went out and bought himself a set of tools and from then on he did the plumbing. He spent his days off with his children. On Sundays, he taught Sunday School, spent time with his family, then did some writing. During the week he was available to civil rights groups, to his friends, and to anyone who called on him. In the meantime, he read everything he could get his hands on, remained the epitome of hope to many Negroes and never failed to encourage them to keep plugging. He is one of the true promoters of brotherhood among black theatre artists.

I first met him when he came to the Rose McClendon Players in 1939. He was from Waycross, Georgia, had attended Howard University, then moved on to New York for further experience. War service later claimed him, then after the war he played the lead in *Jeb*, was featured in *Anna Lucasta*, then worked in *No Way Out*. There followed a succession of small parts as a waiter, a janitor and other bits in Broadway shows.

While working on Broadway one could hear him encouraging Negroes to look elsewhere, emphasizing that Broadway meant money, but theatre meant something much more. Theatre, he often said, belongs to the people, and Broadway does not intend to let them have it. Negroes should certainly seek what Broadway has to offer, but use this to their best advantage. He believed so much in the Negro theatre that he was always there, writing checks not only for his own play, but for other plays by black writers.

Black theatre workers were overjoyed when the news got out that Mr. Davis was writing a new play. People called him and asked to read it. His answer was "Soon, soon." Then one Sunday, Ruby invited a group of people to their house to hear Ossie's play. And the two of them read the first version of *Purlie Victorious*. And they almost lost their house.

John Killens rolled on the floor and banged it, laughing. Julian Mayfield laughed and pounded on his chair, almost breaking it in. Sidney Poitier laughed and hit the wall with his fist, and Tina and Lonnie Sattin stomped their feet. The thought hit me then that if Mr. Davis didn't get his play produced, he was going to have an awful lot of expenses to pay.

The characters in *Purlie Victorious*—supposedly stereotypes— are anything but that. Under the leadership of the Reverend

Purlie Victorious Judson, a group of Negroes set out to claim a building where they want to build an integrated church. They have trouble with Cap'n Charlie, a member of the Southern oligarchy, but the Negroes are victorious in the end. As a matter of fact, Cap'n Charlie's body is the first one to be buried in the integrated church. And since he died in shock, standing up, his casket is standing up.

Some of the lines in the play proved to be priceless: "Running has saved more Negroes' lives than the Emancipation Proclamation." At another point a character named Gitlow has annoyed his wife and she asks: "How low can you git, Gitlow?" There are others: "New York City is so crowded that folks have to stand up to be buried." And, "Being colored can be fun if nobody's looking."

Despite the enthusiasm of his friends and colleagues, Mr. Davis felt he had more work to do on the play. He refused to send it off to the marketplace. Then, one day Howard DaSilva, director of *The World of Sholom Aleichem*, asked to read *Purlie Victorious*. Mr. Davis had been Mr. DaSilva's stage manager during *The World of Sholom Aleichem*.

Somewhat hesitantly Mr. Davis gave Mr. DaSilva the play and reminded him he planned further rewrite. Mr. DaSilva read the play, shouted happily: "This is it! The time is now!" And he took the work to producer Philip Rose who said, "Yes!" Ruby Dee says this is the exact way that *Purlie Victorious* got off her husband's desk. And Mr. Davis privately muttered that he believes his wife got hold of Messrs. DaSilva and Rose and set up the whole thing.

*Purlie Victorious* opened to fine reviews with a cast that included Miss Dee, Mr. Davis, Godfrey Cambridge, Helen Martin and Alan Alda. It ran throughout the season and delighted many audiences.

In the early nineteen-sixties Oscar Brown, Jr.'s *Kicks and Company* proved to be a casualty. Mr. Brown had won considerable acclaim as a composer and entertainer. And he had proved himself outstanding in both areas. He wrote a musical about O. D. Kicks, a devil-figure, involved in, and working against, the Southern "sit-in" movement. It had folk humor, a point of view, and it was satiric. Robert Nemiroff and Burt d'Lugoff set out to produce. Parts of the show were seen on television, and excitement raced through the theatrical community.

The producers engaged Burgess Meredith to star in the show, and Harold Scott for his stand-by. Vinette Carroll was called on to direct, and Lonnie Sattin to play one of the leads. For some reason the company chose Chicago to try out the show. And also chosen was a large, barnlike theatre that put the work at a disadvantage.

There were other problems, too. Dissatisfaction raged and Miss Carroll relinquished her director's role. Script arguments followed. Then, Lorraine Hansberry was called in to serve as director. The Chicago critics didn't like the show and said so in caustic terms.

Of course, it is always a calculated risk to open a show in certain cities before bringing it to New York. Metropolitan jealousies flare, and the local critics' complexes are stirred. They have got to show the theatre people—and the New York critics—that they, too, know theatre. Therefore, they get out forty-two-inch yardsticks and magnifying glasses. And the reviews show it. This, incidentally, is true not only of Negro shows but of white ones as well. There came a point in several shows that involved me where the producers said, bluntly: "Who cares what *these* critics think? *We're* the critics here."

This is not to blame the failure of *Kicks and Company* on the critics. The show admittedly had problems, but it seemed never to have the time to work them out. It closed in Chicago; then the cast held a special audition in New York for David Merrick, Harry Belafonte and others, hoping to gain support. Those actors worked hard at that audition, painfully hard. But the show was in trouble and the easiest thing in the world to do is find something wrong with a play in trouble. Tongues wagged and the cocktail critics criticized, but the play died.

A by-product of *Kicks and Company*'s failure was my involvement with *Ballad for Bimshire*. Composer Irving Burgie—popularly known as Lord Burgess—visited Chicago, and when he returned, he called me up. It was eleven o'clock in the evening and I was sitting around my fireplace, talking with my sons, Tommy and Melvin, about the possibility of Elston Howard winning the batting title. The hours slipped by and the children's bedtime approached. As I bid them goodnight, the telephone rang.

Irving Burgie was on the other end of the wire. "Can you come over here right away?" he asked. "It's important."

I thought immediately of some family disaster. I grabbed my coat and hat and half-walked, half-ran the five blocks between my house and his. I was panting when I rang the bell, but I was relieved when his wife, Page, answered the door. When I asked about their youngster, Page said he was well. In answer to a question about other family members, I was told they were all well. Then, Burgie stepped into the foyer.

"I asked you over because I want to talk to you about a play," he said. "I just got back from Chicago where I saw the premiere of Oscar Brown's play. The critics murdered him."

I stood there, debating whether to pick up one of Page Burgie's chairs and hit him in his head, or grab one of her ornaments and throw it at him. The household furnishings seemed pretty expensive to replace, so I gave up my idea. Then, I thought about telling him in colloquial terms what he and Oscar could both do at this hour of the night. They were friends, yes, but—

He kept talking and interrupting my thoughts. He had been working on the book for a musical for some time, and now he wanted to get back to it. I told him I thought it was a good idea. I had always admired his work, particularly his songs, "Jamaica Farewell" and "Island in the Sun," and I told him he certainly should be able to provide a remarkable score. Then, I reached for my hat and coat. He mentioned that he wanted my help, and I said I certainly would help in some capacity. This was the way of the Negro in the theatre.

I went on back home, and the very next afternoon Burgie was at my house, talking about the book for his musical. We discussed a number of ideas; then the next day he came with other thoughts. We talked some more and then he left.

This was, in itself, not unusual. I had known him a number of years before I lost my mind and bought a house on Long Island. He dropped by frequently, or I dropped in on him. He was a Brooklyn boy, the son of a Barbadian mother and a Virginia-born father. He went to Brooklyn Automotive High School and, after graduation, became one of the first Negroes to work for the Fifth Avenue Bus Company. He was then drafted and sent to Burma, where he began to read a great deal and learned to play the guitar. After the war he decided, to the chagrin of many family members and friends, not to return to the bus company. He went into music, attended Juilliard, the University of Arizona and the University of California at Los Angeles.

After school there followed a number of gigs in various night spots. At one he was heard by writer William Attaway, who called Harry Belafonte and suggested the latter hear Burgie's original compositions. Belafonte did, was impressed and asked for the rights to "Jamaica Farewell." And his recording of this is history. Later Burgie was called to write the title song for the film *Island in the Sun.* His economic situation was now secure and so was his reputation. He wrote "Dolly Dawn," "I Do Adore Her," "El Matador," "La Seine," "Day-O" and 'Star-O."

Many were the times we got together for barbecues, gab sessions and to exchange ideas. So there was nothing unusual about him visiting me. What was unusual was one day at a party a friend told me he had heard that I was collaborating with Burgie on the book for a musical. I said I was not, that I did not collaborate with anyone. That same evening someone else mentioned the same thing to me, and again I denied it. The next day Burgie dropped by my house again and I told him what had happened. He said: "Of course. I thought you knew it. What do you think I've been talking about?"

Initially, like most creators who seek collaborators, Burgie wanted someone to justify his mistakes, to make them seem right even when they were wrong. But he is a very fair, generous, sensitive man, talkative and determined. He can be shown a point if the point has a six-inch diameter.

We became involved in one rewrite after another. Then, Ed Cambridge was engaged to direct the play, and there was another rewrite. Our plan was to create a family entertainment, and we told the story of a seventeen-year-old girl growing up in Barbados, of her dreams, then her love for the land. There were scenes of the island—its society, its bars and its customs. The theme of the play is well stated in Burgie's lyric to the opening number, "Ballad for Bimshire":

> Chorus:
> *I hear my Bimshire callin', callin' to me,*
> *I hear my Bimshire callin', callin' to me.*
> Field Worker:
> *Long time my father told me:*
> *"This is your land!"*
> *And often the land would scold me,*
> *And laugh at my plan.*

*But, I'm comin' along, got plenty to do—*
*Times been hard, but I seein' it through,*
*Gonna hold onto my claim,*
*'Cause when this day is won in the sea and sun,*
*They gonna think well on my name!*

When the written work was completed, Burgie organized a production company, Page Productions. This involved himself, Ossie Davis, Sylvester Leaks, Ewart Guinier and me. Numerous backers' auditions were held, and when only half the needed capital had been raised, Burgie searched for a co-producer.

Here he faced one of the great problems of being a Negro in America. That problem is that Negroes are invariably compelled to associate with many whites whom they would normally ignore. This is true in Civil Service, in the labor movement, and in the freedom movement. Black people have many times declared they have been jimcrowed into working beside low-class whites of poor breeding and little preparation—whites who can't make it with other successful whites. This is one of the unstated subtleties behind the schism between black and white liberals in the Freedom Movement. This is one of the reasons the Communist Party in the United States never had a chance.

I saw this when I was a teen-ager. White left-wingers would rush to Harlem, visit our parties and immediately begin to tell us what we ought to do as Negroes. They had the nerve, too, to show up at concerts at Negro churches in dungarees, sports shirts and white shoes. They also went around to buildings, canvassing for votes. One morning in the nineteen-forties I heard a thundering voice in the hallway. I opened my door and two white youngsters came charging down the stairs. A large black woman followed them screaming. She stopped and looked at me, angrily. "Can you imagine?" she roared. "Long as I been black, them two youngsters gonna interrupt my breakfast to tell me how hard it is to be colored and that I should get out and vote!"

She turned and thundered back up the stairs and slammed the door to her apartment. I went on downstairs to look for my mail. When I reached the ground floor, I heard one white youngster tell another: "You hear that? That's jimcrow in reverse."

They never got the message.

Burgie had lived through these problems, too, so he felt con-

*Hilda Simms and Duke Williams in* Anna Lucasta, *with an all-Negro cast, one of the great Broadway successes of the early postwar period.*

trol of *Ballad for Bimshire* should remain in Negro hands. He discussed this with his accountant, Bernard Waltzer, who agreed to co-produce and raise half the capital.

The entire capital was raised, then the battle for control began. Waltzer had ideas about the artistic end of the venture, and Burgie had ideas that Waltzer should confine his ideas to the business end of the work. Conferences followed conferences and endless meetings occurred. And it became very confusing.

On top of all of that, tempers flared. None of these problems were helped by the failure of the air-conditioning unit to work. All rehearsals were held in the Mayfair Theatre, which is located in the basement of the Paramount Hotel. The heat there was unbearable.

While cast members and crew members continued to argue with each other and with themselves, Burgie, his lawyer, J. Lloyd Grant, and Waltzer continued their debates. The more they debated, the more complicated the whole structure became, and the more it all cost, for time in the theatre is money—a fact well known. There were more arguments. Burgie insisted upon having final control over the work, and Waltzer insisted upon some type of indemnification. It was finally agreed that Burgie would meet the responsibility for all costs over the initial budget.

The show opened with its books splashed in red. I did not help matters because, during the previews, I threw out a number of scenes and wrote new ones. And each time an expensive piece of scenery went with the scene. But the show opened to a majority of good reviews. Critics liked the production numbers better than the book.

All during the run of the show we continued to sharpen and polish the book. And audiences came and supported the show. Eighty-five percent of its audiences came from the Negro community. Nightly thousands of dollars were raised for civil rights groups and civic organizations through theatre parties. Clubs, lodges and associations held nightly theatre parties, then had parties for the cast afterward.

Despite the packed houses and the theatre parties, mounting expenses became insurmountable. The show closed just before Christmas, 1963. Later it opened in Cleveland where it was highly successful.

Among those appearing prominently in *Ballad for Bimshire*

were Frederick O'Neal, Ossie Davis, Christine Spencer, Jimmy Randolph, Miriam Burton, Alyce Webb, Clebert Ford, Sylvia Moon, Fran Bennett, James Trotman, Hilda Harris, Leu Camacho, Albert Grant, Sammy Benskin, Charles Moore and Ella Thompson. Carl Byrd was stage manager and Dick Campbell the company manager. Joe Callaway and Robert Dolphin were the white members of the cast. Talley Beatty and Herman Hickman were responsible for some remarkable choreography.

*Ballad for Bimshire* remains, for me, a show with book trouble. The fault lies in both the conception and execution, and it appears to be a work that was written as an excuse for some good songs. What the play really needs is meticulous imagination, organization and structure. It should have been written first, then had the music added. Therefore, it had to be played at a fast clip with numerous belly laughs so the audience wouldn't have time to think about the story.

With all its faults, it had virtues. It was a throwback to the days when Negroes wrote, produced, directed and managed their own shows. It was a clean show to which parents could take their children without cringing. And Sylvester Leaks and Ewart Guinier brought numerous black organizations to see the show.

Right after *Ballad for Bimshire* opened, William Hairston's *Walk in Darkness* appeared at the Greenwich Mews Theatre. Mr. Hairston had long since established himself as an actor. He was at the Apollo in *Rain,* played *Harlem Detective* on television, and was in the film *Take the High Ground.* He found considerable recognition, but few job opportunities. He turned to writing and *Walk in Darkness* represented his first produced work. He had considerable assistance from Clarence Williams III and Richard Ward in major roles. And his producers were Stella Holt and Fran Drucker, who showed their usual excellent taste.

The play, which dealt with a Negro soldier in occupied Germany, had a limited engagement, then closed. Mr. Hairston went on to direct the next Mews venture, Langston Hughes' *Jericho Jimcrow.* Later he worked with Joseph Papp in producing for the New York Shakespeare Festival.

The next Negro-authored show to appear during 1963–1964 was Langston Hughes' *Tambourines to Glory,* which opened in November, 1963, at the Little Theatre. It had had its problems long before opening night.

Mr. Hughes wrote his gospel drama first as a play, then he adapted it as a novel. He readapted it as a play, and called on Jobe Huntley to provide gospel music for it. The Theatre Guild optioned the play and tried it out at Westport in 1960. Hazel Scott and Nipsey Russell were prominently featured. The play remained under option and off the boards until 1963 when a decision was made to bring it to Broadway.

Louis Gossett took over Nipsey Russell's role, and Hilda Simms appeared in the role originally assigned to Miss Scott. Veterans Clara Ward, Rosetta LeNoire, Lynn Hamilton, and Joseph Attles showed well. And the venture introduced Micki Grant to the Broadway theatre.

*Tambourines to Glory* told of two Harlem women who open a storefront church. In doing so they prosper, but the underworld's influence interferes with their lives. One woman becomes involved with a Machiavellian character, and the result is swindling, chicanery and eventual murder. The play was well mounted, often moving, but the critics disliked it.

An important entry during the 1963–1964 season was Adrienne Kennedy's *The Funny House of a Negro*, which starred Billie Allen and Ellen Holly. Miss Allen is a triple-threat theatrical personality, and in the leading role she proved herself worthy of the glowing notices she received during her stage and television career. Miss Holly was also justifiably praised. Along with Claudia Mc-Neil, Alvin Ailey, Diana Sands and others, Miss Holly had been trapped in the early part of 1963 in a show called *Tiger, Tiger, Burning Bright*. She displayed her artistry there as she had in an earlier inept vehicle called *Too Late the Phalarope*. And both actresses were brilliant in Miss Kennedy's work.

Miss Kennedy wrote *The Funny House of a Negro* during a workshop session at Circle-in-the-Square. When it finally reached the off-Broadway stage, it won respectable reviews even from critics who didn't quite seem to understand it. The talented dramatist's play foundered for a while at the box office, then a well-meaning patron made a substantial donation to the production— a donation that permitted a large number of people to see the work.

*The Funny House of a Negro* reveals Miss Kennedy as a writer of considerable depth, quite introspective and quite knowledgeable of theatrical terms. She has a gift for characterization and dialogue as well as a sense of theatre that will assure future theatrical success. Nor am I impressed with those who call her work personal or individualized. Those who look for every Negro-authored play to reflect their points of view would do well to write their own plays. A play by a Negro is in one sense like a play by a white person—a statement in dramatic terms of that particular author's viewpoint at a given time in history. Since no one expects a white playwright to solve any and all problems in his work, it is unrealistic to expect a Negro writer to do it.

LeRoi Jones' *Dutchman* introduced this poet to New York theatregoers. Prior to its production Mr. Jones had been known primarily as the author of a book about jazz and a book of verse. *Dutchman* marked his entrance to the theatre and it was auspicious. It was a fiery one-act play, and as played by Robert Hooks and Jennifer West, it was particularly stimulating.

*Dutchman* somehow brings *The Respectful Prostitute* to mind, if for no other reason than that both plays seem to continue on *ad infinitum* after the curtain falls. No hope for a change is seen by either Jones or Sartre. The similarity could be that both plays deal with a black man and a white woman—or that both were written by skillful authors who are more concerned with ideas and ideals than with characters.

Mr. Jones' canvas is large and bold. The scene is a subway car. Clay, an ivy-league-suited Negro sits reading. In comes Lulu, a bizarre, sexy white woman. She talks to Clay, taunts him, tempts him, then insults him. Lulu is wild, luring the Negro into the trap of Western world sexuality. Finally, Clay can bear her insults no longer. He springs to his feet, orders her to shut up, then, in direct, unequivocal terms, he tells her what he thinks of her, of all whites, of America, and he starts to leave the train. Lulu stabs him, has his body removed, then looks toward another Negro as the play comes to an end. Mr. Jones is charging that this is the pattern of America—seducing, tempting, insulting the black man, then killing him when he objects. His play won the off-Broadway Obie Award as the best of the season.

Two exciting ventures during the 1963–1964 season were written by white men. Martin Duberman organized *In White America* and revealed Negro history in daring theatrical terms. He offered to theatre audiences a daring dramatic piece, and in it actress Gloria Foster was brilliant.

Augard Fugard's *The Blood Knot* was produced by Sidney Bernstein on the Lower East Side. This two-character play was written by a white South African, and it told of two brothers and the effect of that nation's tragic color policies. James Earl Jones and J. D. Cannon were ideal in the leading roles.

A tragedy known as *Sponomo* was, indeed, tragic. This work by Alan Paton and Krishna Shah opened at the Cort Theatre on April 4, 1964. It was produced by Mary K. Frank with a South African company whose acting level left something to be desired. I saw it along with Marjorie Camacho, Langston Hughes and Raoul Abdul. When the play ended with the good white man and the good black boy reaching for each other's hand, Langston groaned: "Oh, these white liberals! They'd better change that ending or Malcolm will be down here shouting!"

"They'd better change the whole thing," Marjorie said. "That reaching-for-each-other nonsense may be daring in South Africa, but it's tired over here."

The tragedy of *Sponomo* deepened. It created no box office sensation, so producer Mary Frank ran an ad in *The New York Times*, wanting to know, "Where are the liberals? Where are the Negroes?" Later, I met her at a cocktail party given by a group euphemistically known as New Dramatists. She bemoaned the plight of her production. Some good, good soul asked her: "Did you get in touch with Jimmy Baldwin?"

Mrs. Frank shook her head and declared: "I got no support from any Negro writers."

She was grief-stricken and I was truly sorry for her. Mary K. Frank is a very sincere woman, utterly lacking prejudice. She has nothing but good intentions, and she really extended herself to bring a troubling problem to the American stage. The problem, however, is that she did not bring a work of art. And she suffered because of this. In the last analysis, Negroes and liberals are like all other people. They won't buy a badly produced work, even if it favors them.

There were seven Negro playwrights represented on the professional stage during the 1963–1964 season. The seventh to have a play produced was James Baldwin. The flaming, explosive *Blues for Mr. Charlie* was his second play. His first, *The Amen Corner*, was being shown in California at the time *Blues* opened on Broadway.

*Blues for Mr. Charlie* at times seemed more a brilliant series of essays than a play. But, it was theatrically alive and flaming. Emmett Till, a young Negro, and Medgar Evers, a civil rights leader, had both been killed in Mississippi. That state's own brand of justice prevailed—meaning, of course, these crimes went unpunished. Mr. Baldwin based his play on these atrocities.

The playwright took great pains not to romanticize his black characters nor his white ones—sometimes too much. His leading character is hardly idealized. White critics declared Mr. Baldwin's Mississippians are cardboard characters, but since many Negroes have heard words similar to those stated by whites in the play, one wonders if those critics were not looking for self-representation in terms of those roles.

Feder supplied striking, somber lighting and Burgess Meredith directed a fine cast, headed by Al Freeman, Jr., Diana Sands, Pat Hingle, Rip Torn, Percy Rodriguez, David Baldwin and a score of distinguished actors. There were times during the performance when Negroes and whites sprang to their feet, applauded and shouted "Bravo!" And there were times when Negroes shouted and laughed and whites sat silently.

One particularly high point in the play is a soliloquy, brilliantly delivered by Diana Sands. It literally interrupted the action of the play when audiences applauded, vigorously.

*Blues for Mr. Charlie* ended the 1963–1964 season for Negroes. And it ended it with an argument. Closing notices were posted. James Baldwin, who had been out of town, rushed back. He and his brother, David, began a series of arguments with Actors Studio producers. The Baldwins charged the producers had sabotaged the play, had not faithfully promoted it, and that they had ignored the real audiences for this work.

Baldwin and his brother were joined in the fight by a number of theatre people. Full-page ads were placed on theatrical pages. Negro communities were flooded with handbills. And there was a response. Business did become brisk and the play's run was extended. Still, it did not last as long as it should have.

Despite the lack of commercial success of most of the Negro-authored ventures of the 1963–1964 season, many people looked toward the season of 1964–1965 as a fruitful one for Negro productions. Before the summer of 1964 blossomed, such ventures as *Ballad of the Winter Soldiers*, written by John Oliver Killens and me, as well as new plays by Alice Childress, Lorraine Hansberry, Lonne Elder, Douglas Turner, LeRoi Jones and James Baldwin were all announced.

*Ballad of the Winter Soldiers* was more of a pageant than a play. It dealt with freedom fighters throughout history. The term "winter soldier" grew out of Thomas Paine's statement: "These are the times that try men's souls. The summer soldier and the sunshine patriot will in this hour shrink from the service of his country." The winter soldier, the authors felt, was one who did not, who continued to fight for freedom.

Dorothy Pitman produced this work at the Lincoln Center Philharmonic Hall as a benefit for the Congress of Racial Equality. In the cast were Robert Ryan, Shelley Winters, Dick Gregory, John Henry Faulk, Madeline Sherwood, Richard Ward, Sarah Cunningham, Frank Silvera, John Randolph, Alyce Webb, Jimmy Randolph, Ruby Dee and Joseph Wiseman. James E. Wall directed and Perry Watkins was the lighting and set designer. Johnny Richards' orchestra supplied the music, and special accompaniment to Miss Webb's rendition of the Louis Mitchell-James C. Morris number, "Freedom Is a High-Priced Thing" was supplied by Constance Brown.

*Ballad of the Winter Soldiers* was critically well received. The plan was to move it to an off-Broadway house, but the week after its initial showing, the producer and CORE had a devastating battle over policy—a battle that led the producer away from the civil rights organization. And that was the end of the *Ballad of the Winter Soldiers*.

A terrible tragedy followed. Lorraine Hansberry's first play since *A Raisin in the Sun* was scheduled to open. This was called *The Sign in Sidney Brustein's Window*. It suffered a series of setbacks. Harold S. Prince was slated to co-produce and direct, but there followed differences of opinion about the script and Mr. Prince's withdrawal. Next came the engagement of Mort Sahl, who had a series of difficulties with his lines and with the producers. He walked out on the play. No one worried too much about that, but in the midst of rehearsals Miss Hansberry became seriously ill and was hospitalized. This was for the fourth time within a year.

The news of her hospitalization reached me at a time when I was writing for a Harlem newspaper. I telephoned her, and her usually vibrant voice was subdued and soft. I was not prepared for this, for Lorraine Hansberry was never a silent, soft-spoken young woman. She talked in direct terms, never fatalistically, always with hope and encouragement. Now, her resignation flowed over the wire and I had to brace myself.

I tried to be light and gay: "Get up from there," I told her. "Everything is going to be all right."

"I don't know," she said, softly. "This is the fourth time I've been in the hospital this year."

I paused, searching for something to say, then told her: "You've got to get up. The theatre needs you. So—I'll see you when your show opens."

"All right," she said, weakly. "I hope so."

I did see her at her show—at the last preview of *The Sign in Sidney Brustein's Windcw*. She sat directly in front of Marjorie and me. We were enjoying the first act and did not notice her until intermission. She was thin to the point of emaciation, barely able to respond to greetings. She forced herself to offer a smile that must have been painful.

Lorraine left before the last curtain. When we left the theatre, Marjorie and I started for a cocktail party at the home of Dorothy and Bill Pitman. Marjorie was visibly upset, and she asked about Lorraine's health. I told her what I knew was untrue—that Lorraine was going to be all right. On our way to the Pitmans', Marjorie turned and blurted out: "That play was written by a woman who knew she was never going to write another play. That's why she put everything into this one."

This turned out to be the truth. For in January, 1965, Grace Killens telephoned Marjorie to report that Lorraine Hansberry had died. And a part of every Negro theatrical worker died, too. Once again, as it happens in every decade, a prominent Negro theatrical figure died too soon. There had been Bob Cole in the eighteen-nineties, George Walker in the early nineteen-hundreds, Bert Williams and Florence Mills in the nineteen-twenties, Richard B. Harrison in the nineteen-thirties, Dooley Wilson in the nineteen-forties, Canada Lee in the nineteen-fifties and Muriel Rahn and Lorraine Hansberry in the nineteen-sixties.

*The Sign in Sidney Brustein's Window* was a far more mature play on many levels than *A Raisin in the Sun.* It is true that the author introduced a number of problems that did not coalesce, but she spoke of commitment, directly, sincerely and in theatrical terms. The play's death occurred not too long after Miss Hansberry's.

Only three other Negro authors were represented during the 1964–1965 season: LeRoi Jones, Langston Hughes and James Baldwin. Mr. Jones' *The Toilet* and *The Slave,* showed at the St. Mark's Playhouse on the Lower East Side. The critics railed at Mr. Jones. They accused him of being the angriest young playwright to enter the theatre, and they worried about his anger devouring him. Some took exception to his use of profane language. One wonders if some of the objections to Mr. Jones' language aren't really objections to his statements. What he said is that American society is a foul toilet, a slave society. It is as simple as that.

Later in the season came James Baldwin's *The Amen Corner,* brought to Broadway by Mrs. Nat "King" Cole and Frank Silvera. This was the result of a great effort on the part of Mr. Silvera.

Mr. Silvera read Mr. Baldwin's play in 1958, fell in love with it, then took it back to Hollywood with him. All the time he was acting in motion pictures, he dreamed of the day when he could mount the play. The moment was a long time in coming. It was years later that he had the capital and the cast to produce *The Amen Corner.* But Los Angeles was appreciative, and the play ran for more than a year.

The late Nat "King" Cole had been interested in the work. With his death, Mrs. Cole became a more active partner, and she and Mr. Silvera decided to bring the play to New York.

This sensitive, moving play had Beah Richards prominently co-starred with Mr. Silvera, and both poured into the work their complete artistry. The opening was in April, 1965, and the notices were strange, indeed. Many critics seemed to spend more time talking about *Blues for Mr. Charlie* than *The Amen Corner.* Several thought Mr. Baldwin had been a better writer (in *The Amen Corner*) when he was not an angry one. How anyone could sit through *The Amen Corner* and label it anything but angry is mystifying.

Langston Hughes' *The Prodigal Son* opened at the Greenwich Mews Theatre in May, 1965. It ran until September, then moved to Europe. Vinette Carrol directed the Hughes work in a vivid and moving manner. The play itself was rich in feeling, and somehow it brought to mind Mr. Hughes' earlier success, *Black Nativity*. Few people in American letters can capture the feelings of black people as vividly as Mr. Hughes. He loves them and it shows in his work.

These plays ended the season for Negro authors. LeRoi Jones turned his back on the downtown theatre and moved to Harlem. There he started the Black Arts Theatre in a brownstone on 130th Street, just off Lenox Avenue. He revived *Dutchman* for community audiences. There, too, he presented two new one-act plays, *Jello* and *Experimental Death Unit #1*. And there he was to become the center of a controversy that involved the Harlem Youth Unlimited Opportunities and Associated Community Teams—the anti-poverty agency known as HARYOU-ACT.

In the summer of 1965 HARYOU-ACT Executive Director Livingston Leroy Wingate was called on to launch a summer crash program. This was an effort to involve youngsters in work projects, to ease tensions and prevent a recurrence of the riots of 1964. Mr. Wingate responded to this hasty call, and there developed what came to be known as Project Uplift. LeRoi Jones applied for anti-poverty funds for his group to offer free drama on the streets of Harlem. Mr. Jones could be seen twice weekly, visiting the office of HARYOU-ACT. Finally, his group was granted funds for summer work. It should be noted here that the Black Arts group was already in existence when the grant was received. The group offered poetry reading sessions, jazz sessions, painting exhibits and lectures during May, 1965. The charges made by Sargent Shriver and others that HARYOU-ACT brought the Black Arts into existence with Federal funds is simply not true.

But facts have a way of getting lost in the midst of hysteria, particularly when that hysteria involves the Negro community. One fact that was confused and abused was the Black Arts Theatre's policy of not admitting white patrons. The following are LeRoi Jones' exact words, spoken to radio commentator Evelyn Cunningham, in a Harlem restaurant:

"When we moved into our theatre, we did a lot of thinking. And we asked a lot of questions. One thing we found out from old-time Harlem residents is that they resented deeply the nineteen-twenties when white people came up here, had a ball, but Negroes couldn't go downtown. Now, our theatre can only hold ninety people and, with my reputation, half the East Side would be up here just to see what's going on. And we'd be put in the position of possibly having to *not* admit some black people. Can you imagine what the reaction to that would be?"

Miss Cunningham asked Mr. Jones about his antiwhite views. Mr. Jones said there are white people and there are white people. Too many whites place themselves in advisory positions toward black people without really having a frame of reference. "The white man is on top of the hill, looking downwards and the black man is at the bottom of the hill. Whatever symbols that pass between them, commonly known as language, gets bogged down in various frames of reference—and all you get is a whole lot of nonsense."

He did not say *nonsense*, but that is the only alteration in his remarks. Mr. Jones had simply tired of this endless dialogue and he turned to other things—specifically to creating what he termed a true image of black people.

LeRoi Jones is one of the most misunderstood men in America. There have been times when one is tempted to believe that Mr. Jones has welcomed and capitalized on this misunderstanding, but when you talk with him—really talk with him—you see that this is not true. He is a smallish man, thin, bearded, with soft eyes that blaze when he is angry. His shoulders stoop, almost guardedly, as though they have been lashed frequently. His voice is nearly always soft. Actually, you know instantly that this is really a very gentle man, a poet much more than an angry playwright or essayist. The notion persists that had he lived in an era when race relations were less trying, he would have written poetry or a number of scholarly essays in some retreat. But these are turbulent times that have cast many men in roles they would not otherwise play. Therefore, Jones carries with him an entourage, much like James Baldwin does—a fact that prompted *Soulbook's* New York editor Bobb Hamilton to state: "If either of them had been two feet taller, neither would have ever written a line."

Mr. Jones is a brilliant man who appears to me to be more of a poet and essayist than a playwright. He seems to be more interested in ideas than in characters. His characters are ideas, much as Shaw's were. For flesh and blood Jones uses his anger, often strikingly. It has been speculated by many intellectuals that Mr. Jones not only hates white folks, but that he hates himself as well.

Whatever he may be, he is certainly a creative man who commands a lot of attention. And in the classic words of football star Jim Brown: "As Negroes we need everything we can get going for us."

The difficult thing to comprehend is the defensive attitudes about Mr. Jones, the constant need to downgrade him, to accuse him of fomenting race hatred. Yet obviously Mr. Jones did *not* create race hatred. Nor has he said half of the vicious things uttered by William Buckley, Eastland, Thurmond, Wallace or Ross Barnett. Here, then, is the American double standard in its most blatant form. A white man can run for Mayor of the City of New York, and sleekly spout snide innuendoes about Negroes—yet draw a sizable following. A white citizen may say or do whatever he chooses—including murdering three youths in Mississippi or gunning down James Meredith. But a black man who returns "fire with fire" is a hatemonger, a racist and an ingrate. Well, whether whites like it or not, their attitudes toward LeRoi Jones confirm the suspicion held by many, many Negroes—that there is more truth in his words than anyone in America cares to admit.

One of the attacks made against Mr. Jones was that the dramas his group offered in the streets of Harlem were antiwhite. This was a bold misrepresentation. The work seen on the streets was quite mild. It was only pro-Negro. He had a group of Negro children on the streets, reciting poetry about Negro history. Of course, one of the things that became apparent during the attacks on Mr. Jones is that *all* American Negro history is antiwhite for one simple reason: White America has ignored it completely, deliberately, white America fears to see it, particularly on stage, screen or television. White America will put Jones or Baldwin on television to take pot shots at it, but when, oh, when is it going to put on plays written by them? Never. For this would prove to be incendiary.

These are the truths behind the attacks on LeRoi Jones. These are the truths behind Sargent Shriver's attacks on the Harlem antipoverty agency, the truths of Shriver's existence. These truths make mockery of his avowed attempts to end poverty. He is a product of the status quo, dedicated to seeing it continued, and the status quo will not continue if poverty is eliminated!

While LeRoi Jones was making white America shudder, two other significant ventures went unnoticed. Roger Furman, who had in the fifties organized the Negro Art Players' summer stock

company, collaborated with Doris Brunson on a script known as
*Three Shades of Harlem*. And they formed a group known as
the New Heritage Players. This group presented the play to a
community audience at the 125th Street YWCA. And they played
to packed houses.

This effort was performed by actors who would be labeled
"amateurs." But writer-director Furman was wise in his choice of
performers. Professionals might have made the work seem "man-
nered." They would have paused and paced and appeared introspective. Instead, these so-called amateurs brought to the play a
sense of vitality, and the play happened before your eyes.

*Three Shades of Harlem* was a moving, humorous panorama
of the community. It told of the community's problems, of its
hopes and dreams. And it excited audiences. It ran for a number
of weekends, then moved to Walter Cooper's Sunset Ballroom
on 125th Street, where it played throughout the summer.

In Brooklyn producer Kenneth Whitlock organized the Prospect
Park Summer Theatre. His most notable production there was
*A Raisin in the Sun*. The always excellent Harold Scott played
the lead, and the brilliant Gertrude Jeannette was the mother.
In writing of this performance for the *Amsterdam News*, Betty
Goodson said: "It would have torn the roof off the theatre if the
theatre had had a roof." The *Amsterdam News* drama editor re-
fused to believe a Brooklyn theatre venture could be that exciting,
and he refused to print the review. But Abe Stark and Robert
Dowling believed it, for, like Miss Goodson, they saw the show.
And according to their letters to the producer, they intend to
support other efforts by the Prospect Park Summer Theatre.

The New York Shakespeare Festival, under the direction of
Joseph Papp, continued to use Negro actors, and its mobile unit
proved to be particularly noteworthy. Robert Hooks headed a fine
cast that brought Shakespeare to Harlem parks. And Sammy Davis
continued with what can only be described as a personal triumph
in the musical version of *Golden Boy*. It should be added, too,
that in Harlem that summer of 1965 the YMCA produced two
plays which ran for a number of weekends to the satisfaction of
local audiences. The long hot summer—predicted and feared by
experts—did not occur during 1965. Apparently cultural expression, employment and indications of care relieve human tensions
in a manner that can only be described as improbable.

During the season of 1965–1966 actor Robert Hooks became a producer. With Juanita Poitier as his associate, he brought to the St. Mark's Playhouse two one-act plays by Douglas Turner Ward, known as *Happy Ending* and *Day of Absence*. Douglas Turner Ward is known in theatrical circles as Douglas Turner for no other reason than that he has made great strides as an actor. But Ward is his family name and, as a writer, he insisted upon resorting to it. For many years Mr. Ward wrote for various journals under his real name. There came an era—possibly hard to believe for many—when Negro writers couldn't sell anything.

Mr. Ward took acting courses and he was invited to understudy Robert Earl Jones in the Circle-in-the-Square production of *The Iceman Cometh*—the same production that sent Jason Robards, Jr., on his way toward stardom. The play was directed by José Quintero and the stage manager was Philip Meister.

Actor Douglas Turner then played opposite Diana Sands in *A Land Beyond the River*. After that he went into *A Raisin in the Sun*, first in a bit role, but when the show went on tour, he took over the lead. And all the time he continued to write plays. When he returned home Philip Meister attempted to raise funds for two one-actors Douglas had written. The fund-raising proved unsuccessful. That was in 1960.

In 1964, after the run of *Ballad for Bimshire*, actor Robert Hooks decided that the only way to get Negro-written shows on the stage was to produce them. And he took an option on Douglas Turner's two one-act plays. He called on Mr. Meister to direct them.

It was no easy job for Mr. Hooks to raise money for these two plays. But he is a stubborn man and he kept trying. Juanita Poitier was helpful, and so was Godfrey Cambridge; but somehow other big Negro names did not rally to help. And so Mr. Hooks brought the plays into the St. Mark's Playhouse with almost no reserve—and this for nontheatre people means you don't have any money in the bank. If you can't pay, you go out of business the next week.

The Douglas Turner Ward plays were satires. In the first one he tells of two domestics and a militant Negro nephew. The domestics are worried because their employers are talking about divorce. The nephew is less than interested, but when the aunts tell him that his good clothing, his good food and all else that he has is related to their bringing them home from the white employers, the nephew changes his tune. The author here points up, quite humorously, the interdependence of groups in America. Whites depend upon Negroes for their labor and Negroes use whites to promote their future. The question the author raises is: When will both groups learn the truth of their interrelationship and interdependence?

The author continues this in his second play, *Day of Absence.* Here he has Negroes of a Southern city tire of white folks' treatment of them. They all vanish. The white town is left without vital services. Pandemonium breaks loose. And many a comment is made here. The play, performed by black actors in whiteface, brings a new dimension to the theatre.

Both plays opened and received reviews that were, in a sense, charitable. The *not* philosophy of the nineteen-fifties was echoed again, this time without the *not.* Critics used the term *more.* They pointed out, and I quote, "More and more Negro writers are using humor to get things across in the theatre." It is no slight to Douglas Turner Ward for me to state here that in 1898 Bob Cole used humor in *A Trip to Coontown,* as did Jesse Shipp and Alex Rogers in *Abyssinia* in 1906 and in *Bandanna Land* in 1908. So did Frank Wilson in his plays of the twenties, Abram Hill in his *On Strivers' Row,* George Norford in his *Joy Exceeding Glory* in the thirties and Alice Childress, Julian Mayfield and Ossie Davis in their plays of the forties and fifties. The discovery of the Negro writer's use of humor in 1965–1966 can only relate to one obvious and serious fact—that white critics have not really been seeing black drama unfold!

Even so, it is well that they are *beginning* to see it. The only warning note here is this: Don't claim things are just beginning to happen because you didn't know they happened before. That's as stupid as teaching a child that the stars weren't in the sky before the child was born.

The two Ward plays lasted throughout the subway strike and, in the spring of 1966, became truly a "first." For writer Douglas Turner Ward won an off-Broadway, or Obie, Award for his writing, and actor Douglas Turner won an Obie for his acting. This is the same young man whose plays were knocked about, kept off the stage, then—through the courageous work of producer Robert Hooks—reached daylight. And the story is told that director Philip

Meister, who had tried to get money for these shows nearly five years before, called up all of those who had turned him down and said: "Bah!"

Douglas Turner Ward is a polemicist, blessed with a keen sense of humor. He has, in effect, taken what could be two slight jokes and made two plays out of them. Sometimes Mr. Ward's gifts get in his way. A scene gets good to him and he goes on and on with it. This is said here with understanding, for former actor Harrel Tillman once told me: "You never say in one word what you can say in twenty!"

At the Martinique Theatre Gloria Foster played Robinson Jeffers' *Medea* during the 1965–1966 season. This fine actress had in her company the always excellent Virginia Downing and Broadway director John O'Shaughnessy. They brought a fiery reading to the stage, and if sometimes the vehicle demanded a degree of shading, this should be placed at the playwright's doorstep, not the actors'. Both Jeffers' *Medea* and the original seem to start, musically speaking, at high C and there is almost no place to go beyond that. Nevertheless, it was an evening well spent in the theatre, and this is becoming increasingly difficult to find.

The 1965–1966 season saw the mounting of *The Zulu and the Zayda*. Written by Howard DaSilva and Felix Leon with songs by Harold Rome, this play, based on a story by South African writer Dan Jacobson, starred Menasha Skulnik, Ossie Davis and Louis Gossett. It told a touching story of a friendship between a Jewish grandparent in South Africa and a young Zulu. Some might call the work saccharine, "schmaltzy" and other terms familiar to the so-called sophisticates, but it remained a touching work with a cast that was nothing short of magnificent.

*The Zulu and the Zayda* closed on April 16, 1966. With the exception of Mr. Ward's two plays, no other shows continued with large Negro casts. Clayton Corbin appeared in *The Royal Hunt of the Sun* and was later elevated to star billing. Thelma Oliver was brilliant in *Sweet Charity*, and Negroes worked as stage managers, company managers, lighting technicians and as actors with the Lincoln Center Repertory Company. But, generally, they were so integrated that sometimes you couldn't tell they were there. In most instances the Negro theatre artist never shared the spotlight which belonged so completely to the white artist.

Meanwhile, in Harlem a lunatic fringe took control of the Black

Arts from LeRoi Jones and he left the group. That fringe was to later have an encounter with the police. The Black Arts went out of business. And today theatre artists stand on corners or in bars, hoping for the day when they may work again.

Perhaps the greatest commentary on the Negro in the professional theatre was that 1965 and 1966 may well be remembered as "The Conference Years." Black writers conferred all over the place. In fact, many of us talked more than we wrote. I was involved in seven conferences—one sponsored by the American Histadrut Cultural Exchange at Arden House, another sponsored by the New School for Social Research and the Harlem Writers Guild, another sponsored by Dr. Robert Pritchard and Fairleigh Dickinson University, another by the New York Society of Ethical Culture, another at Fisk University in Nashville, Tennessee, still another at Lincoln University in Pennsylvania and one at Gloucester, Virginia. And anyone who thinks I am being supercilious, or that fools learn by experience, will be saddened to know that, at this writing, I am anxiously awaiting forthcoming conferences in Atlanta and two more scheduled for the Midwest in 1967.

The Conference at Arden House was organized by Judd Teller, Executive Director of the American Histadrut Cultural Exchange, and titled "Acculturation and Integration." International figures dominated the scene, and lively ideas exploded from panelists and audience members. Jewish influences and black influences on the majority culture were highlighted. And a remarkable paper was read by Professor Donald M. Henderson of Akron University, in which he noted that we are living in a "time of rearrangement when old loyalties, old myths and old alliances are crumbling."

It was a sizzling conference, with considerable shouting—and I did a lot of the shouting. Matters were not helped at a general session, presided over by gubernatorial aspirant Howard Samuels.

I had gotten to know and like Mr. Samuels and his charming wife, Bobbie. Mr. Samuels was distressed and worried about the tide of black nationalism, particularly that tide which criticizes the white liberal. One of the things I kept trying to tell him throughout the conference was *that being pro-black does not mean one is anti-white*. There have been good white people since time began, in and out of this country. Black people were helped immeasurably by poor whites during the seventeenth-century slave

Who's Got His Own, *by Ronald Milner, at the experimental American Place Theatre in 1966. Left to right: Glynn Turman, L. Errol Jaye, Estelle Evans, Barbara Ann Teer, Roger Robinson, Sam Laws.*

Martha Holmes

uprisings in New York. My own feeling, therefore, is that whites who get involved with guilt complexes need to read and understand the historic roles of white people in the black revolution—a revolution that did not begin in 1954, but in 1619. I tried to tell him that if I were a white man committed to the Freedom Movement, I would stop apologizing for white atrocities while lecturing to Negroes. I would say to my black associates: "I am not a Rankin, Bilbo or Eastland. I want to do something to wipe them out. What can I do?" And the answer to this is one offered by white actress Madeline Sherwood during the rehearsals for *Ballad of the Winter Soldiers*—and the answer was later orchestrated in the Student Non-Violent Coordinating Committee's position paper on Black Power. The answer is that committed whites should stop talking to Negroes who are already committed and *go out and organize the white community* to ally itself with the black community.

At the general session presided over by Mr. Samuels, Mr. Henderson and I were called to the front to discuss the role of the white liberal, and we tried to make our views clear. Someone jumped up in the audience and said: "I thought this was a general session where the audience was supposed to talk. Is this another panel?"

Mr. Henderson replied, sharply: "No, and I don't intend to be on another one." And with that, he walked off the stage and I followed him.

We sat down. And then pandemonium broke loose. Such breastbeating I have never seen on any movie screen. One member of the audience after another jumped to his feet to outline his contributions to the battle for civil rights. A series of long speeches told how each had marched in picket lines, been beaten, spat at, chastised by family and friends because of his belief in the civil rights struggle. And each speech ended with the statement: "No one is going to chase me out of the civil rights fight."

The Honorable Benjamin F. McLaurin, an executive in the Brotherhood of Sleeping Car Porters, rose to try to bring some sense to the proceedings. His remarkable talk was in vain, for the moment he sat down the breastbeating and wailing continued. I do not know how long it lasted because I walked out.

I called home that night and I told Marjorie: "I can see what makes LeRoi Jones give up on trying to talk to whites. I am still not antiwhite, but I wish our friends would *listen* to what we are saying and not tell us what they *want* us to say."

The shouting session continued into April, 1965. That was when I participated in another conference, this one at the New School for Social Research, sponsored by the school and the Harlem Writers Guild. I took part in a panel, "What Negro Playwrights Are Saying," with fellow playwrights Lonnie Elder, Alice Childress, William Branch, LeRoi Jones, Douglas Turner Ward and critics Richard Gillman and Gordon Rogoff of *Newsweek* and the *Tulane Drama Review*, respectively. And contrary to the reports of the white dailies, the majority of the audience. was not *white*—unless a lot of white folks are getting sunburned in early spring.

The battle for America was waged at that conference. If so little dialogue exists between Negro and white intellectuals, it is little wonder that other whites deny Negroes basic human rights. Dr. John R. Everett, president of the New School, spelled it out when he openly regretted the fact that the white intellectual community fails to understand the vitality of the Negro intellectual. And he felt it was the whites' responsibility to listen and create a dialogue.

I viewed the panel "What Negro Playwrights Are Saying" with trepidation. And, frankly speaking, I don't know yet how I happened to be invited to appear on it. Three members of the Harlem Writers Guild and three members of the New School faculty have individually told me he or she plugged for me to appear on that panel. I wish the six of them would plug as hard for me to get my expenses for appearing.

Nor is this offered here as a carp. There is an element in the artistic community that seems to find particular enjoyment when it comes to telling others: "I recommended you for this or that." It is this element that I find particularly repulsive for, when I was struggling to get plays produced, they were flirting with others. I do not need their recommendations *after* the theatregoing public and the Guggenheim Foundation have determined my worth. But I would have loved their support when I was struggling in Harlem, begging people to read my work, to come see it if it got onto a stage. And many Harlemites did—the same Harlemites now denounced by those who currently "recommend me."

At any rate, I was recommended—and I viewed the panel with trepidation. When I saw that playwrights and critics were on the same panel, I groaned: "It's bad enough to have a panel of white playwrights and white critics, but when you put black playwrights up there with white critics, you're lighting dynamite with a blow torch."

Lonnie Elder chaired the panel. He mentioned that Negro playwrights are rarely produced, and he wondered if enough plays had been produced for anyone to determine what Negro playwrights are saying. Alice Childress then echoed the hope for more exposure, but she also called attention to numerous Negro playwrights whose work had been seen in the Harlem area. Next I reviewed the history of the Negro in the American theatre and added what I have been trying to say as a black playwright.

Gordon Rogoff said he hadn't prepared a paper—although why anyone shows up at a Conference without a paper is a mystery to me. Rogoff said he came to talk about theatre, that I had sounded a militant note and that he wasn't going to get into a civil rights debate. He was not, in his own words, "going to be a sitting duck."

William Branch then said he *had* prepared a paper. He spoke of discrimination in the mass media and cited my indignation over his not being called on to write the recent television script about Frederick Douglass. Robert Hooks, who played Douglass, led the applause. Branch noted that only sixteen playwrights have been represented on Broadway in that street's forty-year history. LeRoi Jones followed Branch and read his essay, *The Revolutionary Theatre*, in which he outlined what it is, what it must be, and he exploded many myths surrounding the modern white theatre.

*Newsweek's* Richard Gillman stated only two Negro-authored plays impressed him: Jones' *Dutchman* and Adrienne Kennedy's *The Funny House of a Negro*. He hastily added, to Jones' satisfaction, that he didn't like *Dutchman* for the reason LeRoi wanted him to like it. Gillman declared there was a difference between propaganda and art, and he called for universality in Negro plays. He discounted plays he had not seen, plays that had been produced in lofts and cellars. He then suggested that we might work up to writing a play.

Well, he should have followed Rogoff's example because Douglas Turner Ward jumped him in eloquent terms and told him and white America "like it is." Ward chastised them for being not deaf, but "deef." Questions then poured from the audience, questions directed at Gillman's cry for universality. Alice Childress then took the microphone and put in some vital points, adding that she had seen nothing but bad white plays produced, so why shouldn't some bad Negro plays get produced?

I looked into the audience and saw it break down along racial lines. Negroes applauded when white folks didn't—and *vice versa.* I pointed this out to LeRoi Jones and he said: "What did you expect?" Whites hissed me when I said I didn't have time to waste with Gillman and Rogoff. Negroes applauded me.

Branch then turned to Gillman and Rogoff and said: "What's your name again? I want to ask you how you judge Negro plays when you haven't seen any? How about going up to Harlem and looking at a few? In fact, who in the hell are you to judge, anyway?" Sylvester Leaks jumped up in the audience and roared: "This is like slavery time when Old Master sat up in the big house and didn't know what went on in the slave cabin."

The session adjourned to the home of Zelda and Harry Levine, the radio commentator. And throughout the evening the playwrights echoed this phrase: "I shall seriously question my work and yours the day certain critics like it."

The next conference I attended was at Fairleigh Dickinson University. This one didn't boil into a "shouting session," largely because I delivered my paper, then rushed back to the city.

The next one was at the New York Ethical Culture Society in March, 1966. An *ad hoc* committee—consisting of Actors Equity president Frederick O'Neal, actor Harold Scott, Actors Equity official Ellsworth Wright, actress-director Osceola Archer, author John Oliver Killens and this writer—called this conference on "Enriching American Culture Through Desegregating the Arts."

Desegregation of the arts was clarified in various meetings of the committee. For us it meant job opportunities for Negroes equal with those for whites. It meant, too, something Dr. Esther Jackson, Professor of Theatrical Studies at Adelphi University, pointed out in sharp, direct terms—that the government itself is remiss in its commitment to Negroes. For each Foundation has tax exemption and—although Negroes pay taxes—not one Foundation is rushing to put money into the Negro theatre.

The Committee for the Desegregation of the Arts grew out of this conference, with Dick Campbell serving as chairman. The

Committee noted that, although it is committed to Negroes being given equal job opportunities, it did not want to go on record as simply advocating the casting of roles in terms of Negroes on a "just human" basis. For it was noted that this can be made into a good case against the dissemination of black culture. Indeed, the use of Negroes in "non-Negro" roles is suspect, often considered a gimmick that capitalizes on the Freedom Movement. Such casting does little to assist the Negro's effort to reclaim his heritage or to create a true image of the Afro-American. In fact, a fear might be considered—that a case may be made out for Negroes doing "just human" roles. This would assist in stifling works by and about black people.

Another thing grew out of this conference: Negroes are getting better, varied theatrical jobs—*when* they get jobs. The cold fact remains that more black theatre artists worked during the depression than during this period of alleged prosperity.

The next conference I attended was at Fisk University in Nashville, Tennessee. Alice Childress, William Branch and I were scheduled to participate in a panel, again called, "What Negro Dramatists Are Saying." Branch missed the plane and Childress and I flew to Nashville together. It was a lovely flight, but when we landed, we landed.

We were met at the airport by a station wagon and, along with South African writer Richard Rive and Katya and Burt Gilden, authors of *Hurry Sundown*, we were driven into town. As we approached the campus, I saw what is euphemistically referred to as a "State Store." I suggested that we stop and pick up some supplies.

Mr. Gilden and I went into the store and placed an order. Before I could pay the bill, he very gently placed a twenty-dollar bill on the counter. I said: "Here. I have part of that."

"No," he said with the best of intentions. "I'll take it. I'm sure my book brought more royalties than *Ballad for Bimshire*."

I thought to myself: "Brother, you're going to be in trouble at this conference." And I knew I had landed.

The Fisk Conference was a rock and roll session. John Oliver Killens, Arna Bontemps, Mignon Holland and Fisk University President Stephen J. Wright spearheaded this gathering to discuss "The Image of the Negro in American Literature." David Llorens of the *Negro Digest* wrote excellent coverage of the conference in the June, 1966, issue. In Mr. Llorens' words, it provided "excitement, anger, joy and intense probing."

A significant thing occurred at Fisk. James Forman, then Executive Secretary of the Student Non-Violent Coordinating Committee—known as SNCC or "Snick"—was an active participant. Present, too, was Cleveland Sellers, SNCC program director and other activists. They wanted to know what the civil rights movement could do to assist black writers. We talked far into the night and arranged a meeting in New York City during the summer of 1966.

A number of things happened between the conference at Fisk and our reunion in New York. In May, 1966, SNCC officials met and developed a scholarly position paper on Black Power. This paper, contrary to press reports, is decidedly not anti-white. It is, however, pro-black. Anyone who reads it without prejudice will see that the paper suggests exactly what other national groups have done in order to liberate themselves. The paper commends the role previously played by whites in the Freedom Movement but suggests that whites now become missionaries in the white community and convert bigots. I am not certain that this paper is too far from the Montgomery bus boycott, the Moynihan Report or Puerto Rico's Operation Bootstrap. I am not certain, either, that it is too far from the "black nation" concept that prevailed in the nineteen-thirties.

But the term was deliberately distorted from the time it hit the press. After James Meredith—the man who desegregated the University of Mississippi—was shot while on a voter registration campaign in his home state, civil rights leaders decided to continue the march. It was on that march that Stokely Carmichael, SNCC's new chairman, led the chant for "Black Power."

Now, there were twenty white writers on that march. And not one printed the question CORE official Floyd McKissick raised: "Why didn't your papers send some black writers to cover this march?"

The white writers, led by Pete Hamill of the allegedly liberal New York *Post*, started a series of articles that were overladened with mistruths. It was suggested that Black Power was anti-Semitic. It was intimated that the Black Muslims had taken over the Civil Rights Movement. And, to compound the felony, *The New York Times* carried excerpts from the SNCC paper on Black

Power on August 5, 1966—and right beside it was a distorted piece of reporting that made the SNCC position seem "racist."

One thing the chant for Black Power did initially was to show the naïveté of many civil rights leaders. They did not do what any other group of statesmen would have done when asked a ticklish question—namely, reply: "No comment until we've studied the facts." They rushed headlong into the trap and intimated that Black Power meant Black Death and suggested that it also meant Black Supremacy. They should have walked around America's black communities where this statement was heard all too often:

"White power got white folks and black folks slavery, a dozen or so wars, a terrible depression, trouble with Asia, a newspaper strike, a subway strike, a power failure and more deaths from cars than we lost in all our wars. It's about time to look for some kind of power to offset that race towards hell!"

The Black Power drama roared throughout the summer. The Congress of Racial Equality met and endorsed the concept. And author Lillian Smith resigned from her advisory role in CORE, claiming the Civil Rights Movement was now in the hands of racists, hatemongers and so forth. No one shed a tear, except the white structure, for the latter had been trying to woo CORE, to place it in the position of attacking SNCC, which was just a little too militant. That trick failed and the white structure had to rely on an old gimmick—having dynamite placed, then found by the law in SNCC's Philadelphia office. This is the basis of a court case now raging in the City of Brotherly Love.

These events were reviewed when a group of writers met with Floyd McKissick, Stokely Carmichael and James Forman in August, 1966. Out of this meeting came the civil rights leaders' decision to press for Negro-authored scripts to be seen on television, to press the movie medium for true representation and to bring to white publications the fact that black writers should participate in the handling of things written about the Freedom Movement.

While the argument over Black Power raged all summer, a great institution known as the United States government willingly supported the concept—and knowingly. It did so by funding a number of theatre groups that offered training to young actors, writers and stage technicians. And it turned out to be absolutely worthwhile.

The groups known to me are: The New Heritage Players, the

Gossett Academy of Dramatic Arts and Mobilization for Youth. The New Heritage Players, organized by Roger Furman, had such professional staff members as Walter Julio, Rick Ferrell, Claire Leyba and John F. Payne working with youngsters, producing original plays on the streets of Harlem all summer long. The Gossett Academy, founded by actor Louis Gossett, had such professional staff members as Richard Karp, George Shack, Paul Sorvino, W. F. Lucas, David Smyrl, Michael Ackerman, Melenda Lasson and Kelly Marie Berry giving courses to Lower East Side teen-agers in make-up, acting, fencing, stagecraft, voice and playwriting. Mobilization for Youth had Ed Cambridge directing shows for the street, and one of the actors was Austin Briggs-Hall, Jr., son of the actor—the same actor who has contributed so much to my writing career.

The City of New York also assisted in the Black Power drama. The New York Shakespeare Festival organized a stirring production of *Macbeth*, compellingly played by James Earl Jones and Ellen Holly. Joseph Papp, as has been his practice, had black actors in his Shakespeare productions at the Delacorte Theatre in Central Park. And the New York Shakespeare Festival produced *An Evening of Negro Poetry and Folk Music* on August 15, 1966. This thrilling program was assembled and directed by Roscoe Lee Browne. He surrounded himself with such veterans as Leon Bibb, Gloria Foster, Moses Gunn, Ellen Holly, James Earl Jones, Josephine Premice and Cicely Tyson. And, in the words of *New York Post* critic Jerry Tallmer, "it broke up the place." He closed his notice with: "It was that kind of evening. To remember. And an important one in the cultural history of this city and nation."

The "Conference Years" continued. Gloucester, Virginia, was the scene of a conference on Extending Opportunities for Professional Training Through Education. It was sponsored by the National Association of Dramatic and Speech Arts and the Phelps-Stokes Fund. Its planning committee included many distinguished names—Randolph Edmonds, Frederick O'Neal, Esther Jackson, Joseph Adkins, George Bass, Woodie King, Jr., Thomas D. Pawley, Lloyd Richards, Harold Scott, John M. Stevenson and Ida Wood. Outstanding personalities from various cultural fields met and offered recommendations for what I called "making the artist a first-class citizen."

The Conference held at Lincoln University was spearheaded by Charles V. Hamilton, Chairman of the Department of Political

Science, and librarian Emery Wimbush. It was held on December 3, 1966, and it featured four writers: Ronald Milner, W. F. Lucas, John Oliver Killens and this writer. *Negro Digest* editor Hoyt Fuller served as moderator. Titled "The Writer and Human Rights," this conference was student-oriented. It was a lively affair, punctuated by pungent remarks from students and panelists alike. And one thing became obvious at this conference, as at others—the American student is demanding a day of reckoning.

During my Conference Years I was in and out of New York. And the drama was offstage as well as on. There were evidences of the so-called white backlash, which is really a frontlash that is as old as this nation. This so-called backlash was aided considerably by the powerful communications media which spoke of it as frequently as TV sells products. In short, the communications media is as responsible for the backlash as anyone else.

Stokely Carmichael was accused of starting it all with his Black Power concept. The Conservative Party and the Patrolmen's Benevolent Association teamed up to put the New York City Civilian Review Board to a vote. Their advertising campaign implied that Negroes were synonymous with crime in the streets. The plot to "get Adam Clayton Powell" was being hatched—to get him for doing no more than any other Congressman. And those who "got him," who placed the people of Harlem in the position of being taxed without representation, closed their eyes to Mississippi's racist Representative Collmer, who has gone against his party on numerous occasions. I suppose the Congressional logic was that if Mississippi Negroes have no representation, why should Harlem have any?

If the political signs were ominous, they became downright menacing when Republicans captured a large number of seats. Fingers pointed, all towards the backlash. No one bothered to note that the Republican victory was tied up with the general ineptness of the Democrats. That would have been too close to the truth. Besides, America had its usual scapegoat, the black man. So he took the blame for war, for bungling foreign policy, outright lies, air pollution, high prices, low wages and general incompetence.

The backlash was theatrical as well as political. *An Evening of Negro Poetry and Folk Music* borrowed a title, *A Hand is on the Gate*, from poet Arna Bontemps and it moved to Broadway in September, 1966, at that difficult time of the year when people are paying for their summer vacations, buying school clothing, books, or sending their children off to college. And the work closed all too briefly.

It was, however, gratifying that the American theatre recognized the multitalented Roscoe Lee Browne for his genius. He had been a track star, then a college professor at Lincoln University. There he worked with such professionals as Abram Hill, Ruby Dee and Gloria Daniel. After a few years of teaching, Mr. Browne quit, came back to New York, went into theatre and was acclaimed for his work in *The Cool World, The Blacks* and *The Old Glory* among other ventures. He assembled, directed and acted in *A Hand is on the Gate*, and one looks forward to other work from Mr. Browne.

The next Negro dramatic effort was Ronald Milner's *Who's Got His Own*, which was shown at the American Place Theatre in the fall of 1966. This is a membership theatre, organized by the Reverend Sidney Lanier, and Wyn Handman is the group's artistic director. Under Lloyd Richards' direction Mr. Milner's searing, unrelenting drama unfolded without the "usual Negro humor." Barbara Ann Teer, Estelle Evans and Glynn Tyman played the central roles.

Mr. Milner's badly titled play comes from the Billie Holiday song, "God Bless the Child Who's Got His Own." At the core of his play was the family of Tim Senior, a Negro for whom funeral arrangements have been held that day. And his wife, daughter and son, Tim Junior, go through some soul searching. As Tim Junior understands the genesis of the family's torment, he looks around and declares that nothing has really changed.

Without impugning Mr. Miler's intelligence, it took no genius to see that he was saying that nothing in America has changed in terms of the Black Experience. The critics didn't want to hear this and they went into all kinds of academic jujitsus to find things wrong with the play. They were not unsuccessful and, unlike many other American Place productions, this one did not move to another house and continue for a run. Portions of the play were presented on CBS-TV's *Camera Three* and the following week I joined a playwright's seminar to discuss the Milner work. But as far as I know that is all that happened to it.

On November 9, 1966, William Marshall appeared in Owen Rachleff's *Javelin*, produced in Greenwich Village by Stella Holt. It, too, had a brief run.

On December 6, 1966 Bob Banner Associates brought David

Westheimer's adaptation of his novel, *My Sweet Charlie*, to Broadway. This play, directed by Howard DaSilva, brought deserved stardom to Louis Gossett and Bonnie Bedelia. It was a charming work. Charlie, a civil rights lawyer, got into difficulty during a demonstration. In flight he broke into a summer home where Marlene, a southern white teenager, was hiding because of an unwanted pregnancy. Verbal sparring, getting to know each other, and concern for each other rounded out the well-written, wonderfully comic little play. Despite mixed reviews, the play failed commercially. A theatre that cannot support work such as *A Hand is on the Gate*, *Who's Got His Own* and *My Sweet Charlie* is in serious trouble.

During December, 1966, Alice Childress' *Wedding Band* was shown at the University of Michigan. Ruby Dee headed a cast that included Abbey Lincoln, Clarice Taylor, Katherine Squire, John Leighton, Thomas Anderson, Moses Gunn, John Harkins, Marcie Hubert, Minnie Gentry, Elissa Ross and Lisa Huggins. The reviews were glowing and the play is being discussed for a Broadway opening in the spring of 1967.

At the present writing I know of only one other projected Broadway entry and that happens to be my musical play, *Ballad of a Blackbird*, with lyrics by W. F. Lucas. This work is based on the life of the late Florence Mills.

But if black writers aren't being given a chance to write about black people, white writers are. Arthur Laurents, Adolph Green, Betty Comden and Julie Styne have prepared a musical revoltingly titled, *Hallelujah, Baby*. This is said to tell the story of the American Negro from 1900 to the present. Producer David Merrick recently dropped his option on this work. Mr. Merrick may have made his greatest contribution to black America. In the words of poet Langston Hughes: "You done took my blues and gone . . ."

This is theatre nearly two thousand years after the Christ—an institution false to its founding, waiting, waiting for the millennium, waiting to discover Negroes again, to declare that a milestone has been reached when actually there was one in 1821, in 1826, in the early twenties, thirties, forties and fifties. The eternal search by white America for the Negro millennium is part of its justification for not doing what it should have done 346 years ago—and that is: Guarantee Freedom Now!

Marriage is arranged in Gypsy custom. The bride is sold by her father to a prospective son-in-law for a considerable amount of money—depending, of course, upon how skilled the woman is in performing Gypsy tricks. The language of the group is Romany. It is an unwritten language, spoken in a guttural manner.

The Gypsy stereotype is as ridiculous as other stereotypes. We see them as violinists, crying to the moon. We see them as dirty horse thieves, as swindlers, knife-wielders and as gay, romantic, carefree people. And while all the noted stereotypes fall flat upon examination, possibly none falls flatter than the gay, romantic, carefree people. Too often you will hear them say: "A Gypsy's life is hard, hard." Many of them are cynical, too, about the treatment they are accorded by all Americans. They have a statement written here phonetically: "*O go-rue shoo-dem a geee-shay parley-coa.*" Translated that means: "The bull is kicking dirt over his back, head, and into his own eyes."

This is repeated here because one night a group of Gypsies charged that America represented the bull. Colya Costello, one of the Gypsy leaders, declared this nation is kicking up a lot of dirt, thinking the dirt is flying behind it, but it's going up into the air, over the bull's back and into his own eyes. And blinding him. Costello declared that all the good things America was supposedly doing for the underprivileged people of the earth was simply dirt, and as long as she mistreats minority groups, the dirt will continue to fly into America's eyes.

This was all folklore to me then—very amusing and worth listening to, but with little significance.

But, now—when one looks at the world situation and that of integration in the theatre—I, at least, am compelled to remember the old Gypsy saying.

We have kicked dirt into our own eyes by not doing a complete about-face in terms of race relations, abroad and at home. We know we cannot—yet we tell ourselves we can—have a positive influence over the earth's colored peoples, yet remain pompously white.

The one answer to this is to completely free black people in America. But this is not about to be done, for chauvinism has such deep roots in America that a *white* revolution is necessary—a revolution that will purge white America of its smugness, its arrogance, its pseudobenevolence and its desire to reshape the world in its own image. This means the loud, blabbering, coarse, infantile, scheming, half-male society will have to be turned over on its ears. Its women will have to play the role of women and its men the role of men. And this, specifically, is not going to happen in the near future. America's ruling oligarchy reaps too many profits from the neurosis, the family distress, strain, and the fatherless children spawned out of the duress created both deliberately and accidentally. Every divorce, drug addict, drunk, homosexual, auto accident and violent crime is a deliberate manifestation of the power structure, welcomed by it, maintained by it, often in open or secret alliance with the world's crime syndicate. And there is no evidence that the most radical of radicals wants the complete change that is mandatory toward bringing a new day to this continent. "If you can't beat them, join them" is too widely used in our times for it to have little meaning.

Tomorrow must be seen in terms of today. Since America as we know it shows no indication of a major change, one can only conjecture that America tomorrow will remain the land of the doublecross—a land of high-sounding phrases, but of little human accomplishments. We shall have New Deals, Fair Deals, New Frontiers and Great Societies, but the benefactors will continue to be the present ruling group, plus one or two allowed in the door.

This is the pattern of modern integration, aimed toward a middle-class level—a fact already documented by the Urban Renewal Program. One look at downtown Washington, Philadelphia and Baltimore indicates that middle-class whites are reclaiming the center of the American city. These whites will, of course, permit middle-class Negroes who can afford exorbitant rents to live beside them. As for the poor whites and the poor Negroes—it is once again to the hills of Arkansas or Kentucky, or some outlying ghetto. They will be evicted from the center of the city much like lower-class whites are being moved from the Bowery—much like Columbia University and the Rockefeller interests are trying to remove Negroes from the Harlem area. When these feats are accomplished, we shall have townships of poor whites and poor Negroes *outside* the city.

These poor white and black townships may serve to destroy themselves, for the era known as automation is a reality, and there will be less and less need for human labor. Indeed, there may not be enough work for those who can work. We shall, therefore, have townships that are pockets of poverty where friction will be an increasing factor. Blood will flow in the streets of these townships and pious officials will say: "For shame, for shame!" There will be investigations and platitudes, but more blood will flow, for this will prove to be an inexpensive means of extermination.

Those who think extermination is not a possibility are referred to the numerous Indian tribes that were extinguished—with the finger pointed toward the "barbaric redman." There is another precedent in the incarceration of the Japanese-American during World War II. And this took place under the Roosevelt Administration—a liberal administration! Remembering this prompted historian John Hope Franklin to state on television: "I can't tell you what the future of the Negro or the ordinary white will be in this country. It's going to depend upon the nation's reaction to international affairs."

The difference between the United States of America and what was known as the Union of South Africa dissolves itself into a similarity that is deeper than the identical initials of both countries. But the United States has wisely chosen to develop a black middle class—a class it will absorb and integrate if that group allies itself with the status quo.

This type of integration, or pseudo-integration, is already being felt in the American theatre. Negroes are "integrated" into every avenue of theatre at present, but it has already been noted that more black actors worked during the depression years than during the present years. One need only glance at the figures compiled by Frederick O'Neal for documentation. For the past five years he recorded the following in terms of Negro actors:

|  | 1964-65 | 1963-64 | 1962-63 | 1961-62 | 1960-61 |
|---|---|---|---|---|---|
| Jobs available: | | | | | |
| On Broadway | 74 | 168 | 51 | 123 | 126 |
| Off Broadway | 32 | 116 | 26 | 50 | 29 |
| Number shows employing Negroes | | | | | |
| On Broadway | 22 | 24 | 21 | 14 | 18 |
| Off Broadway | 20 | 27 | 12 | 20 | 9 |
| Number shows with integrated casts | | | | | |
| On Broadway | 15 | 16 | 13 | 10 | 8 |
| Off Broadway | 11 | 11 | 7 | 11 | 4 |

Mr. O'Neal goes on to note: "The drop in the total number of jobs available to Negro actors during the season 1964-1965, as in

certain past periods, is mainly due to the number of shows produced with predominantly, or all, Negro casts. For example,
during the 1963–1964 season, three shows: *Porgy and Bess* (46),
*Tambourines to Glory* (29), *Sponomo* (24), accounted for 99 of
the total number of 168 employed that year. This was all but 69
of the total. That same season three off-Broadway shows, *Jericho
Jimcrow* (20), *Ballad for Bimshire* (26) and *Cabin in the Sky*
(18) accounted for all but 52 of the total employed in that area.
A total of 67 shows were produced on Broadway last season and
63 during the 1963–1964 season."

Mr. O'Neal is apparently pleased, and justifiably so, to note the
increasing number of Negro artists used in roles that are not
specifically designated as "Negro parts." And he notes that casting
as such has held up rather well. He notes, too, with satisfaction
the black playwrights who have had professional productions
within the past ten to fifteen years. He states that the works of
ten black writers have been professionally produced within the
past five years.

Mr. O'Neal is a beautiful human being, a great artist and a
credit to the human race. But he is also not starry-eyed, despite
his optimism. He speaks of the utilization of Negroes in orchestra
pits, among stagehands, lighting technicians and company managers. But he is also cognizant of the paucity of productions. And
therein lies a story.

It is a story that came to the fore when Johnson Publications
ran an article sometime ago: "Are Negroes Monopolizing Boxing?"
They were doing just that, and on Harlem streetcorners you could
hear the sages predicting that soon there would be Congressional
investigations of the sport and it would be declared crooked, cruel
and vicious—which it has been all along. Another sage noted that
in the very near future it was going to be decided that baseball,
football and basketball are *businesses* and that they violate every
anti-trust law on the books—which they probably do. A young
Negro then turned and asked: "Do they have to wait till we get
into these things to find something wrong? Or did they know
something was wrong all the time and decide to spill the beans
after we broke in?"

"Son," an elderly man told him, "we are still getting the left-
overs and the hand-me-downs. We have the Civil Service jobs
now because the white folks have better jobs."

These comments may well supply the answer to the Negro

being integrated into all departments of the American theatre today, for that is not where the *real* work and the *real* money exists today. The question is—how many Negroes are working in television? If we exclude the appearance of Negroes in sporting events, we might possibly watch television interminably without seeing a Negro. James Baldwin and LeRoi Jones are seen at intervals on television, but how many Negroes are writing scripts for that media? With all due respect for Baldwin and Jones, their scripts could say more than their personal appearances. Why not, indeed, show their works rather than the authors? To my knowledge Baldwin has had one work produced and Jones none. And neither has written a Hollywood movie to date.

Television, of course, has no intentions of permitting Negroes to participate in it beyond a cursory level. Networks may have one or two commentators, personnel directors and other "representative" or "token" Negroes to pay lip service to the democratic process, and network officials may editorialize about the validity of the Civil Rights struggle, but they are not going to do more than that. And by more than that, I mean just this: CBS and NBC have too many varied interests and connections in the South and North to permit nonsense toward Negroes. Let the New York Yankees—a subsidiary of CBS—run into trouble and that Board of Directors will scream and cry until there is some type of reconstruction, immediately. The same thing could be done in terms of the treatment of Negroes.

Perhaps the greatest commentary on the networks—apart from the non-participation of Negro artists—lies in its nonbroadcasting personnel. While clerical and technical help involves Negroes, a survey by this writer found these workers were in "hand-me-down" jobs, working under and beside whites whose qualifications do not meet those of the Negroes. And each Negro I interviewed had his hat in his hand, not in order to bow, but to stick it on his head and run out the door whenever a better job presented itself. The same is, of course, true of Civil Service—all of which suggests that the section of the mainstream offered to Negro integrationists is polluted.

None of this is accidental. Television reaches into the American home. Now while a good American white family might sit and watch a story involving a good Negro lawyer, or look on sympathetically at a Negro demonstration being broken up, that becomes *something else* again. The good Negro lawyer shows us

that there are good and bad among all people, etc., etc. The Negro
demonstration shows us how vicious some officials can be and it
is too bad, etc., etc., and it all boils down to a lot of talk without
too much action. But let there appear on television a play about
Negro history—one about Toussaint L'Ouverture or Henri Christophe, or the black soldiers during the American Revolution! That
would really rock the boat, for the white child might ask: Why
didn't I read about that in the history book? And the Negro child
might say: Did my ancestors do that? What am I doing walking
around here with complexes and begging folks to give me something I've already earned?

The television industry isn't half as naïve as we think it is. If it
were, Fred Friendly wouldn't have resigned from CBS.

I believe that real change in America is deliberately a rare
phenomenon. The reality of the present pattern of existence is that
of creating a greater bourgeoisie and a petty bourgeoisie, groups
that will ally themselves with the power structure. The other
groups will dissipate themselves with overburdening problems,
hidden from the most astute observer. These problems will make
the group members introspective, doubtful of themselves, finding
that the fault is always within themselves.

An interesting example of this occurred recently when I took a
taxi from the Hollis-St. Albans middle-class area of Long Island.
At Jamaica Avenue, along 187th Street, we met a particularly
long light. This red light obviously favors the drivers moving east
and west on Jamaica, drivers who are specifically white. When I
mentioned this to the Negro taxi driver, he immediately declared
it was the fault of Negroes. He remembered the day whites lived
in the Hollis-St. Albans area, and they didn't put up with things
like this!

I had seen it all before, heard it again and again. In Harlem
for many years there were bars under the subway turnstiles at
116th Street, 125th Street and 135th Street—bars placed to keep
children from crawling under the turnstiles. These may have existed in other areas of the city, but I never saw them. And civil
rights groups may have complained about them, but I never heard
them. With slums, high rents, discrimination and unemployment
and all the things known to jimcrow living, who had time to worry
about subway turnstiles? These, indeed, became "luxury problems."

One of the greatest of "luxury problems" exists today at 125th
Street and St. Nicholas Avenue. Here stands a major subway stop

on the Independent line. You could catch cold standing on token lines, waiting to be served by booth operators whose arrogance is comparable to Broadway theatre ticket-sellers. There are no token machines on that station platform. Of course, the Transit Authority will probably state in pious terms that it hasn't installed token machines on that station because Harlem youngsters might break them open. But this is questionable because there are always policemen at that station. Unless, of course, the Transit Authority doesn't trust the police.

Endless other problems could be cited—problems that create increased frustrations on the part of individuals that divide them and dissipate their attacks on the major issues of the day. These actually provoke the riots known to Watts, to Harlem, to Bedford-Stuyvesant. When these problems become overburdening and riots occur, the power structure looks at the middle-class of those areas and says, in effect: "Apologize or you won't get *your* civil rights." And that middle class crawls from the power structure's hip pocket, utters pious platitudes and crawls back to safety—all of which explains why the Mau Mau killed more Africans than British.

All of this leads me to the belief that the black American is going to have to do for himself in theatre and outside of it. This is certainly not an effort to rule out white support. Too many whites, from the seventeenth century on, have been allied with the black man's fight for freedom. But the white man is going to have to learn to keep his mouth shut and follow in the Negro's fight for freedom, just as the Negro and others will have to learn to keep their mouths shut when it comes to fighting for the rights of Chinese, Japanese, Puerto Ricans and Jews.

I do not suggest that this is going to be easy. We live in a nation where we have contempt for others. Each one of us knows more about running a government than the politicians. We know more about medicine than our doctors, more about driving than taxi drivers, more about law than our lawyers and more about theatre than our theatre workers. We can cut our teachers to bits because we know more about teaching children than they do. And we know more about rearing children than any other set of parents. It is a know-it-all society, and many of the indignities committed by well-intentioned whites do not reflect subconscious race prejudice as much as they reflect the fact that this white man is also an American. But anyone thinking a white man has a priority on knowing-it-all should walk into a Negro barbershop and sit there for half an hour.

The whole of America often reminds me of a scene in a re-markable Italian movie, *The Difficult Years*. There is a bar scene where a group of men are standing, expounding on the definition of communism and fascism, and while they are talking, totalitarian forces are literally pounding on the door, getting ready to break into the bar!

The cold, historical truth is that it is the divine responsibility of the oppressed peoples to lead the oppressors. This admittedly places a burden on the backs of the oppressed, yet the significant changes in the Western world have resulted from just this phe-nomenon. And if this is true in terms of national and international life, it is also true for the theatre.

The Negro theatre artist is, therefore, going to have to reckon with the fact that he can get a job in the theatre if there is one to be gotten. But there are fewer and fewer shows being produced. The Broadway theatre has become not only a middle-class luxury, but an upper-middle-class one. Foundations have made it clear that all kinds of groups can get money except those in Negro areas. Therefore, the Negro artist and the Negro masses will have to reckon with this, to strike out for themselves.

They will have to reckon with it alone, for the black middle class is still looking for downtown acceptance. The black middle class is no more interested in a black theatre than the white middle class. A black theatre might, and will, rock the boat.

The Negro theatre artist and the Negro masses will have to see that a black theatre is inevitable. White artists, who have much more to gain from Broadway than black ones, are already in a flight from Broadway. They see that once historic street as a center of economic strangulation and artistic stagnation. And so many have gone off to the "hinterlands," to regional theatres which are now flourishing. There now exist fifty such professional companies where there were exactly three ten years ago. Few, if any, of these are Negro theatres, although some have "integrated" black artists. But the pattern is obvious. Just as America raced off to the suburbs in the nineteen-fifties, the theatre is racing from Broadway in the nineteen-sixties. And Negro theatre will have to race off, too.

All of this raises a tantalizing question. Negroes raced, or were driven, to Harlem in the 1900s. They created many styles which

Broadway chased uptown, bought and utilized. Eugene O'Neill and his group created a style at the Provincetown, and Broadway rushed downtown and bought it. The same may be said of the Rose McClendon Players, the American Negro Theatre, New Stages and other groups—including Circle-in-the-Square. The omnipotence of Broadway is to be considered, for it is symbolic of the power structure, able to absorb that which it desires and to frustrate, agitate and destroy that which it hates.

The theatre tomorrow will, therefore, remain much as it is today unless there is a real change in this society. The one hope is that those groups in the ghetto areas—the townships composed of poor whites, Puerto Ricans and Negroes—will create drama as it was intended, as a living instrument that educates, communicates and entertains, an instrument that has a life commitment.

The hope here is that the ghetto or township theatre will spread and that, instead of the barbarians overthrowing Rome this time, these people will march into the center of the city and reshape the American theatre into what that institution ought to be!

This path is paved with difficulty. This is a young country, and Americans do not know their history. The nation has no sense of tradition. It shuttles the old aside and speaks always of today, of the new car, the new gadget, the living present. Its old are pushed into day centers and homes for the aged. The emphasis is on youth to the extent that our society has become ill with the youth-syndrome. You have to be in your twenties to find love in the movies. You have to be in your twenties to seek the finer things of life. Those are your young adult years, and if you don't look out, you'll waste them and find that two thirds of your life is over, so why bother about what happens then?

When you are in your sixties, you are near death, standing around, waiting on the Lord. This is true of whites and it is true of blacks. Our society has committed itself to the young as long as the young operate in our image.

But the young are revolting. All that we taught them about patriotism and national service seems in vain if we look at the anti-draft demonstrations. And they are saying more in these demonstrations than that they don't want to go to Viet Nam. They are telling us in direct terms that we have lied to them, that we have told them things we do not believe and do not intend to follow through on, anyway. And in Biblical terms, the children are rising against their parents.

Youngsters may not know their history, but they are awakening in a fashion that we should look at twice. They have assessed values, and we can talk on and on and ask them what they can do for their country, not what their country can do for them—and they laugh at us. They break into our houses. They dress the way they want to dress. They thumb their noses at us and they smoke marijuana and have drunken parties, and they tell us to drop dead—all because we, their parents, have lied to ourselves and to them!

The hope, therefore, is that this rebellious youth will anchor itself to traditions of truth and honesty while continuing to fire upon the two-for-a-nickel officeholder. The hope is that youth will tell the American oligarchy: No, no, you cannot continue to send me down the road of new discovery through alcohol, drugs, sexual deviation and frustration!

The hope is that the youth from these townships and ghettos will apply the brakes to America's headlong race toward destruction. This is a shrinking world and men fly around it at terrifying speeds. The moon has been hit. And now this shrinking world demands that we deal with each other directly, right now, as brothers, or face total annihilation. One way we may learn to know and to love each other is through the drama. If we see, really see, each other on the world's stages and share common human problems, we may yet achieve a better world.

This, then, is the importance of black drama. It is hope—hope that in the world's most powerful country a minority that has made undying contributions can make its greatest contribution and redeem the majority. This minority stands at a moment in time, poised, with new, vital allies, demanding to be reckoned with. And the world looks on, waiting, waiting.

In the last analysis this nation will have to accept its truly rebellious souls, but not in the sense of doing them any special favors by extending human rights, for these people are not dogs standing at America's door, begging to be let into the house. They have helped to build that house, to preserve it and to revitalize it. And the best way America is going to realize all of this is to have it dramatized on our stages, our television screens and movie screens.

If this is not done, then this history may well remain within the pages of a book that a lonely survivor could possibly find floating on the ocean's waves when human life has been extinguished on this planet!

# Index

237

**A HAWTHORN BOOK**

## DATE DUE

| 6/23 | | | |
|---|---|---|---|
| JUL 1 1969 | | | |
| MAY 9 1972 | | | |
| OC 27 '76 | | | |
| NO 1 4 '76 | | | |
| NO 28 '76 | | | |
| | | | |
| | | | |
| | | | |
| | | | |
| | | | |
| | | | |
| | | | |
| | | | |
| | | | |
| | | | |
| | | | |
| | | | PRINTED IN U.S.A. |